COOP

REVIEWS OF NEIL DRYSDALE'S BOOKS

About *Southern Comfort*:

"Meticulously researched – an informative and comprehensive account" – *The Scotsman*

"A definitive version of why Scottish rugby finds itself on life support" – *Evening News*

"Brilliantly insightful" – *Daily Telegraph*

"An absorbing account" – *Rugby World*

About *Dad's Army*:

"It's not only fluid and fun, but a substantial achievement" – *The Herald*

"A richly evocative and superbly told story" – *The Sunday Times*

"Drysdale's entertaining account of the club's journey does more than tell a story well. It also paints a vivid picture of a bygone world." – *Wisden*

"A tour de force" – *Scottish Cricketer Magazine*

About *Silversmith*:

"A timely and sympathetic portrait of a fascinating figure" – BBC

COOP

THE LIFE OF DAVIE COOPER
SCOTTISH FOOTBALL HERO

NEIL DRYSDALE

BLACK & WHITE PUBLISHING

First published 2013
by Black & White Publishing Ltd
29 Ocean Drive, Edinburgh EH6 6JL

1 3 5 7 9 10 8 6 4 2   13 14 15 16

ISBN: 978 1 84502 637 0

Typeset by RefineCatch Ltd, Bungay, Suffolk
Printed and bound by Gutenberg Press Limited, Malta

To my beloved sister, Jean, who died far too young

ACKNOWLEDGEMENTS

When I initially set out to delve into the career of Davie Cooper, I imagined that many people would have vivid recollections of the myriad qualities which this multi-faceted sportsman brought to the realm of Scottish football during his tragically short life. But I could not have envisaged that such a large number of Davie's former friends, colleagues, teammates, managers and supporters, from across the sport's spectrum, would be so willing to lend me their thoughts and their memories.

Obviously, Rangers was a major factor in Davie's footballing history. But I received a substantial amount of assistance from people connected with his other clubs and even those who worked with him before he joined the professional ranks at Clydebank. In that regard, I would like to thank Stuart Noble, Gordon Robertson, Jim Fallon, Danny Cunning and Ross Alexander for their reminiscences of Coop's early years.

When Davie moved to Ibrox, he made friends on and off the pitch. The former SFA chief executive, Gordon Smith, offered me valuable insights into Cooper's personality, while Bobby Russell, Billy Davies and Jim Bett furnished me with other information, which was appreciated. Other players were willing to talk to me, but requested anonymity and I have respected their wishes, although it seems sad that, more than eighteen years after Davie's untimely death, there should still be so much lingering resentment at how he was treated by the club in the early 1980s. I must also acknowledge the contributions of a wide number of Rangers fans, who made contact with me through the Follow Follow website. The liaison efforts of Mark Dingwall were instrumental in me forging a bond with those who paid their money to watch Davie perform his pyrotechnics week in, week out at Ibrox, even as the club struggled around him. These supporters were, in alphabetical order: Alan Barclay, Scott Blair, Alister Campbell, Terry Clark, Willie Evans, Elaine Hamilton, Ally McGrath, Robert McKenzie, Ian Oliphant, Karen Reid, Gordon Semple, Charles Sharp, Ally Waltham and Colin Wood. In respect to Davie's resurgence at Motherwell, I was helped by the labours of John Wilson and Graham Barnstaple of the FirParkCorner.com website, while the Scotland internationalist, Tom Boyd, was forthright and insightful in telling me how his own career had been assisted by Davie's influence when they were both working in partnership at Fir Park.

In terms of those who ran the show at Scotland level, I am extremely grateful to Sir Alex Ferguson for taking the time to speak to me and, as usual, bringing a humanity and intelligence to our conversation when he had a million other things on his mind. Two other former Scotland managers, Craig Brown and Andy Roxburgh, were equally invaluable in charting Davie's progress from callow Bankie to a man who elicited rich praise from the likes of Ruud Gullit, Sergei Baltacha and Graeme Souness, and were lavish in their tributes to Davie. Indeed one suspects they wish they could have used his talents more on the international stage, because none doubted his ability at the game's highest level.

There were plenty of other people who eased my task in writing this biography and my thanks are extended to: Andy McGilvray at the *Hamilton Advertiser*; Rodger Baillie of the *Sunday Times* and his son, Andrew, a former colleague of mine at *Scotland on Sunday*; Richard McBrearty at the SFA Football Museum; Donald Cowey, the Sports Editor of *The Herald*, who offered insight and information;

the staff at the Davie Cooper Centre in Clydebank, which provides a valuable facility for children with special needs and their families and whose supporters have worked tirelessly to realise their objectives; and I also received significant help and encouragement from a variety of ex-players and journalists, including Alan Rough, William Paul, Stephen Pollock, Ian Angus, Graham Wilson, Russell Kyle, Andy Watson, Bob McKenzie and Gordon McGinn. I would also like to place on record my appreciation for the support and encouragement of John Mowat, who persuaded me to persist with this project when obstacles were put in my path.

I hope that those many Scots who relished Davie Cooper in his prime, regardless of their club affiliations, will feel that I have done his talents justice and that his story, despite its sad conclusion, is still very much worth celebrating. Andy Roxburgh once said, "Football isn't about robots" and he was absolutely correct. It is about heroes and their capacity to brighten up the dullest afternoons with shafts of brilliance, derring-do and magic tricks. Davie had that gift in abundance and none of us who saw him will ever forget that.

NEIL DRYSDALE
2013

CONTENTS

FOREWORD

BY ALLY McCOIST

There is one word which sums up how I feel when I think of the friendship I developed with Davie Cooper while the pair of us were at Rangers together in the 1980s. It is the same word which explains my emotions when I recall being on the same pitch as Davie, even as he produced pieces of genius on a regular basis for the team he adored.

That word is blessed.

Even now, reflecting on his career, I still regard myself as being blessed to have gained the chance to live and work and share football memories with Davie, whether at Ibrox, or when we were in Scotland squads, or just chewing the fat about the game we loved. I used to pick him up at Hamilton and drive him through to Glasgow, and straight from the outset, it was obvious that he had a touch of magic in his personality. But he never made a fuss about it. In fact, I never met a more down-to-earth lad than the youngster who did his absolute best to perform miracles by getting me to turn up for training on time!

There were always myths and misconceptions surrounding Davie, and some people believed that he sold himself short by not spreading his wings and playing in England, for instance. But the reality was that he loved his family, he was true to his friends, he idolised Rangers throughout his life, and it spoke volumes for his determination to stay close to his roots that his whole career was spent at just three clubs – Clydebank, Rangers and Motherwell – in the West of Scotland. Yes, he was an insular guy, in as much as he had his routine and the people he wanted to be around, but what's wrong with that?

In the modern age, some players seem to move from club to club almost on a yearly basis, but Davie was faithful to those he trusted, and he should never be condemned for showing loyalty to those who supported him. In my opinion, it should be quite the opposite. Part of the reason for him not leaving his homeland was his shyness – he just wasn't comfortable with being in the limelight – but the man had a passion for football, and I still remember the look on his face in the tunnel before he took part in big matches. His eyes lit up, he was 100 per cent committed and buzzing, and it made the rest of us feel better when we saw Davie in that mood, because we knew he could do extraordinary things and that knowledge lifted everybody around him in the dressing room.

He was a complex lad, but one of the tragic aspects of his untimely death in 1995 was the way in which he was becoming more outgoing and blossoming before our very eyes. And then he was gone. I honestly believe, towards the end of his playing career, that we were about to see another Davie Cooper, somebody who would have been a terrific coach and inspiration to young players in Scotland, because he was so enthusiastic about football that it rubbed off on all those around him. You could see him growing in confidence, thinking about his future, and not so much coming out of his shell as beginning to realise that he had talents which he could employ to help others. He never talked himself up, and was one of the most grounded boys I ever met, but I noticed a change in Davie after he came back from the 1986 World Cup in Mexico. It was almost as if he had begun to recognise that there was a big, wide world out there and he wanted to be part of it.

I saw him at close quarters for years and reckon Davie was much misunderstood. He had his mood swings, but they weren't an off-putting aspect of his character. If anything, it was an endearing quality when he used to have a grump and a moan to his mates, because it played right into our hands and we ribbed him about it, and that provoked good banter. It also demonstrated how much he cared and how professional he was in his attitude: some people, when they are bestowed with remarkable gifts, take things for granted and fall into the trap of believing their own publicity, but Davie never made that mistake. On the contrary, and having talked to fans at Motherwell and Clydebank who regard him as the greatest player to wear their jerseys, Davie was one of life's perfectionists wherever he went and there were no airs and graces, just a deep desire to be involved in football.

Some tried to argue that he wasn't the most dedicated of trainers, but again, I think that has been overstated. My take on the matter was that Davie liked training a lot more than he let on and it showed in the way that he kept looking to improve his standards during all the years he was at Rangers. He wasn't too keen on the running sessions, but if you threw him a ball and asked him to practise with it, he would be there until midnight and be the happiest man on the planet. We used to joke that Coop couldn't head the ball or use his right foot, but, basically, he didn't need to. Not when you looked at the damage he was capable of sparking with that incredible left peg against any quality of opposition, whether at Scottish club level, in Europe, or when he was representing his country.

I still have the memory of Davie weaving past would-be defenders, or taking sumptuous free kicks. Or of him creating havoc with a wonderful forty-yard pass or making difficult things look ridiculously easy. The conditions never bothered him and I have spoken to supporters who share my belief that he had it all and perhaps never fully appreciated how many of his compatriots were enthralled by the way he could light up any game with a feint, a shimmy or a mazy dribbling run which was worth the admission money on its own. These kinds of people are rare in sport, so they should be cherished. Somebody such as Davie wasn't merely a footballer – he was an entertainer and one of the best.

I feel blessed for another reason. And that is because my sons have the opportunity to enjoy Davie when he was at the height of his powers, thanks to the wonders of new technology. The great goals, the mesmerising artistry, the outrageous pieces of trickery: they are there on YouTube, or on DVD, and I would advise any youngsters with an interest in football to check them out.

Davie asked for little when he came in through the door at Ibrox every morning, except for some tea and toast and a quick glance at his paper. Flash cars, fashion accessories and the trappings of fame, held no attraction for him and that was another of his best attributes. Essentially, he was one of the old school, a modest lad who was happiest on his home turf. A real local hero of his generation.

I have never forgotten Davie Cooper and I never will. The fashion in which he was taken from us at just thirty-nine was very, very cruel. But it does mean that his talent never ages.

ALLY McCOIST
2013

1

GONE BEFORE HIS TIME

Every day, across the world, lives slip away amidst a vale of tears, usually within the confines of a hospital, hospice or in the privacy of one's own home. Sometimes, though, death is destined to happen in the full glare of publicity to young men and women, people with no history of illness or instability, for whom the clock simply stops too soon. David Attenborough described the process well when he observed in sombre tones, "There is always an element of chance in life which an individual can do little about." Yet, no matter how we strive to rationalise the process, nothing can properly prepare us for the moment when suddenly, cruelly, a human being disappears from our existence.

I was working in the old *Scotsman* newspaper building at Edinburgh's North Bridge on 22 March 1995, when grim tidings began to envelop the place, like the knife that ripped through the shower curtain in *Psycho*, spreading the message that something dreadful had happened to the footballer Davie Cooper. Phones began ringing on the sports desk, with inquiries from myriad colleagues, readers and total strangers, asking if we could shed any light on the rumours, and gradually as the hours passed it became clear that Cooper, a special talent, a healthy man with a relish for life, had suffered a terrible trauma. In itself, the details of his demise were tragic enough: the Rangers stalwart and the former Celtic luminary, Charlie Nicholas, had been filming a television series called *Shoot* for STV at Clyde's Broadwood stadium when, all of a sudden, Cooper collapsed and lay prostrate on the turf, the victim of a brain haemorrhage. He was given mouth-to-mouth resuscitation, his heart was massaged and the emergency services did their utmost to drag him back from the abyss, but it ultimately proved a forlorn exercise. One moment, he and his Scotland colleague Nicholas were swapping banter, indulging in practical jokes with the Scotland Under-21 coach Tommy Craig, and the atmosphere was replete with the down-to-earth language of football men enjoying the craic and company together. In the next breath, there was panic and anguish, allied to the screech of ambulances and as Tuesday turned into Wednesday the 23rd, his death was eventually confirmed, even though there were still many people who refused to believe it.

In our office, as in a thousand other places across the country, incredulity was the first emotion amidst that Tuesday heartbreak. "He was happy and relaxed, then the next thing I knew, I saw him lying on the ground," recalls Nicholas. "At first, the kids who were with us at the recording thought that he was clowning around, but, of course, I knew he was dreadfully ill. It was awful." Craig, one of the great unsung heroes of the Scottish game these past forty years, was equally distraught. "There was nothing untoward, no warning, to suggest that anything might be wrong with Davie," he remembers. "He had been as bright and bubbly as ever and we had all been enjoying ourselves that day. Then everything turned black and it was one of the worst experiences of my life."

Gordon Smith, one of Cooper's former Ibrox teammates, who subsequently became the SFA's chief executive as the prelude to returning to Rangers as the Glasgow club's director of football, was one of the first to learn that tragedy had occurred. "I was supposed to be meeting Davie the next day for lunch and I was looking forward to it, because he was in good spirits and he was really excited about starting the next chapter in his career after retiring from playing," says Smith. "Then I received a call from STV, asking me for a comment and it was like a blur: they were telling me that he had suffered a brain haemorrhage and he wouldn't survive and they were wondering if I could pay tribute to Davie. I was hearing the words from the person on the other end of the phone, but I wasn't taking them in. It had happened before to others and it has happened to other people since then, but nothing prepares you for these things. I was just numb."

His words reverberated across Scotland in the next few days. Indeed, even now, there are people who can't make sense of the haste with which Cooper's exit arrived. Years down the line, I travelled to Rugby Park to talk to Ally McCoist, one of Davie's former confreres, and the sense of *recherche du temps perdu* which surrounded McCoist was palpable. It was at odds with the common perception of the man as a cheeky Jack-the-Lad with a superficial gloss and a relentless, joke-a-minute line in repartee. Instead, McCoist chose to talk without his *Question of Sport* flippancy, speaking in hushed whispers whilst he remembered Cooper and contemplated the impending demise of another Ibrox legend, Jim Baxter. "You gradually come to realise there are bigger issues than football and that, when you suffer bereavement in your own household, all the sympathy and condolences in the world can't erase the pain and the loss," said McCoist, who lost his own father in the same year that Cooper died. "When you watch players like Davie and Jim, performing all their tricks on the pitch and loving the thrill of exciting the crowd, you tend to develop this impression that your heroes are immortal. Then you see what happened to Coop and now Jim and you are reminded that we are all too human.

"But, as time passes, you take some comfort from the memories these people have left behind. That is one of the wonderful things about football: you meet people from different walks of life with contrasting personalities and you go through the whole gamut of emotions with them. Davie was a quiet boy in the dressing room, very intense, very determined to do his best, whether it was for

Rangers or Scotland, whereas Jim was larger than life. But they were both special talents and you were privileged to watch them and take pleasure in what they were doing. I suppose that it's an escape from life. And that sensation of waking up on Saturdays and getting yourself psyched up for the kick-off – allied to the jokes and the wind-ups which are part of the daily training routines – are why so many of us love football and why it's difficult for us to call it quits."

In the aftermath of Cooper's death, the Scottish tabloids predictably portrayed him as one of Scotland's greats, a talismanic figure, blessed with every trick in his repertoire and unafraid to parade his skills whenever he had the opportunity. Given the circumstances in which he had been snatched away at only thirty-nine, it was understandable that there should be less focus on the man than the myth, but one had to turn to the broadsheets for more sober, prescient analysis. *The Independent*, for instance, struck the right tone:

Nobody who saw Davie Cooper in action at the peak of his career can doubt that he was one of the most gifted footballers Scotland has ever seen. The former Clydebank, Rangers and Motherwell player had a balletic grace when he embarked upon one of his runs, teasing opponents with an elegant left foot, and his precision at set pieces produced many vital goals. Cooper kept himself fit throughout his career and there was no hint of the tragedy that was to come. He started his playing career at humble Clydebank in 1974, lured on by a signing-on fee of £200, which had been raised by emptying the slot machines in the social club. But his genius was given an appropriate platform when he joined Rangers three years later for a fee of £100,000, and immediately helped them win the domestic Treble. He went on to collect three league titles at Ibrox, as well as three Scottish Cup and seven League Cup winner's medals. His ferociously struck free kick against Aberdeen in the 1987 League Cup final is remembered by many as one of his best goals. He moved to Motherwell in 1989 (for a fee of £50,000 – one of the ironies of Cooper was that, for all his brilliance, he did not command huge transfer fees), with whom he won a Scottish

Cup winner's medal in 1991. For a player of his enormous talent, 22 Scotland caps represented a meagre return, yet he scored vital goals for his country, none more so than the penalty which secured a draw against Wales in 1985 to take the Scots into a play-off and eventual qualification for the 1986 World Cup.

On that night, Cooper and his teammates experienced tragedy in football with the death of the manager, Jock Stein. 'It wasn't the best penalty I ever took, but, to be honest, everything about the night had been totally ruined,' he said at the time. He moved back to Clydebank on a free transfer in 1994 as player and had been set to retire at the end of the season, after twenty years in the professional game, where he shone at the highest level.

As a person, he was liked and respected by all those who came into contact with him, and a future in coaching or the media seemed likely. Graeme Souness, the former Rangers manager, rated Cooper as a more naturally gifted player than Kenny Dalglish and was convinced that he could have achieved worldwide fame if he had moved to Italian football. However, Cooper's skills transcended the great Glasgow divide as even the Celtic supporters recognised his great talent. The real tragedy of the death of Davie Cooper is that he was still playing the game. He wasn't a legend of yesteryear, finishing his days as an old man, but somebody revered for the player and person he was in the present. That is what makes his untimely death all the harder to accept.

The unvarnished tone of this tribute contains hints of the frustrations and contradictions which lurked beneath the surface with Cooper. If he had been born with more arrogance and less self-deprecation, he might have advanced his reputation, but he preferred to remain close to his roots, despite the fact that it hampered his progress. Even when he served up feats of individual lustre for his beloved Rangers, there were always supporters at Ibrox ready to criticise his work ethic or what they perceived as a tendency to drift out of matches, although for a long period of his career, he was their best and occasionally only hope.

In and around the emotional scenes which shrouded his funeral at Hillhouse Parish Church in Hamilton, Walter Smith, a man capable of recognising the burden which Cooper had borne, spoke movingly of his tristesse, whilst expressing the opinion in his eulogy, "God gave Davie Cooper a talent. He would not be disappointed with how it was used." Perhaps some in the congregation had not fully appreciated his gifts or recognised the routine derring-do with which he had sustained Rangers when they were languishing in the doldrums in the early stages of the 1980s, but Smith didn't make that mistake. On the contrary, he had been enraptured by Cooper's powers and subsequently made his feelings clear that he regarded him as a character with talent to burn. "The pressure on him must have been enormous, but the arrival of players such as Souness and [Terry] Butcher allowed Davie the freedom to play and he responded wonderfully well to the challenge. You can discuss his many match-winning displays and go into all the details, but all that really needs saying is that Davie was a magnificent footballer."

Yet if he possessed a swagger on the pitch, Cooper was plagued by self-doubts away from centre stage. In the early days, following his transfer into the goldfish bowl of Glasgow tribal rivalry – other-wise known as the Old Firm – he was quickly branded the "Moody Blue", a monicker which stuck, as a consequence of his refusal to be dragged into delivering pat quotes to the media. To some extent, this was because he had absorbed the lessons of how the newspapers – particularly in the aftermath of the ill-starred 1978 World Cup campaign in Argentina – were inclined to put their heroes on plinths, then chip away relentlessly at their pedestals, almost on a whim. More pertinently, he was shy, and whether feeling intimidated upon his entrance at Ibrox or worrying whether he would become tongue-tied during an interview, the young Cooper constantly fretted about his place in the grand scheme of things, as Gordon Smith explains:

"I was used to having stick flying around, and it was a normal part of the training sessions that if you made a mistake, you could expect to get pelters from the rest of the guys – it came with the territory and most of the comments were tongue in cheek. But Davie had a problem with the criticism and took it personally, and felt that he didn't get any respect from the older boys at Rangers. And he definitely went into his shell, which only made things worse. It wasn't vindictive, but Davie hadn't experienced anything like that before and he thought the lads were making a fool of him, which seems incredible when you think how much talent he had. Yet there was a shyness there, and insecurity, and it needed people like me and Bobby Russell to bring him round to the fact he was well regarded by the rest of the Rangers lads and they were simply having a laugh.

"The bigger problem for Davie was that he spent his whole career playing in Scotland, where you were considered a liability if you weren't a tackler and he was operating in an environment where it was still the norm for teams to hoof the ball up in the air and play at 100mph without anybody putting their feet on the ball and creating space for their colleagues. If Davie had come through in almost any other system, he would have run the midfield and he proved he could do that job excellently when he went to Motherwell. By playing him on the wing, his opportunities to parade his skills were limited, because you can't dictate a game from out wide, so it was a shame that he didn't spread his wings because I honestly believe that Davie Cooper, in his prime, would have fitted superbly into a Manchester United or Liverpool set-up and if he had been offered that chance, it wouldn't just have benefited him but the Scottish national side.

"At one stage, Alan Mullery tried to sign both me and Coop, and take us to England, but [the then Rangers manager] John Greig would only let him sign one of us and Alan probably made the wrong choice! Don't get me wrong, Coop loved Rangers, he relished being part of one of the biggest clubs in Britain, and he regularly demonstrated his gifts for his club, his country . . . wherever he went. But nowadays, he would be a midfield libero, he would be asked to bring vision, tricks and skill to the party and he would be a superstar. So yes, it is a source of regret that the place he played his football didn't do him any favours."

Those readers under thirty, or anybody who lived before the advent of the Internet and other technological innovations, might have only a vague recollection of Cooper's ability to conjure up wondrous exploits with a ball at his feet. Sometimes, he could drift through would-be tacklers as if they were cardboard cut-outs. On other occasions, he possessed the requisite vision and control to plot a course to his target like a chess grand-master thinking six or seven moves down the line.

During the 1979 Drybrough Cup final against Celtic at Hampden Park, he concocted a goal, straight from the pages of *Roy of the Rovers*, with an almost bewildering amalgamation of the outrageous and the unexpected. Collecting a pass from Alex MacDonald, Cooper nonchalantly flicked the ball up and over Roddie MacDonald, waltzed past Murdo MacLeod and Tom McAdam, then, as his foray gained momentum and the Ibrox aficionados began to sense they were witnessing something special, he confounded Alan Sneddon with another delicate chip, as the prelude to rifling a shot beyond Peter Latchford, who had no idea only fifteen or twenty seconds earlier that his line was about to be breached by a dazzling piece of sustained dexterity. Even Cooper subsequently described it as a once-in-a-lifetime strike, yet those who had followed his progress en route from Hamilton Academical to Rangers weren't unduly surprised by the apparent simplicity with which he dismantled Celtic. This, after all, was a fellow with the capacity for mastering feats which others could only dream about.

It's amazing how some individuals can leave starkly contrasting impressions on those who encounter them. Prior to my first meeting with Cooper, I had been forewarned by various people that he was "hard work", "an awkward bugger" and a "block of ice." Those of the Celtic-supporting persuasion went further and argued that he was one of the old school of Rangers acolytes, who was comfortable with the sectarianism which surrounded the Ibrox club, as well as the more positive aspects of the Old Firm's rivalry. In the event, I found him a genial, self-deprecating character who seemed more at home in a saloon bar watching horse racing than dressed in a suit and tie with a hundred flashbulbs popping in his face. By the stage he moved to Motherwell and discovered a renewed lease of life away from the spotlight, Cooper had come out of his shell and could twinkle when the occasion demanded, even if there was little doubt that he much preferred playing to being dragged to media functions.

In the bigger picture, he detested the whole religious backdrop to the antagonism between the Glasgow behemoths, and his attitude was summed up when he remarked, "I don't like Celtic and I don't like going to Parkhead, but that doesn't mean I don't like the Celtic guys. I do. And I have the greatest respect for men like Charlie [Nicholas], Roy [Aitken], Tommy [Burns] and Danny [McGrain]." Of the latter, Cooper declared, "At the peak of his career, he was one helluva of a player and he made my life a misery on a regular basis, because he was one of those full-backs who always liked to attack and he was forever going off on an overlap. That didn't suit me at all, because it meant that I had to chase back with him and whatever other attributes I might have had, chasing and tackling were not among them."

So, if he was a nugget, he was a nugget with an earthy response to adversity, who was always galvanised amidst the frenzy which habitually surrounds an Old Firm clash, without losing his sense of proportion. He needed that pragmatic approach throughout his years with Rangers because, despite his deep affection for the Govan organisation, he was often forced to bite his tongue or moan volubly to his teammates rather than to those who fielded him out of position and squandered his talents.

Graeme Souness, a man blessed or cursed (depending on your point of view) with the capacity to turn any minor kerfuffle into a full-scale row, labelled Cooper "Albert Tatlock", after the *Coronation Street* character, which brings to mind the words "pots" and "kettles", but at least Souness recognised the ability and advised his compatriot to test himself in a higher league. John Greig, however, another chap who amply fulfils P. G. Wodehouse's definition of a Scotsman with a grievance, was suspicious of Cooper from the outset, and the antipathy between the men was mutual. Long before one was master and the other servant, Greig had knocked lumps out of the teenage Cooper when Rangers tackled Clydebank and it was as if these diametrically opposed customers had decided from that juncture there was no point wasting breath on pleasantries or discussing the minutiae of total football.

All the same, that was no excuse for the fashion in which Cooper was made to feel increasingly isolated when he should have been at the peak of his career at Ibrox. Yet, oblivious to the fact that he was one of the few reasons why the hard-core support still shelled out their admission money, Greig marginalised one of his star perform-ers, boxed Cooper into a corner and, rather as Souness subsequently did with McCoist, seemed to think that if he could generate suffi-cient friction a brassed-off player would eventually demand a trans-fer. It didn't work, and did neither party nor their club any favours. On the contrary, according to one former Rangers player whom I contacted – and who requested anonymity – matters reached the stage where Greig wouldn't even deign to speak to Cooper as their relationship mouldered while Rangers hit the skids.

"You have to understand that John couldn't handle the situation where he had to risk falling out with the supporters, so he got other people to do the hard parts of his job. This was a time when the club was really, really struggling to keep pace, not just with Celtic, but Aberdeen and Dundee United as well, and the crowds just vanished. There were some nights where you could have heard a pin drop at Ibrox, until the booing started at the end and five seasons passed without Rangers winning the title, which seemed like an eternity for everybody at the club.

"Basically, John was out of his depth, and the worse the results got, the more irritable he became. Coop was a natural target, because

John felt that he should have been working harder than he was, but the gaffer didn't seem to understand that you can't keep dropping somebody like Davie and expect him to perform miracles on the few afternoons he got onto the pitch. By the end, I remember that John wouldn't bother telling Coop that he was being dropped – instead, he sent his assistant, Joe Mason, down to the dressing room to pass on the bad news and, as you can realise, that just made the atmosphere worse between the two men.

"This was when Davie was twenty-six, twenty-seven, twenty-eight . . . it was a period when he should have been the key man in the Rangers side and becoming an automatic pick for Scotland. But for much of these five years John walked by him in the corridor without speaking to him and Davie knew that his face didn't fit with the boss. Looking back, it all seems very petty and small-minded. But you also have to appreciate that John was given the job before he was ready for it and he had barely walked in the door before he talked to the board about money and found he was in a no-win situation. The board didn't have loads of cash for new faces and a lot of the team were going over the hill. So Greig was in a difficult position from day one. He wanted hard men around him, guys who would play the way that he used to do and would pretty much rely on perspiration, not inspiration. Well, that was never going to suit Coop, was it?"

In which light, it was a testimony to the player's professionalism that he kept his head down, ignored the recurring references to "Moody Blue", and persevered in the thankless role of entertainments convenor within an increasingly barren milieu as the great Rangers squad, assembled by Jock Wallace – who was both a sergeant major *and* a surrogate father to Cooper – was scattered to the wind, either through players being transferred to England or further afield or simply running out of gas.

By the mid-1980s, Rangers were a rabble, and their deficiencies had been exposed by Alex Ferguson and Jim McLean at Aberdeen and Dundee United, but although there must have been a temptation to cut and run, Davie clung to the wreckage, awaited redemption and, as his former teammate, Billy Davies – another proud son of Lanarkshire – told me, that dedication beyond the call of duty was one of the reasons why he revered Cooper:

"Davie was his own man, but he helped me an awful lot when I joined Rangers in 1980. I was only fifteen and it was a life-changing experience when I suddenly found myself standing next to all these international players, but I spent a lot of time with Coop and he took the trouble to encourage me and we became good mates, on and off the pitch. The thing about Davie was that he liked his own space, he had his own way of doing things and you got used to that if you knew him. For instance, he never turned up for the pre-season photographs – he really wasn't comfortable with people fussing about him – but he was a manager's dream, because he cared passionately about his football and never let anything else get in the way of doing his best for Rangers throughout his career.

"Looking back, Davie did have a problem with the press. He didn't hate them, but he was misrepresented by the tabloids in particular and his attitude was that he wasn't prepared to help them if they were going to knife him in the back. I respected that. As far as Coop was concerned, some of the journalists had an agenda, and it wasn't positive, and he just wouldn't rise to the bait or get involved in their games. He was never a big party animal in any case, and preferred spending time with a few friends, so he was never going to be relaxed in the company of strangers, but as he grew older, he mellowed and I think he recognised that the press had a job to do and he would trust them to do it in the right way. If they didn't, well there was no point in dealing with folk you don't trust.

"In that respect, I suppose he was a hero to me. He couldn't stand bulls*** and he was a straight-down-the-line guy. He sat me down when I was wet behind the ears on a tour of Canada in 1980 and told me how to handle the media and deal with the distractions, and his message was that you should count your blessings to be getting paid for playing football and cherish the experience. Some folk tried to portray him as dour or miserable, somebody who was in the game for what he could get out of it, but that's garbage! Ask the kids he was coaching on the last day of his life. Ask the Motherwell youngsters whom he helped at every turn when he came to Fir Park in 1989. Ask the fans for whom he signed hundreds of autographs. Basically, he was one of the most grossly misrepresented men I have ever known, yet he would have done anything to help those who needed it, whatever their background, and that is how I will always remember Davie Cooper."

Whether for his club or country, he could scintillate and motivate those around him, but once again the feeling persists that Cooper was born before his time. In the 1980s, with the likes of Jock Stein and Alex Ferguson at the helm of the national team, the Scots remained in thrall to physicality over any notion of sophistication. Almost everybody I spoke to whilst writing this book expressed surprise or even amazement that Cooper only mustered 22 caps, but there again, as some observed, he was never inclined to wrap himself in the Saltire or regard international recognition as anything particularly special. This wasn't due to lack of patriotism or problems with the SFA, but simply a question of pragmatic common sense for a young man from Hamilton, who knew that Rangers paid his mortgage, and his first loyalty was therefore to Ibrox, rather than Park Gardens.

In any case, after the folly associated with the 1978 World Cup campaign – a catalogue of errors which now strikes one as comic, with the late Ally MacLeod running the show about as efficiently as if Basil Fawlty had been installed as the manager of the Ritz Hotel – there had been a change of emphasis and downplaying of expectations, following the conclusion of the Argentine post-mortems. Cooper wasn't alone in believing that MacLeod hadn't been up to the job in the first place, but nor was he convinced that one man should have been made the scapegoat while the SFA continued on their have-money-will-travel junkets. Ultimately, therefore, whereas he might just have provided solutions on the road to Argentina,

Cooper's brand of virtuosity and trickery didn't have the same appeal for those in Stein's mould who were seeking to restore the country's credibility, first during the 1982 World Cup and thereafter to the 1986 event.

Craig Brown was among the "Big Man's" backroom staff, as the former Celtic boss brought his management skills to bear on his homeland. It wasn't pretty, and Stein grew frustrated at the stop-start nature of his job, where friendly matches were fitted in to accommodate the SFA's financial requirements, rather than for the benefit of the players, a situation which led to increasing call-offs from Scotland duty by those Scots at Liverpool and elsewhere, ostensibly due to niggles and strains, but principally because such luminaries as Alan Hansen and Graeme Souness knew that their club could reign in Europe, but their country was never going to be a threat on the international stage.

And yet, as Brown argues, there should have been greater scope for somebody with Cooper's gifts to have established himself as an integral member of the Scotland line-up in the 1980s, particularly given the abundance of evidence that he was eminently capable of raising his level of performance when surrounded by other quality personnel:

"It's all summed up for me by the fact that when I was coaching at Motherwell, we took an interest in Davie and one of our scouts went to have a look at him. In these days, you got a mark out of 10 in ten different disciplines – such as heading, tackling and ball control – and Coop only scored 58 out of 100. What these marks couldn't point out was the sheer brilliance somebody like him was capable of with the ball at his feet, and that exposed all the flaws in the report system. It didn't cater for somebody who had the ability to ghost past defenders and create something out of nothing, as Davie did throughout his career, whether it was for Rangers, Motherwell or Scotland.

"It was a similar story at the 1986 World Cup, where we needed to beat Uruguay in our final match and Alex Ferguson plumped for Eamonn Bannon over Cooper. It wasn't a stupid selection – Eamonn was a tireless performer, although he didn't have the inspirational qualities of Cooper – and Alex's preference was for tough lads, because he knew the South Americans would be taking no prisoners in that match. But they were reduced to ten men in the very first minute, and, with hindsight, it was pretty obvious that all they were interested in after that was getting a draw. There were a few question marks over Coop's work rate, but not from me – I always thought he had an excellent work ethic – and it wasn't until late in the game that he was introduced and immediately showed what we had been missing. Unfortunately, he didn't have enough time to unlock the Uruguay defence, but it was definitely another case of what might have been.

"The sad thing is that Davie was almost too honest for his own good. It cost him caps and limited his international appearances, because he never wanted anybody to accuse him of not giving 100 per cent for his country. In the build-up to the 1990 World Cup in Italy, three of the contenders were struggling with injury – John Robertson, Richard Gough and Davie Cooper – and Andy [Roxburgh] asked them all, 'Are you going to be fit for this tournament? Not just one or two games, but the whole event?' Gough said that he was, but no sooner had he gone to the World Cup than he was crocked and I never picked him again after that; whereas Coop told us that he wouldn't be fit for the Costa Rica game, but he would be ready for the Sweden fixture. And that meant that he was ruled out of competing in what would have been his last stab at World Cup glory. But you couldn't blame the lad – he was being as straight down the line as he always was.

"In fact, that summed up Davie for me. He was a consummate professional and he didn't want to earn any reward through deceit, unlike one or two other players I could mention. Andy Roxburgh once made a video tribute to Coop and some of the things he could do with a ball were quite extraordinary. But he had practised them for hours, growing up as a kid in Hamilton, and he had something of Jimmy Johnstone about him, in that he could beat players through sheer skill and artistry and he could do it inside or outside you, which made him such a dangerous opponent. The likes of Willie Henderson were hard to play against, but the bottom line was he usually had to depend on his pace to create chances. Whereas with Davie, he could leave you bewildered and beaten with skill and he was in love with tricks and constantly trying new things. Of course, they didn't always come off – that applies to any footballer – but the fact that he only gained 22 caps says more about the environment he was playing in than it does about Davie himself and I think he could have won another ten or twelve caps if he had been more dishonest."

What an indictment this is of the prevailing culture in Scottish football. And yet, eighteen years after his death, one suspects Cooper would be even more disillusioned with the state of the game in his homeland. At least, in his heyday, the SFA's finest made a habit of reaching the finals of major tournaments, even if their results once they arrived there suggested that they were simply along for the party. Nowadays, though, there is a genuine sense of drift and disillusionment, a consequence both of the plummeting standard of the Scottish Premier League and a failure by the sport's administrators to address the difficulties from the ground floor. We have had reviews, Think Tanks (although whether that was ever actually delivered is a moot point), political initiatives and cross-party displays of concern at Holyrood, without anything happening to stop Scotland's unhappy toboggan ride down the Cresta Run of the FIFA rankings.

Yet Cooper saw this scenario looming on the horizon, even in the 1980s. He denounced the "hammer-throwers" masquerading as footballers, berated the Scottish obsession with guts and grit over skill and precision and, quite correctly, lambasted the philosophy within Scotland's so-called premier tournament. His critics might argue that Rangers didn't exactly help in developing youth by snapping up the best talent from other clubs and – while English sides were banned from Europe – importing the likes of Terry Butcher, Chris Woods and Graeme Roberts from south of the Border. But that doesn't negate Cooper's candid assertion, made in 1987, that the Scottish game needed to adapt or face the consequences, something which it still stubbornly refuses to accept.

After all, who among us can quibble with this damning assessment?

As Cooper told a *Record* journalist is 1987: "Any decent player gets the ability kicked out of him, whereas in Europe, you are given more time on the ball and, therefore, there is a greater chance of the finer points of the game flourishing. That isn't the case here, where a fair number of our matches are like the games we had at school, when it was thirty-two-a-side and everybody charged about like headless chickens. Not only that, but they are really tall headless chickens, and I sometimes wonder if a lot of our players are only in the game because they are over six feet tall. Height and strength seem to be considered the right qualifications, whereas skill and ability are almost secondary in many places. Some of these guys would kick their grandmothers and it's difficult, with the best will in the world, to see how a Diego Maradona or a Michael Laudrup would survive in that company. It all leaves me a bit frustrated and I am sure there are other players who feel exactly the same way."

From this distance, these appear remarkably prescient words from somebody who endured as much grief from troglodyte defenders as anybody in his domain. In one respect, they merely reinforce the impression that Cooper, no matter how much we might admire his skills and relish his penchant for cabaret performances in the midst of a dogfight, and for all that we might empathise with his decision to stay loyal to his friends and family and ignore the lucrative offers he received to venture to a bigger, better league, was ultimately confounded by the mediocrity with which he was surrounded. That wasn't his fault, or at least not if you value such qualities as camaraderie, pride in family, and a refusal to become obsessed with pound signs and the trappings of fame. But when he embarked on a love affair with Rangers, the club he had supported as a wee boy in Hamilton, and the organisation to whom he offered yeoman service for more than a decade, it was hard not to feel that most of the passion went in the one direction.

Perhaps that explains the outpouring of grief at his untimely demise and the shared melancholia between the rival factions of Glasgow's blue and green tribes: the thought nagging away subconsciously that Scotland never fully appreciated Cooper's class until it was too late to tell him, hence the lachrymose scenes on that chill March day at Hillhouse Parish Church. He wouldn't have been comfortable in the spotlight, or at least not once he was off the pitch, and he might have laughed sardonically at some of the tributes paid to him, but his name still evokes images of a young man, weaving in and feinting out of centre stage, as he left an army of bewildered defenders in his wake.

It's not a bad way to be remembered even if he was gone too soon. But, for the moment, we have to press the rewind button back to a February day in Hamilton in 1956.

2

A STAR RISES IN THE WEST

Joni Mitchell was right. Sometimes you don't know what you've got till it's gone. When Davie Cooper was born in Hamilton on 25 February 1956, he entered the world at almost the same time as a whole generation of gifted Scottish footballers, who were destined, at least on international duty, to become synonymous with hard-luck stories, quirks of fate and embarrassing anecdotage. Frank McGarvey came a month after Cooper, and others to arrive kicking and screaming in the same year were Steve Archibald, David Narey, Tommy Burns, Davie Provan and Paul Sturrock. In fact, when one casts a glance over those names from the mid-1950s – Willie Miller, Gordon Strachan, Bobby Russell and Graeme Souness were all born within eighteen months on either side of Cooper – the biggest surprise wasn't that Scotland should have enjoyed a prolific period of qualifying for World Cups from 1974 onwards, but that they achieved so little success at the finals of major tournaments. As we will discover, it wasn't for lack of individual talent.

On the contrary, their homeland in that period was awash with football and little else to occupy the minds of working-class children. Cooper, the son of Jean and John, and little brother to John Jnr, grew up in surroundings which were typical of the time: a luxury-free zone where men worked on Christmas Day, women engaged in a bewildering array of household tasks and child-bearing which left many of them old at forty-five, and the notion of mortgages, cash machines and colour televisions, let alone the Internet, Twitter and Facebook, were the stuff of science fiction, and of the far-fetched variety at that.

In these circumstances, it was hardly surprising that the Coopers were a close-knit, down-to-earth family, with a passionate regard for football in general and Glasgow Rangers in particular. Davie's father was employed at the Lanarkshire Steel Works in Motherwell, and his mother, once the boys had gone to school, found herself a job behind the bar at the Lariat hostelry in their hometown. If it sounds a modest background, it was no better or worse than that experienced by tens of thousands of Scots as they adapted to the demise of rationing and the creation of rock'n'roll. When Davie was born, he and his parents stayed in a flat at 4 Barrack Street in Hamilton; later, in the early 1960s, the four of them moved to a similar dwelling at 25 Brankholm Brae in nearby Hillhouse, which was the sort of unprepossessing industrial landscape where nobody noticed how poor they were, because everybody else in the street was in exactly the same situation.

As somebody who vaguely recalls these days, the first observation worth making is that football was the glue which brought both social cohesion and an escape from drudgery and day-to-day routines, even if the Old Firm's sectarianism baggage in the west of the country inflicted myriad scars whenever the clubs locked horns. For those of us who weren't blessed with Cooper's skills, any patch of blaes or, praise be, grass, still offered the opportunity to dream of wearing a Scotland jersey and scoring the winning goal against England (who, despite the proximity to the end of the Second World War, were usually the enemy, and especially after they had collected the World Cup in 1966). With hindsight, considering that every weekend there was hardly an inch of unused turf throughout Glasgow, as countless teams vied for supremacy at junior, juvenile and amateur level, the emergence of a Celtic collective, capable of winning the European Cup in 1967, the same year that Rangers lost in the Cup Winners' Cup final to Bayern Munich, owed less to good fortune than the tireless endeavours of an army of peripatetic scouts, unpaid volunteers and other grassroots stalwarts who loved the game and relished the chance to unearth, encourage and support fresh talent. Back then, Scottish football was a truly democratic environment, where those with promise would earn an opportunity at some level to advance to a more exalted plane. And although it would be absurd to pretend that Cooper and his compatriots were living in any bounteous land of milk, honey and half-time oranges, his international confrere, Alan Rough, paints a vivid picture of how these formative years offered an escape route from the alternative career options of working in the collieries, steelworks, shipyards or as a council tradesman:

"Every Saturday and Sunday, wherever we could find pitches, the only thought in our minds was to organise matches of six-a-side, or twenty-two-a-side, and the weather, the state of the facilities or the prospect of looming exams were irrelevant. If it snowed and then froze in the winter, as it frequently did, we would use mounds of sand to mark out impromptu pitches; if it rained (as it even more frequently did!), we would clamber over walls and sneak into car parks and kick lumps out of one another on slabs of concrete. Luxuries only went as far as the occasional present of a new strip or a leather ball, but that didn't matter to us in those days. We had football and our mates and from the moment the bell rang at school and the two best players assembled everybody else together, picked their best pal, and then gradually moved down the line until there were only two kids left, who usually wound up as the goalies, nothing else entered our hearts or minds, because the lot of us were just happy to be in our own little world.

"I don't exaggerate: football was my life, as it was for thousands of us. Youngsters in Scotland nowadays have grass surfaces, Astroturf pitches and community centres with floodlit facilities, but we had none of these things and we didn't care. Our matches were fought out on red ash or on a variety of gravel and blaes pitches and we competed on that stuff, week in, week out. I can remember many afternoons where I would be sitting in a tiny dressing room, picking bits of grit out of my legs and the wounds were stinging, and it must have been worse for the likes of Davie Cooper, because he was trying to get past great hulking defenders who had quickly worked out that the best way to stop tricky wee lads was to kick them up in the air until they got tired of the pain and ran away home. But although it was a tough environment, we never thought about complaining."

Right from the outset, there was never any question that Cooper and football would go together as harmoniously as Rodgers and Hammerstein. There is a picture in the *Hamilton Advertiser* archives of the toddler, at eighteen months, holding a ball, with a beatific expression on his face, and even once he moved from Beckford Street Primary School to Udston Primary when the Coopers flitted to Hillhouse, his focus was always on sport rather than unduly worrying about arithmetic or English. In some respects, he fitted the stereotype of the working-class boy with more brains in his feet than his head, but this was an overly simplistic interpretation, because even from an early age there were facets of Cooper's personality which diverged from the normal and demanded analysis.

Firstly, and strikingly, in view of subsequent events, he was introverted from the earliest days, a quiet child, who seemed happier to stay indoors and play with his toys than venture outdoors into the harum-scarum milieu of the park and sand pit. Sometimes, it is the youngest of the brood who is allowed to forge his own path in life and develop an outgoing, gregarious nature, but, in this case, John Cooper, three years older than Davie, was the roaring boy who rushed outside and into scrapes and mischief, adopting the attitude that the best means of surviving in a community such as Hamilton was by getting your retaliation in first. By comparison, and as he admitted, Davie was a timorous bairn, who preferred the security offered by being close to his parents and was "more or less a mummy's boy", which meant that if the choice lay between the risk of getting his hands dirty or pushing his Dinky cars across the living room, he plumped for the latter.

None of this was especially unusual, yet it demonstrates that the notion that Cooper turned into a "Moody Blue" was simply absurd. Instead, he was always uninterested in the notion of strutting around the playground or indulging in the recreations which might have pushed him into trouble with his teachers, and eventually matters reached the point where the bold John decided it was high time that his brother came out of his shell. Even in terms of launching his football career, it was a wise step, given that until he was eight or nine, the sport ranked low on his list of priorities and surprisingly, given his ball skills, Davie was initially shoved in goal in order to make up the numbers – where, perhaps unsurprisingly, he performed with all the natural athleticism and balletic poise of a couple of tanked-up members of the Tartan Army trying to sprint up an escalator.

But gradually, as he embraced the soccer culture and forged friendships with those who populated the Hamilton youth circuit, Cooper not only grew in confidence but began to serve notice of his burgeoning skills between the age of ten and twelve. Physically, he had filled out, and switched between left-half and inside-left for the Udston Primary team with sufficient élan that he was installed as captain: the sort of psychological boost which allowed his talent to flourish even as his early indifference metamorphosed into an obsession with everything football. Stevie Bollan was one of his contemporaries who witnessed the transformation and, even now, describes it as inspirational to behold:

"Davie was one of those boys who practised away for hours and was never happy unless he was close to a football and he could work on his dribbling or his keepie-uppie, or see if he could get the ball to come back off the kerb when it was too wet to play on the grass pitches. It was funny, because when you think of how much he eventually achieved during his career, he took a while to catch the football bug, but once he had got it, there was no stopping him. I remember that the word started to go round Hamilton that there was a young lad who was really talented playing for the Udston team and they went from strength to strength while was there. One year, they won the Shinwell Cup – which was a big deal in the town – after beating Low Waters Primary 4–2 in the final at Douglas Park, and although that was the first time that he had played in front of such a big crowd, he was in his element, scored one of Udston's goals and basically ran the whole show.

"Sometimes you find in youth football that the late developers are the best players when they get to their teens, but Davie never made any grand claims for himself. One or two of the other laddies thought they were the bee's knees, and it swelled their heads a bit, but that was never the case with Davie. If anything, when some of the rest of us started taking an interest in girls, he only had one thing on his mind and that was football. This was in the late 1960s and you had The Beatles and the Rolling Stones on the go, and a lot of the girls had a crush on Davie, but he couldn't be bothered with any of that stuff when he was at school. Instead, he rushed home every day, was in and out to get his football, and he was the last to go home for his tea. Then, within ten or fifteen minutes, he would be scooting back to the park and moaning when it got dark too early for his liking."

When he wasn't involved on the pitch, Cooper's weekends were occupied in following Rangers, and he was as delighted as anybody else in thrall to Ibrox when they triumphed in the 1972 European Cup Winners' Cup against Moscow Dynamo. It was a reminder of the standards which Scottish clubs aspired to in that period, and even if some people continue to argue with some justification that the Old Firm have had a malign influence on their country, there was no denying the jinky *joie de vivre* with which Davie and his father walked down to Burnbank most Saturdays to get a lift from a regular at the Lariat Bar, who just happened to be called John Stein. On other occasions, Davie sometimes travelled alone on the pub's supporters' bus, and these excursions to Glasgow were the first time that Cooper came to realise what it meant to be involved with Rangers. He loved the atmosphere of the stadium, ignored the more queasy connotations of some of the chants from the terraces, and revelled in the exploits of performers of the calibre of Colin Stein and Willie Johnston. Yet there was no trace of him being star-struck or of copying those he was watching. Far from it. Others in the Udston ranks sought to imitate their heroes, but Cooper wanted to blaze his own path and that individualistic, slightly cussed streak had both positive and negative effects.

On the plus side, he continued to work tirelessly on his game, oblivious to his mother's warnings that he would give himself indigestion if he didn't slow down, and his repertoire of tricks was expanding sufficiently to attract the attention of a number of youth scouts, who purred with delight at the young maestro's feints and dummies. But, rather less auspiciously, when Cooper advanced from Udston Primary to St John's Grammar, he was discomfited by the switch, told his mates that he detested the place – and school in general – and there was a brief sign of the indecision and mood swings which occasionally troubled him through his life. Most of his resentment towards St John's stemmed from the fact that they had no organised football until third year, but one also detects a frustration where even small things conspired to leave him raging at the world. As for the reports in some quarters that he was bullied at the new school, this wouldn't have been an uncommon occurrence for a twelve-year-old boy in a tough area – and I recall how scared I was during my first week at Whitburn Academy when some of us were greeted to the place by having our heads stuck down the toilet! But one of his former classmates who spoke to me in confidence told me that part of Cooper's problems was his reluctance to go with the flow and fit into the new schedule: once again, that maverick streak which drove him on was also driving him up a cul-de-sac of vulnerability:

"Davie Cooper was a perfectionist, pure and simple. He ate, breathed and slept football and couldn't give a stuff for anything else, which was all right for him, but not for the rest of us, who had to worry about passing exams and trying to make something of our lives. There was one night where Davie tried to get us to come out and play football – this was a couple of days before our exams – and he was actually crying in frustration because we told him we were too busy studying. Tears were running down his cheek, and he even started swearing at us, which was unusual, because Davie wasn't into using bad language for the sake of it. But he got really depressed and cheesed-off during that first year.

"There were other things going on as well. Davie started noticing the girls and got himself distracted. He was trying to keep his head down at a school he hated and carry on his football, but his body was changing and he was trying to do too much too quickly. What came out of it was his impatience with people who weren't prepared to help him and his frustration with rules and regulations at school. I think if somebody had come along and offered him a full-time contract at twelve, he would have signed on the dotted line and never worried about education again in his life. But, of course, that wasn't an option, and when you are desperate to do something and you think you are being held back from doing it, two years can seem an eternity. So, Davie was miserable for a while."

Salvation and portents arrived in equal measure. Two friends of his parents, Bill and Rose McKenzie, decided to establish a youth team, called Udston United, and one of their first recruits was Cooper, all bristling purpose and tireless industry. When he wasn't involved in training and playing, the teenager helped sell raffle tickets, knocked on doors to let the local people know about the club's foundation, and generally demonstrated that when he believed in something, Davie was happy to muck in with his comrades. By this juncture, football was his be-all and end-all – any ephemeral interest in other things, such as education, tennis or athletics had been rapidly extinguished – and, as he progressed from the Udston ranks to Hamilton Avondale, another local organisation, run by a pair of brothers, Alan and Stuart Noble, Cooper already began stacking up honours in the lower leagues. Despite being one of the youngest lads in the Under-16 (and subsequently Under-18) team, he was now courting attention from senior authorities and there was a sense of inevitability when he was selected to represent Scotland's Amateur League side.

Gone was the petulance which had bedevilled him at St John's, and in its wake was a burning determination to seize these opportunities with both hands. This, let's remember, was a period when the Scottish game was enjoying a halcyon period, hot on the heels of Celtic and Rangers' European successes and the improving fortunes of the national side, who were in the process of qualifying for the 1974 World Cup finals in Germany, even as Cooper was involved in three home international youth fixtures against England, Northern Ireland and Wales. At sixteen, Cooper's globe was spinning on its axis and even though he heeded his father's advice and accepted a job as an apprentice printer, working in the Nobles' office in Hamilton, nobody seriously imagined that he would have to fall back on a trade when he was garnering rave reviews and widespread attention.

Nonetheless, he was wise to exhibit his application away from football. After all, Davie had witnessed at first hand how the game can swallow you up and spit you out without a second glance. His older brother, John, had displayed sufficient soccer ability to command interest from south of the Border, but when he travelled down to Hull City at the age of sixteen, his experience was the opposite of the high life he might have anticipated. As a mercurial winger with an instinctive touch, he was optimistic that he would cut the mustard in the professional ranks, but these were the days when defenders were able to scythe through their opponents like Old Father Time without seeing yellow or red and John couldn't handle the constant niggle, allied to the incessant glare of publicity from the local press, and gradually became horribly homesick in his modest digs.

In some ways, this was the worst possible scenario that could have materialised, not only for John, who returned to his roots after two traumatic years in England and joined the junior ranks at Larkhall Thistle, but also for Davie, who used his brother's privations as a reason to stay close to his origins for the rest of his career, even though he acknowledged, privately, that he was more dedicated and talented than John. However, that recognition sat uneasily with his own inner feelings and, given that he had developed into a local Hamilton hero, it was relatively straightforward to linger in his backyard.

Still, that didn't deter the scouts. Up they came from Coventry City, from Crystal Palace, and from Southampton and they tried out their various sales pitches, working on the assumption that Davie would be persuaded by some glossy brochures and smooth talking. What they couldn't have predicted when Cooper listened politely to their overtures and then declined them all was that he had no intention of going anywhere for the foreseeable future while there were opportunities to prosper in Scotland. From a neutral perspective, it is difficult not to believe his approach was overly parochial and that he might have done himself a favour, on and off the field, by leaving the nest. Yet when you are a grand poisson in a small pond, the motivation to move elsewhere can prove elusive.

At any rate, Cooper maintained he had time on his side. There was a trial with Clyde and an offer of £4 a week, followed by a liaison with Motherwell and their manager, Ian St John, of "Saint and Greavesie" fame. (He reckoned that Cooper required beefing up, and proposed farming him out to the Juniors, at which point the conversation was terminated abruptly). Next up, Clydebank entered the bidding stakes and, initially at least, Davie was concerned about the rivalry which existed between them and Hamilton.

To those with less talent, his procrastination might seem remarkable, but we have to bear in mind that despite all the glowing reviews, Cooper wasn't wholly convinced that he could make the transition to the senior ranks and his response to learning that

Rangers were interested in his services in 1973 speaks volumes about the man's innate caution and low self-esteem. Where others would have danced with joy, Davie rejected their invitation on the basis that he believed there would be such a production line of players whirling in and out of Ibrox that he would never gain an opportunity to make a favourable impression. Celtic, too, approached him in a bid to commence negotiations, after tracking his progress at Hamilton Avondale and, considering that these were the days when Jock Stein was trying to recruit new blood to fill the boots of his nine-in-a-row league-winning side, Cooper's declaration that he wasn't prepared to hang around in the reserves didn't make a positive impression with the Big Man. It was hardly a Micawberish philosophy, nor an especially courageous stance, but there again the bars of Glasgow are packed with characters who once had a trial for the Old Firm and have been supping their pints on thoughts of what might have been for the last thirty or forty years. Whatever Cooper's future, he had resolved that it would be in Scotland and it would be on his own terms or not at all.

And, amazingly, for a while, it looked as if it might actually be the latter. As he advanced beyond his eighteenth birthday and became too old to participate on Avondale's behalf, Davie began to drift out of the game and focused on his employment with the Nobles. He enjoyed a flutter on the horses, flirted occasionally with tennis and was comfortable – too comfortable, in some people's eyes – with being a few minutes away from his parents. Even those who have no truck with the contemporary ambition of so many youngsters to acquire so-called "celebrity" might blanch at the dexterity with which he edged out of the spotlight and settled into a domestic routine, which revolved around a small inner circle – John and Jean, Bill and Rose McKenzie and his older brother. But there again, this was the same boy who had ventured on holiday to Rimini when he was twelve and instead of delighting in his first foreign sojourn, spent most of the ensuing vacation, amidst the heat, sea and sand, worrying about his pet dog, Scot. In which light, his subsequent admission, "I guess I am essentially very family-orientated and don't like to stray too far from my domestic scene," encapsulated the peculiar brand of dynamics at work with this fellow. It was as if he was a child of the 1930s, not the 1960s.

Thankfully, from a footballing perspective, the Nobles kept reminding Cooper that his talent wasn't something to be wasted and that he would regret it later on in life if he passed up the opportunity to test himself on the professional circuit. Yet by the time he reached eighteen, he had finished his apprenticeship, was barely involved in sport whatsoever – apart from having a punt on the Grand National! – and claimed to be savouring his day-to-day work involved in printing tickets, programmes, pamphlets and other publications behind closed doors in the firm's Almada Street offices. Stuart Noble was aghast at the situation and, unbeknown to his employee, decided to pursue matters on his own initiative by making contact with the Clydebank chairman, Jack Steedman.

"Davie was a mass of contradictions," Stuart Noble recalls. "On the one hand, he had what is often described in Scotland as a 'guid conceit of himself'. He had made up his mind that he wasn't going to spend his time slumming with a lower-league club, because he thought he was better than that. Looking back, he was right. But on the other hand, he created some problems for himself because he didn't seem to understand that every club had a pecking order and you couldn't just expect to waltz into the first team at a high-level organisation.

"I remember one Monday morning, where he had turned down all these offers from English teams, and he walked in with the attitude that he could afford to wait: sooner or later, he would secure the deal of which he was worthy. This situation had gone on long enough that he had actually stopped playing the game, so I eventually said to him, 'Davie, where do you want to play football?' He looked at me and replied, 'At Rangers, Celtic or Hibs. And in that order.' Well, I knew the Old Firm had already tried to sign him up and he had turned them down, for one reason or another, so I phoned Hibs and asked to speak to their then-manager Eddie Turnbull [one of the Easter Road side's illustrious 'Famous Five']. At first, he didn't believe that Davie hadn't already signed for the Old Firm or one of the big clubs in England, but when I told him that he was a free agent, he said, 'That's brilliant. Tell him to come over to Easter Road.'

"But Davie was Davie. He had his own way of doing things and expected others to understand that, without spelling it out in words. When we told him about the response from Mr Turnbull, he assumed that it meant he was going to be playing for the First XI the following Saturday. And because Hibs were away to Morton, Davie fixed up a lift with one of his mates so that he could make the trip to Greenock. The reality was that Mr Turnbull wanted him to turn out for Hibs Thirds against Gala Fairydean and when Davie didn't make the trip that was the end of Mr Turnbull's dealings with him. I could see where Davie was coming from – he knew he was good and he wasn't going to waste his time with amateurs or junior football, or even in reserve teams. But it was definitely a gamble on his part. In the event, it worked out for the best, but there were a lot of us who were worried that he was going to end up with nothing because of his attitude."

Finally, though, after an excessive amount of swithering, Davie was persuaded to have a chat with Steedman, one of those wily operators who rivalled Arthur Daley for *chutzpah*, sharp wits and thinking on his feet, and who deserves credit both for igniting the spark which ignited Cooper's career, and for transforming his club into a force to be reckoned with on the Scottish circuit. In the days leading up to their meeting, he spoke to the Nobles and Bill and Rose McKenzie, while taking the trouble to learn about Davie's past and astutely concluded that the best way of sealing the deal was to combine class, panache and hard cash into an offer which couldn't be refused. It was an alluring combination, and from the moment Steedman arrived outside the print works in a resplendent new Jaguar and began painting a rosy tableau of how the teenager could become a star in the game, his protégé was transfixed. He grew even more interested when the older man took an envelope out of his pocket, crammed with £5 and £10 notes, and said, "Here, son, there's £300. That will be your signing-on fee, and we can talk about the rest of your wages later." The story went the rounds thereafter that Steedman had used the takings from the "puggy" – the fruit machine – in the Bankies' social club to fund the deal. But whether this is true or apocryphal, it was a master-stroke on his part, because any reservations harboured by Cooper suddenly evaporated and were replaced with pound signs in his eyes, akin to a scene from a *Loony Tunes* cartoon.

The consequence was that a previously sceptical Cooper had been converted, despite his early objections. He couldn't drive and was worried about the heavy schedule which he was entering, but after thirty minutes in the Jaguar, he shook hands with Steedman and began a new chapter in his life. One can only imagine the reaction of Rangers and Celtic when they discovered the mercurial talent they had attempted to sign had pledged his allegiance to lowly Clydebank, but none of that concerned Davie as he parted company with his new boss. "I'll see you in five or six weeks, when the new season begins, and we'll send you out a letter with your contract details," concluded Steedman. It was an adroit piece of business for the pair as the dawn broke on Davie's senior career.

3

TAKING IT TO THE BANK

Most provincial clubs in Scotland have enjoyed their season or two in the sun, or at least provided memories of coruscating Cup performances and giant-slaying acts which their aficionados can cling to when they slip into less auspicious periods. Even today, more than thirty years after Davie Cooper signed a professional contract with Clydebank and subsequently embarked on a golden period for the team, there are scores of supporters who recall these days with affection and can reel off the names of their leading players, be it Cooper or Jim Fallon, Gregor Abel or Peter Kane, and the likes of Jim Gallagher, Sam Goodwin, John Gilmour and Jim Lumsden . . . redoubtable characters who combined to ensure that the Steedman brigade climbed up the divisions with a string of fine results which, however briefly, turned Kilbowie into a minor centre of excellence.

Nobody pretended they were ever going to be able to challenge the Old Firm in the West of Scotland, or Hibs and Hearts on the other side of the country, but the Clydebank collective of the mid-1970s boasted an effervescence, *esprit de corps* and sense of community pride which combined to send them on a hot streak towards the highest echelon in the Scottish league game. There were no prima donnas in the ranks – and anybody who even attempted the hint of an air or a grace was swiftly brought down to earth with a blast of industrial language – but even though Cooper and his confreres were forced to train on an ash pitch and lacked everything but the most basic facilities and amenities, they didn't grumble, but instead knuckled down to working with their coach, Bill Munro, a kenspeckle figure with the knack of making his charges feel special even though they were working in the football equivalent of a doss house. This was, let's remember, a time before Astroturf and floodlights on training nights, and yet, despite their privations, the little-leaguers transcended their setting with a luminous glow.

At the outset, Davie was still employed by the Nobles in Hamilton and his typical day saw him engaged at the print works before catching a train to Glasgow Central Station, scoffing a bag of chips on his way to Kilbowie, running round the corner to Queen Street and journeying to Singer Station, where he invariably was the last man to pitch up in the changing room. If any of these connections failed, he was stuck, even though he only lived a few miles away from his destination in the grand scheme of things, and the routine caused him all manner of problems. He was loath to ask anybody for a lift, couldn't afford the taxi fare on any kind of regular basis, and former colleagues recalled him turning up with a face like fizz, bemoaning his choice of club and swearing under his breath . . . and this was even before he had adapted to the tedium of running round and round the track on the sort of treadmill which can dispirit the hardiest of souls. However, once he had a ball at his feet, he was transformed and fine-tuned his dribbling skills, his corners and free kicks, until he had attained the lofty standards he was seeking.

Fortunately, if these training sessions too often veered towards the mundane or robotic for Cooper's liking, he relished the encouragement offered to him by such totemic figures as Steedman, who pulled the strings effectively behind the scenes; Munro, whose words of wisdom originated from a deep-rooted love for everything connected with football; and Fallon, one of the most faithful servants of his club in the history of Scottish football, a fellow who eventually turned out for the Bankies on more than 600 occasions.

Even today, the latter works at the Sports Health and Injury Clinic inside Hampden Park and speaks about Cooper with unvarnished praise for his former comrade in arms:

"I was captain of the side when Davie joined us and it was a tremendous fillip to have somebody of his quality in the squad, because it showed that we were ambitious, that we weren't happy just to hang around in the old Second Division, and it was a fantastic time to be involved with Clydebank, a few years where we thought almost anything was possible and the spirit between the players and fans was brilliant. We used to have to train between a wall and railway line – we weren't allowed on the field – but even in that environment it was obvious Davie had a huge amount of talent and the longer we all worked together, the more optimistic we became about our prospects.

"He was a quiet boy, a very quiet boy. He generally kept himself to himself. But he wasn't aloof or anything like that and he had a droll sense of humour once you got to know him. One of the things was that he didn't act as if he was just passing through on the way to Rangers, even though we all knew that he supported them like crazy. And the fans loved him for the commitment and determination he put into his time at Kilbowie. Mind you, we had a good team and we enjoyed a wee purple patch, which meant that he was given the chance to meet the big Scottish clubs on a fairly regular basis between 1975 and 1977. It definitely toughened him up, because these were the days when defenders were allowed to tackle really hard and you had to be a resilient character to keep charging down the wing in these circumstances. But he knew that if he got into trouble, there were guys in our side who would make sure he got back out of it."

On the field, Clydebank started to reap the fruits of their labours with an accomplished series of displays, both on league assignments and within the Scottish Cup, a tournament which offered Cooper his initial taste of jousting with giants. He made some effective contributions when Munro's men sealed a creditable 2–1 victory over Dunfermline – who were a division above their opponents at that stage – and that success was the catalyst for a fourth-round away tie with Celtic, who might have slipped a little from the side which had registered nine league titles in a row, as well as the European Cup, but who retained sufficient menace to provide an acid test of the teenage Cooper's qualities.

Understandably, considering Davie's support for the Ibrox club, the tie represented both an opportunity to confront the enemy head-on and an induction to the seething cauldron of partisan bias which epitomises match days on the Old Firm's turf. At the Lariat bar in Hamilton, Cooper received plenty of advice on how to approach the contest – and one or two of the pub regulars placed bets on him scoring at Parkhead – but the youngster himself was underwhelmed by all the fuss and told his friends that he was focusing more on Clydebank's league programme than on worrying about the Celts. Behind the scenes, he was as nervous as one might have anticipated, but it wasn't in the Cooper family's genes to betray their emotions in public and, in any case, as Muir and Fallon had pointed out to their teammates: this wasn't a game they were expected to win, so there was little or no pressure on the Kilbowie personnel as they made their way to Glasgow.

On paper, at this distance, it shouldn't have been a gruelling mission for the hosts, who included such illustrious names as Kenny Dalglish, Danny McGrain, Harry Hood, Jackie McNamara, George Connolly and Dixie Deans in their line-up. But these Cup occasions tend to level things up and from the beginning the outsiders performed with pride, resilience and a bonnie panache as they seriously tested Celtic's mettle. Indeed, Clydebank took the lead with a goal from Joe McCallan midway through the opening half, and Cooper gave the renowned McGrain a torrid afternoon, increasing in confidence as the proceedings raged on, and even drawing grunts of approval from the home fans. It wasn't enough to dent the strut of the hosts, who responded to falling behind by upping the ante and peppering the Clydebank ramparts with a sustained salvo of shots and headers which eventually pushed them well in front, with Dalglish pouncing for a brace of goals and McNamara and Roddie McDonald completing a relatively comfortable success. But nonetheless, Davie's display rightly earned plaudits from the newspapers – the *Sunday Mail* reported, "Young Cooper showed a lot of skill, composure and confidence on the ball" and *The Sunday Post* singled him out as a player to watch.

In the final analysis, he and his colleagues had served notice that they were no longer content with lower-league anonymity and battles waged in front of a few hundred supporters. Instead, with Steedman confirming his determination to aim for promotion and the Bankies pledging themselves to full-time football for a number of their squad, Cooper was caught up in the excitement as much as anybody else, oblivious to the English scouts and managers who still continued to make overtures without winning him over. His maiden season might have advanced in fits and starts – his Scottish League debut arrived on Saturday, 31 August 1974, when his side lost 3–0 against Queen of the South – but there was ample evidence, amidst his twenty-nine starts and two appearances as a substitute, that he was the real deal, while his five goals – the first of them against Alloa Athletic in December – exhibited his ability to influence games in every department.

Off the pitch, by the summer of 1975 he had started dating Christine McMeekin, after the pair met at an ice rink, and Cooper was feeling happy about his life. He had his family, a steady girlfriend and a close-knit circle of friends, with whom he played darts, placed a bet on the horses at the bookies in Hamilton and enjoyed a pint or two, without falling victim to the bevvy culture which has destroyed many promising careers before and after him in Scottish football. Even if he was uncomfortable when asked to carry out media engagements, he enjoyed a rapport with the Clydebank fans and was happy to sign autographs whenever he was approached "in the right manner", as explained by Steve Scroggie, one of those who cheered him on from the terraces:

"Davie was old school. He had been brought up by his folks to say 'Please' and 'Thank You' and he didn't like being taken for granted. One time, a group of us were waiting to try and get his autograph and it was a perishing winter's evening in Clydebank, so a wee bit of impatience started to set in. Eventually, the players came out of the stadium and when we caught sight of Davie, one of my mates, Billy, walked over to him, handed him a pen and a piece of paper and said, 'Hey, Davie, we've been waiting for you.' Well, it wasn't the right approach to take at all. Davie immediately handed the stuff back and said, 'It's Mr Cooper to you, son.' And then he started marching off into the distance. One or two of us were a bit shell-shocked, I suppose, but Billy shouted after him, 'I'm sorry, Mr Cooper, it's just that we're freezing oot here.' And within a couple of seconds Davie turned round and replied, 'That's okay, son, what's your name?' He then stood and signed all our books and had a chat with us about that afternoon's match.

"It was the same when he used to come out of the training sessions. Because Clydebank had to practise on a patch of open ground, it was very easy for youngsters to watch the sessions and, unsurprisingly, once the team started climbing the leagues and becoming well known, a lot of boys and girls started to take an interest in the likes of Davie. He was friendly towards us, but if anybody ever tried to take his photograph, he didn't seem pleased to be the object of so much fuss and usually bolted away as quick as he could. It was nothing to do with him being big-headed or thinking he was a star or anything like that. It was the opposite, if anything. My dad told me that he used to meet Davie in the bookies and he would stand and talk about horses and jockeys for hours on end and he would get involved in swapping banter with the rest of the punters, because they took him at face value and he responded in kind. You wouldn't see that happening today with somebody of Davie's quality, but it summed him up. Money wasn't a big deal to him, and he went out of his way to avoid the spotlight. All that mattered was football."

That and family were Cooper's two main preoccupations when it came to f-words. Thankfully from his perspective, Clydebank, bolstered by the back-stage machinations of Steedman, were aiming for the stratosphere and when the 1975–76 campaign commenced, they waltzed into the limelight with a superb sequence of results which more than justified the chairman's investment in the club. Straight from the outset, they dominated the championship, and the statistics speak for themselves, with Cooper scoring all of twenty-two goals in forty-nine matches, in addition to making a massive contribution as a creative midfield presence and slippery customer on the wing. He notched up his first hat-trick on the senior stage in a 3–1 victory over Alloa Athletic and, fittingly in the circumstances, broke the deadlock (from the penalty spot) to clinch promotion with a 2–0 win over Forfar at Kilbowie, a triumph which illustrated the potent blend of grit and glamour which had been established at the club. By this juncture, Cooper's abilities were gaining increasing prominence and there was a predictable reaction from opponents, who deduced that the best means of halting him in his tracks was booting him into the nearest casualty ward. In fact, such was the level of aggravation aimed in his direction that Clydebank started monitoring the infestation of awful tackles on their star man, as Davie subsequently related: "One newspaper actually had a writer counting the number of times I was fouled, and Jack Steedman helped him out by telling him it was thirty-six times in three games. He reckoned that I was the most-fouled player in British football. Mind you, he also thought that I was the worst trainer in the world, so what did he know!"

These were heady months for the Clydebank faithful. Beneath the surface, they must have recognised that Cooper wouldn't be in their midst for very long, but they were resolved to treasure him while they could and he reciprocated where it mattered. They feared the worst when it was revealed that Aston Villa, under manager Ron Saunders, had tabled a £65,000 bid for the twenty-year-old, but despite being offered more than treble what he was earning at Kilbowie, he brushed aside the offer and stayed put.

All of which makes it perfectly understandable that those who paid their admission money, week in, week out, revelled in his trickery and their team's triumphs. Gordon Robertson, who is now the chairman of Junior club Clydebank FC, was one of the throng whose lives were illuminated by Cooper's contribution to the cause.

"There are a lot of us who are now in our mid-forties and early fifties who will never forget that period and how Davie brought a bit of style and charisma to a small provincial club," says Robertson. "There was a real buzz among the fans and a genuine sense of anticipation and excitement before we went to matches because, quite honestly, he shone like a beacon, and that was even though he was surrounded by some other good players.

"One of the most memorable aspects of these years was the understated way in which he used to leave defenders clutching at fresh air: he didn't care about making fools of them, he was just in his own wee world, testing himself to the limit and seeing whether or not he could make the most outrageous things work to Clydebank's benefit. If he had been selfish, he wouldn't have been so popular, but Davie was always prepared to take the stick that was dished out and he suffered some fearful clatterings before dusting himself down and getting on with things, and the supporters loved that effort and commitment. You have to bear in mind that, prior to him joining up with us, we had never been out of the bottom division in our history, so we were in uncharted territory and it was fantastic when we began climbing the leagues and taking on the likes of the Old Firm. Suddenly, Clydebank were being taken seriously and a large part of that was down to Davie, pure and simple."

The eulogies speak for themselves, but the question remains whether Cooper's obdurate refusal to contemplate any relocation from his roots stunted his growth as a footballer. Quite apart from the Aston Villa offer, it was estimated that at least a dozen other clubs in England made serious bids for Davie's services between the beginning and end of 1976. From the youngster's perspective, the cash involved in these deals was immaterial and he told several of his Clydebank teammates, "England might as well be Outer Mongolia as far as I am concerned." Fallon, meanwhile, watched his club colleague refine his skills and had no doubt that Cooper was one of those individuals who never liked to fly too far from the nest. In the wider picture, he eventually risked veering down a one-way street, but the West of Scotland was where he was most comfortable, where he could enjoy a night out with his mates, and it was futile lamenting his insular outlook and especially when, as Fallon concluded, "He didn't have a mercenary bone in his body."

Essentially, Clydebank benefited from his homespun philosophy and the wider world of Scottish football revelled in Cooper's prodigious gifts the longer the 1970s progressed. Indeed, he and his Kilbowie teammates enjoyed another successful campaign in the 1976–77 championship season, where they and a talented St Mirren collective, managed by a young maverick with fire in his nostrils called Alex Ferguson, battled for supremacy on their way to the top flight the following year. Week after week, the Bankies flourished with their mix of youth and experience, grisly muscle and gallus sleight of foot, and the goals arrived in sack-loads, along with some major revisions for the record books. East Fife were trounced 6–0 at Bayview, then visitors Arbroath were demolished 8–1 – an unprecedented winning margin in Clydebank's history – with Cooper notching another hat-trick, and they went seventeen matches without losing between December 1975 and October 1976. Suddenly, anything seemed possible and no opponents were unduly feared.

This included Rangers, when the clubs squared up in the quarter-finals of the League Cup in what gradually unfolded into a marathon tie, featuring as many twists as the collected works of O. Henry. The reigning Scottish champions, bossed by the relentlessly ambitious Jock Wallace, had secured the Treble the previous season, and, even while they achieved some creditable European results, were in the process of sizing up a number of youngsters in their domestic competitions, with Cooper at the front of the queue. Yet although it might have appeared a comfortable draw for Wallace's ensemble, they soon found themselves embroiled in a dogfight when the first leg began in Glasgow.

For his part, Davie, who had often visited the stadium as a supporter, was granted little time to soak in the atmosphere, let alone enjoy the experience, before he was sprawling on the turf, as the contest started with a maelstrom of flailing limbs and bone-crunching tackles, with Rangers and their principal hatchet-man, John Greig, clearly determined to ensure they wouldn't be embarrassed by Cooper's much-touted trickery. As a microcosm of the acrimonious relationship which developed between the two men during the best part of the next decade, it could hardly have been bettered with the younger of the protagonists focusing on skill and inspiration and the man who was subsequently voted his club's greatest-ever player relying on ferocious, bone-crunching committment. "Two minutes into the match, I learned the ground rules according to John Greig," recalled Cooper. "The man who later became my gaffer waded in with the kind of assault that Jack the Ripper would have been proud of, and then, just to rub salt into my wounds, growled, 'If I get another chance, I'll break your leg.'

"There was no doubt about it, Greigy gave you that warm, it's nice-to-be-wanted feeling. Not that he was alone, for it seemed to me that he and big Tam Forsyth took it in turns to put me up in the air, wait for me to come down again and then repeat the process." However, if they were hoping these tactics would dishearten Cooper and his colleagues, there were mercifully mistaken as spurts of football broke out amidst the violence, with the little-fancied visitors savouring their participation in a cracking encounter. They grabbed the lead through Mike Larnach, and although Derek Johnstone equalised, the Bankies regained the initiative with a Billy McColl penalty, as the ebb and flow continued, whilst Wallace stood on the periphery with a face like curdled milk, his exasperation punctuated by staccato bursts of rapid-fire invective. Yet even when his half-time tirade appeared to have effected a turn-around in the proceedings, with Alex MacDonald and Johnny Hamilton finding the net to push the hosts 3–2 in front, parity was restored when Cooper conjured up the winner to earn his men a deserved draw.

It had been a frantic collision of styles, temperaments and strategies between two clubs divided by a few miles and a couple of million supporters, but for the sprinkling of Clydebank fans such as Steve Scroggie, who witnessed their heroes' refusal to be pummelled into submission, this was a night which would never be forgotten:

"Davie was immense, but then so were the rest of the Clydebank boys. It was clear at the start that Rangers had decided they were going to beat us by any means, and some of those early challenges on Coop would have been straight red cards these days. But he just kept getting up and continuing as if nothing had happened and it definitely had an effect on Greig and the rest of his defence. Basically, instead of concentrating on stopping the other Clydebank players, they spent most of their time chasing Davie round the park, and it messed up their system and allowed our other guys to create chances and come close to beating them in their own back yard. It was terrific for us, but I suppose it was a bit depressing that Rangers, with all the cash they had at their backs, should have felt the need to resort to kicking and lunging at anything that moved in their direction.

"All the same, we were pretty jubilant at the end. We hadn't expected to win, and even when we were 2–1 up at the interval, we weren't getting carried away because you always expect the Old Firm to come roaring out of the blocks and Rangers had enough quality in their team to put the match out of sight if it hadn't been for the efforts of everybody in the Bankies colours. We were ecstatic when Coop scored to make it 3–3, but most of us knew that it would probably end up with Rangers signing him because they had already made Davie an offer, and we guessed they would simply keep upping their price until Jack Steedman had no option but to sell him to Ibrox. But you have to realise that when you are supporting a provincial club like Clydebank, you can't afford to waste too much time thinking about what might happen next week or next year. You have to enjoy the good moments while you can and we had a ball that night."

These months towards the conclusion of 1976 were auspicious both for Fallon's men and Cooper in particular. As somebody who was already acclaimed around the Kilbowie environs, Davie's reputation was spreading further afield, whilst his performance against Rangers had persuaded Bill Munro to draw comparisons between his young charge and George Best, and it wasn't a surprise when he was selected in Scotland's Under-21 squad for an international clash against Czechoslovakia in Pilsen. To his credit, Cooper wasn't inclined to believe the hyperbole which had heightened around his name and he was self-deprecating in his reaction to being likened to Best – "Being mentioned in the same breath was enough for me" – but it was obvious that the next stage of his career was beckoning at a gallop, even if his initial instinct was to lap up his local-hero status.

Ultimately, though, small-town loyalties don't sit well with international aspirations. Under their coach, Andy Roxburgh, a new generation of talented Scots were thrusting themselves into the picture, and although they were held to a 0–0 draw by the Czechs, which was in itself a creditable outcome, Cooper acquitted himself well, in the company of a veritable phalanx of future stars. (The team was Bobby Clark, George Burley, Pat Stanton, Roy Aitken, Arthur Albiston, John Wark, David Narey, Tommy Burns, Davie Cooper, Davie McNiven and Paul Sturrock.) Granted, he was still enjoying life at Kilbowie as part of a side which would go on to gain promotion for a second successive season, and when the Bankies entertained Rangers in the return leg, they once again provided a thrilling display to secure a 1–1 draw, with the incisive Cooper levelling matters after Greig had broken the deadlock earlier. But the bottom line was that these goals were simply raising his profile, increasing his value and Steedman, a shrewd observer of the market, steeled himself for inevitable transfer negotiations.

The talks began even as the '76–77 season was weaving towards its climax. On the pitch, Clydebank held Rangers for a third time, but were eventually edged out when the teams convened for a fourth meeting at Firhill – where another Cooper goal wasn't sufficient to prevent defeat through strikes from Derek Parlane and Bobby McKean. In the league race they were eventually pipped by St Mirren, but sealed their ascent to the top rung with a point against Dundee at Dens Park, despite the best efforts of the latter's gifted young firebrand, Gordon Strachan. This was a marvellous achievement for a club with Clydebank's modest resources, but there was also a sense amongst the fans, including Gordon Robertson, that they would shortly be bidding farewell to their star man.

"We went to all these League Cup matches and Davie was dynamite," recalls Robertson. "It is impossible to overstate how influential he was for us and you could notice the fear in the Rangers ranks whenever he got hold of the ball. His confidence filtered throughout the team and when you think that we were playing opponents who had won the Treble the year before, it was brilliant that we more than matched them over the course of four games. Some of the supporters felt that we should have tried harder to retain his services and if we had managed that, who knows how we might have fared in the top tier? But, while it would have been nice to hang on to him, we knew that offers were being tabled for Davie and once he started to get Scotland recognition it was only a matter of time before he left. That didn't make it any better when he departed, mind you. Some of us had grown up with him over these years from 1974 to 1977 and we were genuinely heartbroken at the end, which explains why when Clydebank set up a Hall of Fame in 2007 the first two inductees were Jim Fallon and Davie Cooper. That's how much they meant to us."

Rangers, who had struggled to contain Clydebank in their quartet of Cup jousts and who were trounced by Aberdeen when the clubs locked horns in the semi-finals of the same competition, were on the look-out for an injection of new blood. Yet it speaks volumes about the fashion in which football has changed – or perhaps not, now that matters have turned full circle at Ibrox – that when the Glasgow giants sought to agree terms with Jack Steedman, they started the bidding at £50,000 for Cooper and only advanced in segments of £10,000, as if convinced that the lower-league organisation would leap at any sum, no matter how paltry. The discussions continued thereafter for a few weeks, although since both parties were only concerned about price – Cooper was on his way and that was the end of it – the to-ing and fro-ing rather resembled a cigarette vendor trying to flog cheap fags (purchased across the Channel) to customers at the Bathgate Market on Friday mornings. Davie, for his part, continued to leave the contract negotiations to his elders, preferring to focus on the good news surrounding his football – which culminated in him being selected by the Scotland manager, Ally MacLeod, in the senior squad for the 1977 Home Internationals and that summer's tour of South America, designed to act as a fact-finding exercise for the following year's World Cup.

It was a meteoric rise from where he had been eighteen months earlier and he had clearly graduated into the major league. But there were still elements of amateurism about the fashion in which Cooper's move to Ibrox was transacted. Neither party had concluded the matter prior to Steedman going on holiday with his wife Margaret to the south coast of England, so, even as the couple attempted to enjoy the sun, Jack nipped in and out of his hotel to keep in contact with Willie Waddell, the Ibrox general manager, while the transfer fee inched up towards the six-figure mark which both clubs knew was the asking price in the first place. Eventually, at the end of a significant amount of phoney-war haggling, Rangers made their offer of £100,000, and all that remained was for Cooper to sit down and discuss personal terms with his imminent new employers. He was just twenty-one, he was in prime form with the world at his feet and had already gained international recognition. In which light, he should have been able to dictate whatever he desired.

Instead, however, there was a rather shambolic breakdown in communications between the respective parties. Firstly, Davie received a telephone call from Wallace, in which the latter stated his intention to come to the Coopers' home in Hamilton to seal the deal. Then within half an hour the instructions were changed and the player was advised to make his way to Ibrox at his earliest convenience. Since he still hadn't learned to drive and thought it might look peculiar if he turned up at the stadium in a taxi, Davie had to ask his father to give him a lift into Glasgow and he and the two Johns, father and brother, made the journey in a Fiat 125 Super which had been presented to Davie by Clydebank FC.

On the road to Govan, all manner of questions were swirling through Davie's mind – Was he ready for the challenge? What should he ask for at the interview? Could he cope with the pressure of joining an Old Firm institution? And would he get on with Wallace, the martinet with a notoriously short temper and a penchant for sand-dune-based training regimes? – and it was only as he was pulling into Ibrox that he realised his only previous experience of what a transfer entailed lay in brown envelopes stuffed with used banknotes, which meant that he was completely unprepared for what ensued when he arrived in Govan.

As if that wasn't enough of an impediment, he was barely through the portals at Ibrox before he was standing face-to-face with a triumvirate of Rangers legends, men with sharp suits, firm ideas on the traditions of the organisation which they had represented and unbending notions on how business affairs would be conducted. There was Waddell, Wallace and Willie Thornton, the assistant manager, and they were sitting in a row in front of Davie, even as the two John Coopers sat outside the fabled Blue Room.

Predictably, it was less a meeting of equals than an interrogation. Yet Cooper's own account of the proceedings reinforces the impression that he would have signed on the dotted line, whatever the salary: "I felt like a schoolboy up in front of the headmaster – only there were three of them. What I didn't feel like was a professional footballer who was in reasonable demand and who should have been holding all the aces in transfer talks. But I wasn't genned up on that kind of thing and the deal was concluded within an hour of me arriving at the ground. Initially, Rangers offered me a signing-on fee of £5,000, but I think even Messrs. Waddell, Wallace and Thornton were a bit embarrassed by that, because it didn't take much negotiating from me to get the figure doubled.

"At that point, I was led to believe that, after tax, I would end up with something like half of the money and that didn't seem too bad. I went out to have a word with [his brother] John, but he was so keen that I should sign that he would have let me accept a tenner, never mind £10,000. The basic wage was around £150 a week and there were bonuses per point, which all helped. I don't suppose it was a fortune compared with what clubs Down South were offering, but I was happy enough at the time. But in retrospect, I got stung a bit because, at the end of the day, the taxman took £6,500 of my share, to leave me with just £3,500. I learned my lesson from that and I vowed to myself that I would do better in a new contract. But I was just pleased to sign on the dotted line."

In this, as in many other respects, Cooper was living on his wits and learning on the job. He left Clydebank with the approbation of the crowd ringing in his ears, his final goal for the First Division side scored against Raith Rovers in a 2–0 victory on 23 April 1977. A week later, he turned out in his swansong and, at the denouement of a 4–2 success over Falkirk at Brockville, offered his thanks and said his goodbyes to Steedman, Fallon and diehard supporters such as Gordon Robertson and Steve Scroggie. Nobody could have blamed him for seeking higher challenges, but there was still an air of tristesse around Kilbowie, and the prevailing mood was amply summed up by the faithful Fallon:

"Davie never offered anything less than 100 per cent for Clydebank and his contribution was immense. I remember there was one match against Albion Rovers where he kept getting fed passes by Jim Lumsden and was causing havoc with their defence, and it was obvious that the Rovers boys were on the verge of losing their rags when Davie came up to us with a worried expression on his face and said, 'Guys, please stop giving me the ball. This defender is getting really angry and I think he is going to kick me!' He was like that: he loved doing tricks with the ball but didn't want to make a fool of anybody. Mind you, if he had been more arrogant, heaven knows where he might have finished up." Once again, that reverie of what might have been hung unspoken in the air.

4

ON THE TREBLE TRAIL

At first glance, Davie Cooper and Jock Wallace might not have come across as one of life's natural double acts. The former was an introverted character, a lad who shunned the limelight and who preferred to let his feet do the talking. The latter was a grizzled individual with a cantankerous personality and a predilection for earthy language which made him a fearful figure in the King's Own Scottish Borderers, who could reduce grown men to quivering wrecks with the stringency of his punishing training regimes and his philosophy that his players might fail for lack of talent, but they would never be bested for dearth of application or effort, irrespective of the quality of the opposition.

Yet when Cooper, a callow twenty-one-year-old, shook hands with Wallace, twenty years his senior, at Ibrox in the summer of 1977, it marked the beginning of a friendship built on mutual respect and admiration, which endured until the two men died within eighteen months of each other in 1995 and 1996. They might not always have agreed on tactics or on the merits of pounding the sand dunes at Gullane as preparation for important matches, but both shared a passionate attachment to Rangers FC and their contrasting qualities complemented each other, to the point where they could exchange dialogue with a grunt and a nod and turn those basic gestures into the equivalent of a fifteen-minute chat with anybody else.

Indeed, even before the deal was done to bring Davie to Ibrox, the duo had amply demonstrated that their reverence towards the Govan-based organisation didn't extend to forgetting who was paying their salaries elsewhere. In 1967, Wallace, as both manager and goalkeeper of Berwick Rangers, had been the catalyst for the lowly ranked club's remarkable Scottish Cup success over their Glasgow rivals, one of those results which had *Grandstand* presenters biting their nails over concerns that they might have been the victims of a wind-up. Cooper, for his part, was thrilled at being granted regular opportunities during his spell at Clydebank to test his mettle against Rangers in various Cup fixtures and not only rose to the occasion in these visceral contests, but drifted and darted through the grasp of international defenders such as John Greig as though he was the Scarlet Pimpernel and they were a flailing pack of addle-headed Frenchies.

It was, in short, a partnership founded on the basis that their similarities were more important than their differences, and the pair quickly emerged as pivotal figures in what was to prove a momentous season for the Ibrox collective. Wallace had already earned the plaudits of his supporters for ending the long-time hegemony established by Jock Stein's Celtic, but, in common with all the best football managers, he recognised that nothing stood still in the game and that constant regeneration was the only way to maintain a stranglehold over your opponents. Hence his decision to bolster his squad for the 1977–78 campaign by recruiting a trio of youngsters, who went on to form their own alliance of free spirits amidst the often stern edifice of Ibrox. Obviously, Cooper, at twenty-one, had talent in abundance and a capacity for joyous self-expression wherever he travelled, but he couldn't and wouldn't have been the presence he was in the Rangers ranks without the encouragement and mickey-taking offered by Bobby Russell, twenty, who joined from Shettleston Juniors within a few weeks of Cooper and Gordon Smith, at twenty-three, the senior member of the triumvirate, the man nicknamed "Casper", who ghosted

51

away from Kilmarnock and spirited his path to Glasgow for £65,000 in the summer of '77.

Sometimes these things happen by accident or owe more to good fortune than any master plan, but Wallace possessed sufficient savvy to recognise that there was nothing to be gained from assembling a regiment of clones. It might be simplistic to define these three musketeers as the shy and retiring type (Cooper), the gregarious man about town (Smith) and the bright-eyed roaring boy (Russell), but they established a rapport almost from the moment they started training together as the young pretenders amidst the established order who boasted the ambition, resolve and variety of gifts to rattle cages and stake their claims for promotion without worrying about putting noses out of joint.

Davie was the most talented: nobody disagreed with that assessment. But equally, he soon discovered that he couldn't merely stroll into Ibrox and demand to be treated like royalty. There were hierarchies and cliques within the squad, one or two high-profile players nearing the end of their shelf life, who were kicking and screaming against the dying of the light and who decided that if they couldn't command automatic selection from Wallace, they would do their best to discomfit and discombobulate the fresh-faced terriers in their midst. It didn't work with Smith: then, as now, he rolled with the punches and delivered well-timed jabs to silence the antagonists. It didn't work with Russell, who allowed the invective to sweep over him, while he grinned at those dishing out the abuse. But it paid dividends with Cooper, who returned home from his first few sessions at Ibrox with a fraught countenance and a litany of anxieties. Who were these people swearing at him and calling him a "lazy c***"? Weren't they all supposed to be pulling in the same direction for the greater good of Rangers? At this distance, it might seem surprising that a fellow with Cooper's qualities could be so badly affected by some name-calling, no matter how vociferous the gibes, but this wasn't some gentle joshing, but rather a calculated act of psychological warfare designed to sort out the men from the boys. After all, if he couldn't handle the vitriol from his own team-mates, what use would he be when he was thrown into a cauldron of loathing, such as a typical Old Firm tussle!

Thankfully, however, his comrades were on hand to lend him support and remind him that he had earned his chance at Ibrox on merit and the only person who really mattered in the bigger picture was their redoubtable gaffer, Wallace. Straight from the outset, as soon as the duo had clapped eyes on each other, they forged a bond, epitomised by their initial exchange, as recorded in Cooper's auto-biography *True Blue*:

Wallace: You don't give the ball away very often, do you, son?
Cooper: Only when I want to, Mister Wallace.

The latter remark was delivered with the most posthumous of pans, but the older man, much as Jim Taggart used to do after examining the latest batch of recruits to the force at Maryhill Police Station, was quietly impressed without blinking an eyelid. It should have served as an auspicious omen for the newcomer because Wallace usually dispensed compliments the way Steely Dan released new albums. (That's around once every decade or so.) Yet, in the initial weeks of his induction to life amidst the Old Firm, first Russell, then Smith, who marched into Ibrox after the club had surprisingly lost their opening league encounter, felt it necessary to spring to their confrere's defence as the tension increased around the Rangers personnel, with the old stagers and would-be fresh princes jostling for ascendancy in a febrile clash between the twenty- and thirty-somethings.

Smith's words encapsulate the nature of the sniping for territory which ensued: "When you have players on the one hand who are hard workers, who are always prepared to get stuck in and graft for the good of the team, and you have individualists on the other who have that touch of class but, rightly or wrongly, are perceived to be picking and choosing their moments, then of course it creates a bit of resentment, especially when you have somebody like Davie, who never blew his own trumpet and who believed that the only thing that mattered was Rangers FC. Some folk alleged that he was aloof or didn't mix well, but that was nonsense, yet he was definitely affected by the stick he received from certain players in the squad when he arrived at Ibrox. He thought that it was vindictive, that some of these players didn't want him to be at Rangers and, at the start, he even imagined that they were laughing behind his back and making a fool of him. The thing was that I had been involved with a full-time professional club at Kilmarnock and you took it as read that when you joined the set-up, the guys who were there would try to work out what made you tick and what cheesed you off, and as you might expect when you bring together a group of young, mostly working-class males, it isn't a place for the faint-hearted. You have to go in there with the attitude that sticks and stones might break your bones, but, basically, it is all water off a duck's back.

"It was new to Davie, however, and he didn't really know how to respond to it at first. It annoyed him, it got him down, and he took the criticism personally, he really did. I spoke to Bobby Russell and he told me he had noticed it as well, so the two of us started chatting away to Davie, having a laugh with him and encouraging him to throw in his tuppenny's worth, and we ended up becoming close friends. We were all new to the Old Firm and I'm not sure anything can prepare you for what it is like when you leave a small club and walk into the goldfish bowl, but gradually, day by day, week by week, Davie came out of his shell. He didn't fundamentally change as a person – right from the outset, you could tell that he was a quiet lad, somebody who was never going to make a big song and dance about how good he was – but he settled down after a few weeks and I think he recognised that the only thing which really mattered was what he did on the pitch."

Smith's comments are what one might anticipate from a stalwart of the glory game: whether offering nuggets of acerbic wisdom as a BBC pundit or laying the foundations for a wind of change to blow through the stuffy corridors of the SFA, he has never been afraid to wade into controversial waters, even when there were instances where it might have helped him to click his brain into gear before opening his mouth. Russell, though, watched Cooper squirm in those early days at Ibrox and grew to appreciate that, whatever transpired in the future, he was a man who not only cared deeply about football, but felt crushing disappointment when his form dipped below his lofty standards.

"Davie was a perfectionist and that pretty much applied to him in his later years at Rangers the same as when he started out. He was an introverted personality, but if he was expecting any favours when he joined Rangers, he quickly got a rude awakening. I can understand the reaction of the older guys when the three of us walked onto the training pitch, because these players had won the Treble under Jock Wallace in the 1975–76 season and the squad was packed with internationalists, so they were entitled to think, 'These boys want our places and it's up to us to make them fight as hard as we possibly can.' Obviously, when they noticed that the abuse was hitting a raw nerve in Davie's case, that only spurred them to throw more of it in his direction, but it was nothing that didn't happen at a lot of other clubs. We were the new kids on the block and, with hindsight, we probably were a bit cocky and took it for granted that because Rangers had paid good money to sign us up we were automatically guaranteed opportunities when the bottom line was that we had to go out and prove we deserved the chance.

"The fact was that Davie cared an awful lot about his levels of performance all the way through his career. If you are a defender, you defend and rely on those around you. If you are a striker, you attack and hope that if you don't find the net on any particular day, goals will come from elsewhere or you will benefit from a piece of luck. With Davie, though, he knew, as a creative player, that he was expected to produce pieces of magic and conjure up wee bits of something special every time he walked out onto the field, and it is simply impossible to reach these standards 100 per cent of the time.

Other more selfish or less committed characters might have been happy to play the percentages – there is no footballer in the history of the sport who has been at the top of his game every match they have played, and we are all human, we all experience highs and lows, and that is nothing to be ashamed about. But Davie felt wretched when he fell below the standards he had set himself and you could see it in his body language, even on occasions when we had won, but where he felt he had underperformed. He was his own harshest critic, and it needed a certain type of manager to get the best out of him. But fortunately, for both Davie and for Rangers, Jock knew how to pull the strings and we all benefited from his wisdom."

Everything was new to Cooper that summer. The expectations of the supporters, the professionalism of the backroom staff, the quality of the training facilities, the pages of Old Firm comment, speculation and reportage . . . it all added up to a different world from what he had experienced at Clydebank. Yet, fans are the same the world over, and if Davie believed he would receive any sort of honeymoon period, he and his colleagues were in for a rude awakening when the hostilities commenced.

Aberdeen, at Pittodrie, were first on the schedule – always a hazardous assignment in these days – and although Rangers offered debuts to Cooper, Russell and Billy Mackay, they slipped to an emphatic 3–1 defeat, a result which certainly didn't flatter the hosts. That was bad enough, but in their next match, despite Smith having been recruited to the cause, Ibrox fell ominously silent throughout a 2–0 defeat at the hands of Hibs, the muted grumbling from the terraces only a portent of what was to come when a smattering of angry supporters decided to stage a demonstration outside the stadium at the climax of the game. Even by Old Firm standards, the abuse aimed at the Rangers players when they exited the ground, just 180 minutes into the season, might have seemed OTT, but if the youngsters in the ranks hadn't realised the new pressures they were under, the sight of sections of their own followers flinging expletives in their direction surely rammed the message home.

To their credit, though, the spectre of these early disappointments was rapidly exorcised and the malcontents melted away like snow on a spring afternoon. Rangers possessed quality through their team, bolstered at the back by such luminaries as John Greig, Tom Forsyth, Sandy Jardine, Alex Miller and Colin Jackson, whilst the likes of Tommy McLean, Derek Johnstone and the fledgling trio, Smith, Russell and Cooper, brought menace and a cutting edge further up the field. It required time for the component parts to gel, and even when Davie notched his maiden goal for Rangers at Love Street against St Mirren on 17 September, the visitors could only manage a 3–3 draw. Yet, as the weeks elapsed and the Glaswegians gained cohesion, they began to carve out victories on a regular basis and establish supremacy at the summit of the league, in addition to proving their worth in the country's domestic Cup competitions.

There was to be no success in Europe – despite eliminating Young Boys of Berne in the preliminary round of the European Cup Winners' Cup, the Dutch club FC Twente knocked out the Scots in the next round – but, on their home patch, once the teething troubles had been remedied, Rangers cranked up the gears and didn't so much beat many opponents as pummel them into the dust, including successive wins over Aberdeen, the first by 3–1 in the championship, the second a comprehensive 6–1 trouncing in the League Cup, with Smith securing a hat-trick and Johnstone, Alex Miller and Alex MacDonald also getting on the score sheet. As Cooper said in a rare newspaper interview – he tended to shy away from these assignments the way a vegan might skip Sunday lunch with Clarissa Dickson Wright – he really started to feel he belonged in this company during a heady autumn, where Wallace's men sparked into full flow. By this juncture, he had become a familiar figure at Ibrox and scored his first Ibrox goal for his new employers against his old employers Clydebank, amidst a clinical 4–1 triumph as the visitors rued the fashion in which Cooper had started to weave his mazy menace all over his new environment.

Naturally, one of the critical tests lay in how he performed against Celtic and he received his first opportunity to lay down a benchmark in September. In the build-up, both teams had appeared uncharacteristically fragile, but the tribal rivalry was as ferocious as ever, and in many respects Rangers' heart-stopping 3–2 victory set the template for the rest of the season. They trailed 2–0 at half time, a consequence of Tommy Burns marauding on the left flank and creating chances for the tall Icelander, Jo Edvaldsson, who caused all manner of problems for the home defence – who had started without their talismanic presence, Greig – and propelled headers past the despairing Peter McCloy in the eighteenth and thirty-first minutes.

Unsurprisingly, Wallace was livid at his interval, possibly recognising his own tactical error as well as the deficiencies of his rearguard, and he lightly incinerated his personnel, as the prelude to replacing Parlane with Greig for the second half and throwing Johnstone into attack from his starting position at centre-half. Celtic responded, somewhat bafflingly, by pushing Edvaldsson back into defence and immediately surrendered the initiative in a match, where momentum can be so important.

Smith reduced the deficit in the fifty-third minute, and with the visitors increasingly penned into their own half, there was a sense of inevitability when Johnstone seized the equalising goal with twenty-five minutes remaining. Yet, for a while Peter Latchford threatened to salvage a point for his side with a string of excellent saves as the clock ticked on and the bombardment continued. Cooper stated in the aftermath that he couldn't believe the noise which was reverberating around Ibrox in the closing stages – "They were willing us on, and even though we were tired by the end, we had to keep on going for the fans" – and these voluble supporters gained what they were seeking when Latchford let a shot squirm from his grasp in the drizzly conditions and the ubiquitous Smith tapped in the winner.

Once again, two misfiring ensembles had generated a white-knuckle ride of thrills, and Davie and his team supped up the adulation, doubtless some of it from the same people who had called for Wallace's head a few weeks earlier. It was Cooper's first taste of how speedily fortunes can be transformed, for better or worse, between these traditional adversaries, and he celebrated as lustily as the majority of the fans, not least because he remembered how he had watched these fixtures as a youngster and left the stadium with tears in his eyes when Rangers slipped to defeat – as often happened – in the 1960s.

Those memories had moulded his upbringing, but it shouldn't be imagined that he had any truck with the bilious sectarian nonsense which habitually enveloped these clubs. On the contrary, Cooper admired the pride in the breasts of such opponents as Roy Aitken, Tommy Burns and Danny McGrain and went on record with his unambiguous response to those who claimed that the Wallace-managed side was fuelled by bigotry.

"I have any number of friends who are Roman Catholics and we go out and enjoy each other's company. There is never any suggestion of hassle and while I try to steer clear of the religious implications in an Old Firm match, I suppose everybody gets caught up in the general atmosphere. You realise that some people simply want to see the Protestants beat the Catholics or vice versa. But me? I just want to beat Celtic at every opportunity, regardless of whether they have a team full of Mormons, Protestants, Muslims or atheists. My reason is simply that I play for Rangers and Celtic is the enemy in Glasgow in a footballing sense. There is no more to it than that. There are players at Celtic who feel the same way and Tommy Burns, for example, has never hidden the fact that he dislikes Rangers intensely. That's fine, it never extends beyond the match, and I can't blame people if they get more affected than usual about scoring goals against each other.

"Maybe things like that are down to the tension of the game and that perhaps makes it more understandable, if not acceptable. Players are always incredibly nervous during an Old Firm match simply because they are really frightened to lose. We all know the score and what we can expect if we get beaten and there is absolutely nowhere to hide. On the one hand, you get your own fans giving you stick for being beaten by your main rivals and, on the other, you get Celtic supporters gloating and winding you up because they have won. It seems like everybody in the world wants to give you abuse for one reason or another and I rarely leave the house on the night after we have suffered at the hands of the Parkhead club. It isn't worth all the bother and aggravation and I knew quite a few of the Celtic boys who feel exactly the same as I do and behave in the same way."

Cooper had little to worry about on that front during the 1977–78 campaign. Despite their early travails, Rangers gradually settled down into an efficient groove, whereas Celtic endured a miserable time of it. As autumn progressed into winter, Wallace's personnel acquired the priceless knack of winning, even when they were below their best, and maintained a stranglehold over their domestic rivals which continued for the remainder of the campaign. For the most part, Cooper was satisfied rather than ecstatic with his general quality of performance – he was never a person given to dramatic mood swings or Capraesque flights of fancy – but it is a testimony to how swiftly he established himself in the Rangers' first team that he appeared in fifty-two of their fifty-three matches during his first year at Ibrox. Away from the field, he remained happiest when he could get back to Hamilton as quickly as possible, but bolstered by the friendship of Russell and Smith, he emerged slowly but surely from his shell, even if he eschewed the golfing trysts which occupied his colleagues' minds when they weren't involved in training or playing.

Instead, Cooper continued his love affair with gambling and basked in the banter of the bookmakers. It was never an addiction, yet even as a teenager, Davie had grasped the minutiae involved in laying bets across a range of pursuits and he could work out odds and calculate potential winnings with the rapidity of *Countdown's* Carol Vorderman. On one occasion, while his Rangers confreres enjoyed a golfing trip to St Andrews, he placed his stake money on a quartet of horses in a roll-up wager and was glued to his hotel television as, one after the other, his choices romped to victory. With the first three selections safely in the winners' enclosure, he was joined by Russell, Colin Jackson and the rest of the squad, and they collectively bit their nails and uttered silent prayers as the decisive race was poised to start. At that juncture, Cooper thought he was in trouble when Willie Waddell strolled into his room to discover the source of the commotion and, given the general manager's reputation as a devil for discipline, this was one of those situations where he might have been expected to crack the whip. But, in the event, Waddell was caught up in the frenzy, took off his jacket, and sat down with the other Rangers employees, cheering on Davie's horse, a short-odds favourite called Weth Nan, which duly romped home to provoke a mass cheer in an otherwise tranquil Fife milieu. Once the dust had settled, Cooper's winnings totalled £567, which represented the best part of a month's wages for him, and it also helped him bond with the rest of his colleagues.

That camaraderie oozed through the ranks, irrespective of the opposition or whatever competition in which Rangers were involved. They still weren't entirely convincing and, despite beating Dunfermline to reach the semi-finals of the League Cup, the Ibrox men were given an awful fright by lowly ranked Forfar Athletic, who led 2–1 until late in the proceedings, before Derek Parlane equalised, as the prelude to Alex MacDonald, Parlane again and Derek Johnstone scoring in extra time to lend the score a gloss which didn't reflect their side's struggle.

However, one of the ingredients which stamped out that Rangers collective as being formidable adversaries was their ability to dig deep, and whether rallying from a 2–0 deficit to defeat Motherwell 5–3, with Cooper among the scorers on his twenty-second birthday, or gaining the upper hand – just – in their hard-fought scraps with Aberdeen, who were starting to develop into a formidable force within Scottish football, Rangers were a team moulded in Wallace's image: resilient, tenacious when under the cosh and tireless in their pursuit of apparently lost causes. All the hours spent yomping in the sand at Gullane paid dividends the longer the season advanced and Cooper, much as he might have disliked the rigours of those Army-style exercises, was one of the principal benefactors. Other clubs ran out of steam or crashed into a wall, whereas Rangers maintained their intensity and thrived amidst the mud and glaur.

They also capitalised on some dubious refereeing decisions, which sparked controversy in the press and incurred the wrath of rival fans – *plus ça change* . . . ! – and one of the most notable incidents happened in the Old Firm match at the beginning of January, as recounted by Gordon Strang, a long-standing Rangers aficionado who emigrated to Canada in 1985 and who watched the pivotal moment in near-disbelief:

"We had taken the lead through a brilliant goal from Gordon Smith, but Celtic came hard at us, because they pretty much knew that if they didn't get something from the match, it would spell curtains for them in the league – and neither of the Old Firm ever likes to be out of the title race that early in the season. Well, they had us under the cosh and Joe Craig bustled his way through our defence and was blatantly pushed by big Bomber [Jackson] inside the box. I sunk my head in my hands, because I knew it was a stonewall penalty and there was this huge crescendo of noise from the Celtic fans, who probably just assumed that they would get the chance to draw level. Anyway, I wasn't able to look for about five or six seconds and then, suddenly, the mood in the stadium grew really nasty and I realised that the referee hadn't given the penalty. I was cock-a-hoop, but you should have heard the racket from the Celtic lads . . . if they could have got onto the pitch, heaven knows what they would have done. And their players completely lost the plot.

"They crowded round the ref and were screaming in his face and they were so caught up in their protests that they didn't seem to realise that he had awarded Rangers a free kick. It was a terrible decision, to be honest, but one of the first things you learn in football is to play to the whistle and the Celtic guys forgot about that and gifted the game to us.

"They were still complaining even when the ball had broken to us in the middle of the park and you had this weird sight where all the Rangers outfield players were pouring forward and the only Celtic lads who were trying to stop them were the goalkeeper, Peter Latchford, and Franny Munro. The other nine were still flinging abuse at the officials, but when did you ever see a referee change his mind in these circumstances? Never! So it was pretty dumb behaviour. Eventually, with their defence posted missing, John Greig had the chance to tap in the easiest goal you will ever see and, of course, that simply increased the sense of injustice amongst the Celtic players and their followers. But there was no way back for them and we won fairly comfortably [3–1] in the end."

Predictably, the press reflected and accentuated the Parkhead club's grievances. "Robbed" declared one headline the following morning. "Why No Penalty?" was the question asked by most of the football writers. Even Cooper admitted in the *Daily Record*, along with the majority of his teammates, that Rangers had been extremely fortunate and that it was the pivotal moment of the tussle. But irrespective of the furore and particularly with the passing of time, it simply become another Rangers success in a campaign where, despite their occasional vulnerability, men such as Cooper grew up quickly amidst the constant buzz and publicity which surrounds the Old Firm.

The epithet "Moody Blue" soon developed common currency. In the early stages of his career, there was certainly no doubt that Davie was uncomfortable in the media spotlight and although he was forced to participate in several PR activities, designed to furnish the Fourth Estate with preview material for the bigger matches, he soon recognised that the shorter his answers, the less he would be bothered for quotes or insight. This didn't mean that he was rude or unpleasant in his dealings with the papers, but according to Rodger Baillie, the veteran journalist who wrote for the *Mirror* and *Record* in the 1970s and 1980s and who had worked more recently for the *Sunday Times*, it allowed him to focus entirely on football without being side-tracked by requests for interviews:

"At the outset, Davie was very difficult to interview and the legend of the 'Moody Blue' came into being, although my own experience was that he was a self-conscious young man who found it a bit embarrassing to be confronted by a crowd of slavering hacks. But later on, when he was at the centre of a contract row with Rangers, I remember being invited out to his home in Hamilton with a photographer [the *Record*'s Eric Craig], and it was as if somebody had turned on a tap and he was happy to speak about anything and everything. Maybe at the start he was worried the media would twist his opinions or land him in trouble with the Rangers management, but the longer he was at Ibrox, the more he came to realise that we didn't bite and that we could actually be helpful in putting his side of the story across when it came to handling such matters as contract negotiations.

"You come across people in any walk of life who are introverts, who are shy and want to keep themselves to themselves, and I think Davie fitted that description in the early years. While he was on the football pitch he could control what he was doing and he had a terrific amount of ability, so he usually attracted good reviews from the journalists and the crowds, even if there were always critics who questioned his work ethic and his tackling, things like that. The bottom line was Jock Stein and Jock Wallace both held him in high regard and you would have to say that they were pretty good judges of what makes a quality footballer.

"My own opinion is that he was unlucky to be playing at a time when wingers were supposed to run themselves into the ground, stick to their positions at No.7 or No.11, and do nothing but attack or defend – a lot of Scottish football folk were suspicious of anybody who wanted to spend time on the ball or conjure up pieces of magic through skill rather than pace. It was a debate which continued throughout Davie's career and I heard more than one person remark that they could never be sure they were going to get a full ninety-minute performance from Davie Cooper. Maybe we should have been focusing more on the fact that he had the ability to turn matches round in the space of five minutes, but he was operating in a different world from the one of today."

He was also plying his trade during a revolutionary period in the Scottish game. Enough verbiage has already been expended on the riches-to-rags saga of Scotland's participation in the 1978 World Cup, but a seismic shift was also occurring on the domestic circuit, with the emergence of Aberdeen and Dundee United, the self-styled "New Firm", who benefited prodigiously from the ambition and motivational skills of Alex Ferguson and Jim McLean. Neither club was quite able to wrest any major prizes away from Rangers' grasp in the 1977–78 season, but there were sufficient indications that the status quo was being transformed in the north-east of the country and those Old Firm diehards who assumed that they would dominate, come what may, for as long as they liked, regardless of the ambitions of their opponents, were gradually disabused of that notion.

Indeed, the hunt commenced in earnest, even as Rangers kept their opponents temporarily at bay. In the championship race, they finally wrapped up the title with a 2–0 victory over Motherwell at Ibrox, the goals coming from Colin Jackson and Gordon Smith, but the Ibrox men only finished two points clear of Aberdeen, on 55 to the latter's 53 – this from thirty-six matches with only two points awarded for a win – and it was a measure of how the balance was shifting that Celtic languished back in fifth place, ending up behind Dundee United and Hibernian, and only averaging a point a match.

Such impoverishment might sound unfathomable to those who grew up during the Old Firm's supremacy from the end of the 1980s onwards, but a decade earlier, the rest of the Scottish clubs had no inferiority complex when they tackled the Glasgow duo, particularly when the latter had to travel away from their tribal citadels.

And with good reason! Because, when one studies the decline which followed Jock Stein's departure from Parkhead and twins it with the similar reversal of fortunes which befell Rangers as the 1980s began, it was obvious that these were vulnerable organisations, still saddled with sectarian baggage, unhelpful links to Ireland, and officials who seemed to believe that they could carry on merrily as they had done for the previous half century. And if that meant having the occasional, bloody riot on the terraces and a string on murders, serious assaults and mayhem in A&E departments on a Saturday night across Ayrshire, Lanarkshire and the fastnesses of wild West Lothian, then so be it.

Nearly everybody colluded in the process – I can still recall one of my teachers at Whitburn Academy laughing off a rammy with the response that the release of violence was a useful safety valve for those on either side of the religious divide – but eventually the clubs themselves found themselves increasingly detested at home and isolated on the European circuit.

Even such a marvellous talent as Cooper was capable of stirring conflicting emotions with the ball at his feet, but these usually amounted to nothing more upsetting than cries of "Hun bastard" from those who watched him dazzle in the spotlight with his full repertoire of artistry, vision and insouciant improvisation. He heard the abuse, inwardly vowed to make these people eat their words, and was often successful in the early stages of his career. Yet, there was less he could do about the vultures who continued to hover over Ibrox.

However, none of that mattered to Davie when he collected his maiden piece of silverware for Rangers with victory over Celtic in the League Cup final in March 1978. He and his teammates prepared as usual with a trip to Largs, where they split into their own little groups. Cooper typically stayed close to Russell and Smith, enjoying a few frames of snooker with the other new recruits, and never missed the opportunity to peruse the *Sporting Life* and place a few pounds on his fancied horses. Unlike his colleagues, he also spent significant amounts of time on the phone to his mother, Jean, who listened patiently while her son, mustard keen about football but less comfortable with the day-to-day anxieties of life around the Ibrox environs, poured out his thoughts in a splurge of contrasting sentiments which would certainly have surprised those who had bracketed him with Garbo and Harpo Marx in a list of least favourite interview subjects.

"Davie was never comfortable being away from his family," recalls Russell. "Sooner or later, he would grow restless and wonder whether he couldn't get back to Hamilton and it was clear that he had his own routines and favourite places and he got homesick very quickly without themIt used to be the same in the off season or whenever we had a few days off – he was always happy to see us and talk to us, but we always had to meet him in Hamilton, at the same hotel, pub or bookmaker's, and he was a creature of habit. Maybe it coloured his judgement, or perhaps he was just happy to stay close to his roots. Whatever, I don't remember it having any negative influence on his time at Ibrox."

As the final tussle beckoned, Wallace assembled the squad and spoke of the challenge which would face them from opponents, who were still smarting from the controversy surrounding the New Year fixture. Moreover, with Celtic out of contention for any other honours – they lost as many league matches as they won (15) in the championship – the manager warned his players they would be up against wounded men, individuals who had been criticised mercilessly in the media and throughout the pubs of Glasgow for the previous six months and who would be desperate to gain redemption of sorts, even if the League Cup was small potatoes compared with the other trophies up for grabs. His speech, a mixture of rhetorical flourishes and anti-Celtic invective – think Churchill, as spoken by Mark McManus, with a soupcon of the Reverend Billy Graham thrown in for good measure – hit the mark in galvanising his troops, most of whom, in any case, required no incentive to perform at full pelt whenever the Old Firm locked horns.

In which light, it was hardly surprising that Rangers began at 100mph and cranked up the gears thereafter. Cooper was as excited by the task as he was exciting to behold and some of those who surveyed him that day still believe that this was the afternoon when the boy grew into a man. "He must have covered every blade of grass and he was like a cat on hot bricks," recalls Stewart Paterson, a long-term Ibrox supporter. Another in the crowd at Hampden, Dave Smith, recollects that Davie had a "wee bit of a mad glint in his eyes" as soon as the nettle commenced. "He was usually quite laid-back and there was one game in his Clydebank days where he actually strolled off the pitch and waved at one of his mates, telling him to get the beers in at the Lariat! But in that final he was like a man possessed. It was the biggest game of his life and he played like he knew it was."

His Celtic adversaries soon grasped what they were up against, especially when Gordon Smith cut the ball back into Cooper's path and the latter dinked the ball past Peter Latchford in the thirty-eighth minute. Instantaneously, Davie went into raptures, screamed and jigged and overdosed on emotion for a few seconds, and later confessed that it was just as well that the gates were closed at Hampden, otherwise he might have sprinted all the way to Ibrox in his ecstasy. It was a sweet feeling, ample reward for pounding up and down the dunes at Gullane, and he winked to his gaffer, Wallace, as if delivering the message: "That was for you, Boss." Yet the redoubtable Jock, who instinctively realised that these were dangerous times for any team, simply told his player re-focus on the match. It was a timely reminder, because Celtic were determined to regain the initiative and scrapped and fought with such unstinting intensity that few could have begrudged them the equalising goal from Edvaldsson, which dragged the contest into extra time. However, as if to illustrate the problems which had afflicted the rest of their season, the Parkhead men could not maintain the same momentum for 120 minutes and with Wallace ringing the changes, introducing Alex Miller and Derek Parlane for Cooper and Johnny Hamilton, the prolific Smith emerged with the clinching goal as fatigue set in on both sides.

At the finish, Cooper leapt out of his seat and embraced Wallace with the warmth one might expect from a father and son being reunited, rather than two fellows who had been seated a few yards away from one another for the previous forty-odd minutes. Yet that symbiosis emphasised how close these two characters had become in the space of less than a year. A decade later, when Davie reminisced about that first Cup triumph, he spoke in matter-of-fact tones about the post-match celebrations, first in the Blue Room at Ibrox, then with his parents and his girlfriend, Christine, inevitably in the circumstances at the Avonbridge Hotel in Hamilton. But his conversation grew more animated when he recalled the scenes in the immediate aftermath of the success at Hampden.

"The look on the manager's face at the final whistle was fantastic: you could see how much it meant to him, but although he was bursting with pride, he was more concerned with congratulating his team and there were no favourites, nobody bigger or better than the rest, he treated us all the same," recalled Cooper. "It made it all worthwhile to see him at the end. And what that experience also did was to make me even hungrier for more medals and the chance to be involved in big matches like that one on a regular basis. These things are what you are in the game for. And if you are with the Old Firm, you have to get used to these matches and take the pressure in your stride, because nobody else can do it for you."

Between the joy of this achievement and the elation of cementing another League Championship title, Cooper's entrance on the big stage had turned into a momentous season in the sun. Yet, if there was to be further reason to toast the club's health as the climax of his debut year loomed, there was also cause for alarm in events behind the scenes. On a positive note, the Double became a Treble when Rangers, who had earlier snuffed out Berwick, Stirling Albion, Kilmarnock and Dundee United, faced up to their closest challengers, Aberdeen, and eventually won 2–1, breaking the deadlock through Alex MacDonald, adding to their lead with a goal from Derek Johnstone – who subsequently picked up a clutch of Player of the Year prizes and commendations – and were deserving of their victory despite conceding a bizarre late goal when Peter McCloy, normally so stoical and phlegmatic, embarked on a hanging-from-the-crossbar routine, while Steve Ritchie narrowed the gap for the Dons. But, in the event, it had little bearing on the outcome and the Ibrox men's litany of achievements was followed by a series of revelries, from the Blue Room, to the Popinjay Hotel in Rosebank and the Avonbridge in Hamilton, all the way to impromptu parties at the homes of Tommy McLean and other members of the victorious squad.

Somewhere in the midst of this, it was noticed by one or two of the celebrants that Wallace, normally a larger-than-life presence on these occasions, was muted in his rejoicing, but he explained that he wasn't as young as he used to be and, as he pointed out, it had been a long, tortuous season, where he had been forced to blood new-comers, accept the wrath of his own fans and generally work as if his life depended on it. And, of course, as the man in charge of an institution, he couldn't afford to be complacent.

Instead, the hangovers had barely been cured before he was sitting down, planning for the future, and trying to fathom how to replace several pivotal members, such as Greig, McCloy, McLean and Jackson, all of whom were in their thirties. Greig, for so many Rangers fans a talismanic character, was thirty-five, and his best days were clearly in the past. But these were big, big shoes to fill and Wallace knew that it couldn't be done easily or cheaply. He required money, and significant amounts of it, and, as somebody who had attained two Trebles in three years, was entitled to believe that he would be rewarded for his exertions, both personally and with a transfer budget.

In the event, he received neither, even when it was staring the Rangers board in the face that their continuing success required an urgent injection of new blood. And ironically, considering how often the Ibrox club's followers have rejoiced in the "biscuit-tin" mentality at Celtic, it was the parsimonious attitude of individuals such as Waddell, which proved the catalyst for the shock announcement on 23 May 1978, that Wallace had resigned as manager of the country's most successful footballing organisation.

It was one of those moments when football ends up on the front pages of the Scottish newspapers and, almost as if realising the propaganda shambles into which they had blundered, Rangers sought to appease the fans and only compounded their initial mistake with another by appointing Greig as the new manager, with immediate effect. At a stroke, a man with a wealth of tactical nous and coaching expertise was replaced by an ingénue in these departments. And in the blink of an eye, Wallace was off to Leicester, with barely enough time to say goodbye to his personnel before the revolving doors at Ibrox bade him adieu and hastened in one of the darkest periods in the club's history.

5

MYSTERY, MAGIC AND MR GREIG

Heaven knows how many tens of thousands of Rangers supporters were struck dumb by the news of Jock Wallace's resignation, but there was certainly vexation and a dossier of questions awaiting the Ibrox directors as the dust settled on Jock's departure. In these days, the Old Firm and smooth public relations went together like Jeremy Clarkson and political correctness, and conspiracy theories proliferated in the taverns and hostelries throughout the West of Scotland as the fans – and tabloid journalists – did their best to comprehend the reasons behind Wallace's abrupt exit from the manager's post.

Most people agreed that it couldn't have been based on his track record in the job, not given a trophy haul, comprising a brace of Trebles in the previous three seasons, even if Rangers' failure to make any impact on Europe in that period exasperated those who believed they should have been building on the Cup Winners' Cup triumph in 1972. There were plenty of Ibrox aficionados inclined towards the notion that the club's handling of the Wallace episode proved that their directors couldn't have organised a sponsored silence in a Trappist monastery, but there was never any satisfactory explanation offered for the manager's departure. Was it, as some claimed, because Jock had wanted to recruit Paul Hegarty from Dundee United at a time when Rangers remained committed to their policy of not signing Catholic players – and yes, there were exceptions but not high-profile cases prior to Maurice Johnston switching from Parkhead to Ibrox in 1989? If that was truly what occurred and Wallace had found himself at loggerheads with Willie Waddell, his decision to resign deserved greater exposure in public, and might have helped break down barriers, more than a decade before Johnston's arrival in Govan, flanked by David Murray, Graeme Souness, and half a million flashbulbs.

However, it was more probable that Wallace had simply grown fed up dealing with people who wouldn't give him the requisite funds to guide his ensemble to the next level. In 1977, even as he witnessed the impressive rise of Aberdeen and shuddered inwardly at the fashion in which Rangers were thrashed 4–0 at Pittodrie on Christmas Eve, he must have mused on the Scrooge-like tendencies of those who ran the show in the boardroom, and particularly Waddell, whose fiscal dealings meant that he was never in any danger of being confused with Andrew Carnegie. Earlier in that same year, while recognising the pressing need to recruit some fresh legs to a creaking defence, Wallace had done his best to persuade Rangers to invest in a talented twenty-two-year-old, who was still learning his craft in Glasgow. Yet when he went into the boardroom to put his arguments to Waddell and insisted that the proposed £100,000 transfer fee would turn out to be one of the bargains of the century, he was told that Rangers would only pay £80,000. Thus it transpired that Alan Hansen was snapped up by Liverpool a few weeks later – for a fee of £110,000 – and Wallace was left to rue another opportunity squandered through the tight-fisted approach of officials who seemed more interested in bricks and mortar than they did in furnishing the investment which was necessary to bolster their team's resources.

Many, if not all, managers have problems in these departments. But when one considers how Wallace brought Cooper, Gordon Smith and Bobby Russell to Ibrox for a grand total of £165,000, it was hardly surprising that he grew disenchanted at the intransigence of those above him in the pecking order. What *was* surprising was the fact that, even though the redoubtable Jock had forged a close alliance with that aforementioned trio, they only discovered that he had left Rangers upon scanning the tabloids on 24 May and were as perplexed and annoyed as any of their supporters on the periphery. Cooper especially couldn't believe the news, as he subsequently revealed in *True Blue*:

"The first I knew of the Big Man's decision to quit came when I read the news in the morning paper [*The Daily Record*] and there is no doubt that it was an absolute bombshell. He had just led Rangers to the Treble and he was at the peak of his career, so it seemed inconceivable that he should just turn his back on it all. I immediately phoned Bobby Russell to see what he thought about it. Like me, he was flabbergasted. It's a strange thing that in circumstances such as that, people always expect the players to know quicker than anybody else, but generally we are the last to hear and this was one such instance.

"All sorts of thoughts ran through my head after I got over the initial shock and since Jock never explained why he quit, we can only guess at the reasons. One, without question, was money. Rangers did not pay well at the time and clearly Jock felt that he deserved more in view of the tremendous success rate he achieved. The club, presumably, felt he didn't and, rather than it becoming an interminable stalemate, Jock got up and chucked it in. I dare say there were other factors and questions have always been asked about how he and Willie Waddell got on, but, in my opinion, it boiled down to basic, straightforward finance. I was very sorry to see him go, because I thought that he had done a tremendous job at Ibrox. He always did his own thing, and while he respected other people's views, he would stand or fall on his own judgements. He also treated everyone the same way. In that season, he had senior players such as Colin Jackson and Alex MacDonald alongside mere novices, like myself and Bobby Russell, yet we were all the same in his eyes. He had no favourites or at least if he did, he didn't show it."

The upshot, though, was that John Greig was installed as the new manager, and from the board's perspective, it probably made a lot of sense. As somebody with Rangers in his blood and who would eventually be voted the club's greatest-ever player, the move ensured a swift transition and guaranteed that, no matter their reservations over the manner of Wallace's parting, supporters and players alike would be prepared to grant Greig a prolonged honeymoon period.

With the benefit of hindsight, it is easy to cast doubts over the whole appointment process – and tempting to draw parallels with other occasions such as the elevation of Alan Shearer, whose revered status as a Newcastle icon didn't count for much when his beloved United were relegated at the end of the 2008–09 season. But it would also be wrong to draw a veil over the reservations sounded by many Rangers supporters at the time, those people who lamented Greig's dearth of managerial experience, and queried the rationale of throwing a thirty-five-year-old player with close connections to several figures in the dressing room, who were nearing the end of the shelf lives, into a situation where tough decisions had to hold sway over sentimental considerations. The bottom line was that there had never been any love lost between the artisan, Greig, and the artist, Cooper, and it should have been obvious that the former would be suspicious of the latter, particularly given how he had kicked him up in the air on their first meeting. And yet, for a while at least, they acquiesced in the other's company. It couldn't last – and beneath the flimsy carapace of comradeship, there was always a serious personality clash – but both men, in their different ways, were besotted with Rangers and privileged to be involved with them. The problem, if anything, was that they loved the club too much to recognise they might have fared better elsewhere.

Yet according to his former colleagues, this possibility never entered Cooper's head, even when he was in and out of the ranks, and was regularly denied the chance to orchestrate a Rangers revival even as their fortunes gradually deteriorated under Greig. In the short term, there was little reason to be overly pessimistic about his tenure, with the Old Firm continuing to spar for supremacy in the 1978–79 season – oblivious to the burgeoning ambitions of their opponents at Pittodrie and Tannadice – and the new manager recovered from a poor start, where Rangers failed to win any of their opening six league fixtures, to record a string of positive results, both on domestic duty and abroad, with the highlight being their tremendous victory over a star-studded Juventus team in the autumn of 1978.

On the plus side, this outcome was a vindication of Greig's tactics and team selection and nobody could quibble with a hard-fought 2–1 aggregate success against such illustrious adversaries as Dino Zoff, Antonio Cabrini, Marco Tardelli, Claudio Gentile, Roberto Bettega . . . serried characters from Serie A, who featured in Italy's World Cup-winning squad and whose exploits remain the stuff of legend in the football annals. Yet, if this success confirmed that Greig knew how to send out a side to scrap for their lives and deny their rivals any space whilst relying on pace on the flanks and a muscular approach in the midfield, it also highlighted the fragile nature of Davie's place in the new man's grand plan. He wasn't included in the ranks, either home or away, and although he accepted that Greig required different teams for different situations, this proved a microcosm of the relationship between the pair.

There were no showdowns or histrionics, tantrums or teddies-out-of-pram routines, but equally there was little mutual understanding of the other's qualities. It could have been resolved earlier if Cooper had chosen to spread his wings and follow the likes of Hansen and Kenny Dalglish down to England, but that option was constantly ruled out by his determination to stay in Scotland. "He never wanted to go anywhere else. Davie loved Rangers, but he also loved his folks and his home life in Hamilton and that was the end of the debate," said Bobby Russell with a mixture of admiration and bafflement. As for the fans, who had relished Cooper's gifts in his maiden season at Ibrox, the likes of Gordon Strang grew mystified at the negative tactics employed by Greig:

"It was fair enough when you were playing a team like Juventus or PSV [Eindhoven], to concentrate on keeping things tight at the back and not allow them time on the ball, because the Italians had nine World Cup [squad] players in their side and they were capable of ripping anybody apart if you let them dictate how they wanted to play.

"John got it spot-on during these European matches and we came away from these nights feeling that he might be the right man for the job after all. But then he became more and more cautious and started picking teams to avoid losing rather than guys who would actively pursue victory and I guess it was just the way his mind worked. It was a backs-to-the-wall mentality and he had worked his arse off for the previous fifteen years to bring trophies to Rangers and he obviously thought he had to depend on the old guard to bring him the results he wanted. But when you had a talent like Davie Cooper at your club, somebody who could take opponents to the cleaners and wasn't afraid of anybody he came across, it always seemed a bit daft to leave him on the bench, or, as happened too often, not select him at all. We were gobsmacked by the situation, because there was never any real indication that Greig and Cooper did not get on, but these were desperate times for Rangers and as the years passed by and the manager's new signings began walking through the door at Ibrox, most of whom didn't have any of Cooper's qualities or class, a lot of stuff happened which didn't make sense. It all went to hell, basically."

In the short term, Greig gained cheers from the majority of Rangers supporters on the strength of his European successes over Juventus and PSV. The latter was a classic confrontation and it appeared that the Scots had blown their chances when they could only draw 0–0 at home, but despite slipping behind in the early stages of the return leg, Rangers produced one of their classic performances in adversity, first taking the lead through Alex

MacDonald and Derek Johnstone and then, after the Dutch side levelled again at 2–2, applying the coup de grâce with a stunning goal from Bobby Russell, who had quickly developed into a coruscating presence amidst Greig's team. This was the first time that Eindhoven had tasted defeat at home in Europe, and although the Scots were subsequently eliminated at the quarter-final stage of the competition by Cologne, who capitalised on their opponents' lengthy injury list to edge to victory by 2–1 on aggregate, there was no disgrace over their exit. On the contrary, the twin triumphs signalled definite progress from some of the reverses which had been inflicted on Wallace's men.

On the domestic front, there were further reasons to be quietly optimistic, even if some observers queried Greig's insistence on splitting up the prolific partnership between Johnstone and Gordon Smith because he wanted to deploy the former as a centre-half. However, there were scant grounds for being overly critical as Rangers mounted bids in every competition and for much of the campaign looked capable of collecting another Treble. The League Cup was secured with a 2–1 success over Aberdeen in the final, courtesy of goals from the veterans MacDonald and Colin Jackson, while the Scottish Cup was also retained, though only after a tortuous sequence of tussles with Hibs, who were chasing their first victory in the competition since Paw Broon was a young man. The first contest ended goalless; and so did the second – this was football as tedious attrition without regard for entertainment value, a state of affairs which eventually came to encapsulate Greig's spell as manager. But eventually, the teams shrugged off their defensive strategies with sufficient vigour to generate a pulsating third leg of the battle, which Rangers won 3–2, with a brace from Johnstone and an own goal from the unfortunate Arthur Duncan proving just enough to edge out the Easter Road side.

Cooper was involved in both competitions and provided sprinklings of quality which were often at odds with the frantic, up-and-at-'em nature of these Cup forays, where all that mattered to Rangers was the outcome. It frequently made for stuffy, unedifying viewing, but it has to be borne in mind that the winter of 1978–79 was a dire one and when pitches weren't turning heavier and muddier, they were freezing up altogether, leading to a scenario where Rangers participated in only three league fixtures between 23 December and 14 March. In these circumstances, Greig plumped for pragmatism and used his more skilful personnel sparingly, but usually to good effect and Rangers, albeit without exhibiting the effervescence and flair sought after by a section of their support, scrapped away with Celtic as the winter chill froze into the waters of March.

Unfortunately, from Cooper's perspective, one or two developments were starting to cause him unease at Ibrox. At twenty-three, when one might have anticipated that he would be growing more comfortable in his own skin, he was struggling to cope with flitting in and out of contention and these problems were accentuated by the rapid progress of his club colleague John MacDonald, who had already burst through into first-team contention at the age of seventeen. Whether it was true or not, Davie believed that Greig was guilty of "playing favourites" more than had been the case with Jock Wallace, yet even if this was justified, Cooper's attitude was at best over-sensitive, at worst positively neurotic.

On some evenings, he returned home to Hamilton and complained bitterly to friends that the club he loved was "kicking him in the teeth" or "trying to flog him to another club", and on these nights he was difficult to console. At other times, where he had enjoyed practising his tricks on his confreres – he used to enjoy dribbling past Tom Forsyth whenever the pair locked horns on the training pitch – he would tell anybody who cared to listen that he had 100 per cent confidence in his own abilities and he would prove as much on the next occasion he received the nod. These contrasting emotions were to plague him for the next five years, but it wouldn't be fair to traduce Greig and cast all the blame on his shoulders for the stand-off which developed between these two proud characters.

On the contrary, both dug in their heels, resolved to defend their positions, and the consequence was that John MacDonald waltzed through the middle without a word of complaint.

In the midst of these backstage developments, Cooper and his colleagues were doing their utmost to cling on to their league title, despite the close attentions of Celtic, and it was with a sense of inevitability that fate decreed the outcome would be resolved between the Glasgow behemoths at Parkhead with the visitors requiring only a point to take the spoils. Yet if such an equation suited Greig, whose instincts told him to cling on to what he had and leave Celtic to worry about scoring, those very tactics suited his rivals down to the ground and this was one of the afternoons where powerbases shifted, reputations were enhanced and diminished and where Cooper experienced his first genuine taste of disappointment and found what it meant to lose to the other half of the Old Firm.

There was no hint of what lay in store when John MacDonald opened the scoring, especially once Celtic, already in arrears, were further hindered by the sending-off of Johnny Doyle, and the match predictably teetered on the precipice between a triple-X video nasty and a firestorm for the officials. Yet, even when Roy Aitken and George McCluskey shrugged aside their team's early travails to push the Bhoys in front, Rangers remained very much in contention, especially once Russell had equalised, briefly silencing the vociferous home support. It was a scenario which cried out for Rangers to be adventurous, to use their numerical advantage to press for a third goal and take the fight to their traditional rivals. But instead, with Greig judging that his men should sit on what they had, they retreated deeper and deeper into their own territory, ceded the initiative and the momentum to the hosts, and there is only so long that anybody can keep the ramparts intact when all these factors come into play. So it proved!

Maddeningly, though, for the small number of Rangers aficionados in the ground, they were undone not by the brilliance of the opposition, but through their own deficiencies in clearing their lines when Colin Jackson scored an own goal which effectively handed the title to Celtic, with Murdo MacLeod's effort on the final whistle merely the cherry on the parfait. At the death, all the glory was in one camp and all the misery in the other, and although they couldn't have guessed it at the time, the haunted expressions on the faces of the Rangers personnel was to become a regular feature of Scottish football in the years ahead. Nor was there much comfort to be gleaned from the shell-shocked fans, many of whom blamed the manager for what they perceived as overly negative tactics, though it has to be remembered that if Rangers had weathered the onslaught and emerged with a 2–2 draw, or even snatched a victory against the odds, Greig would have been viewed as a hero, with this the latest triumph which could be appended to his already illustrious CV. In short, perspective flew out of the window, as it often does when these clubs meet.

Cooper, as one might expect, was inconsolable. Until now, he had known only triumph, whether in winning promotion or titles with Clydebank and Rangers and even when he had endured defeat in Old Firm encounters, these hadn't been anything but minor upsets in a grander campaign. His words in the aftermath reflected his black mood. "It was a real horror show", "one of the worst days of my football career", there was "no consolation whatsoever in the Cups we had won, because the championship was the main prize", and, even as some of his teammates arranged elaborate plans to drown their sorrows by getting away from Glasgow, almost if they were devising an escape from Colditz, Davie retreated back to Hamilton, met up with his family and never ventured near a pub, hotel or any other public place for the next forty-eight hours. In these periods, he *was* a moody blue and didn't really care who knew it, but at least when he was surrounded by other Rangers followers they could wallow in each other's despondency and allow the wider world to carry on regardless.

"I was gutted," he told me more than a decade later. "Nothing had prepared me for what it would feel like to have a whole season's effort snatched away in the space of a few moments. "It doesn't matter what you do or how hard you try to put the result to the back of your mind. It sticks with you and you know that there is no hiding place anywhere in the West of Scotland. I spoke to the likes of Roy Aitken and Tommy Burns when we won the league in similar circumstances and they agreed with me that you just want to emigrate as soon as you have got changed and walked out of the ground. It is like a spectre which haunts you for weeks."

If that was a depressing episode in Cooper's life, the temporary blip didn't prevent English clubs from maintaining their interest in attracting his services. As the summer of 1979 passed, the likes of Newcastle United, Coventry City and West Bromwich Albion made tentative inquiries as to whether he might fancy a move south, but the response was always the same. In one sense, this loyalty was admirable, but it also meant that his managers at Ibrox knew that, come hell or high water, and irrespective of the size of the transfer deals on the table, Davie would not be going anywhere. As one season merged into another, it not only limited his horizons, but led to behind-the-scenes tension with the club over his earnings and bonus payments, and Cooper later admitted that he should have been more flexible in his approach. Yet, for all that he might moan about his lot to his friends in Hamilton – one of them told me, "Davie didn't lose the rag very often, but when he did, everybody knew all about it" – he never lost his passion for football.

Occasionally, it looked as if he was carrying the weight of the world on his shoulders, and nobody would associate the words *joie de vivre* with the years of austerity and underachievement which befell Rangers in the early 1980s, but Cooper remained one of the shining lights in the darkness and I like to think that whenever people sit down together throughout the world and muse on the greatest goals in the history of football, they will cast their gaze – courtesy of YouTube – over a litany of moments when Davie transcended the prosaic and soared into poetic realms with the quality of his play.

One of these was orchestrated – it would be doing it an injustice to describe it in anything other than artistic language – during the Drybrough Cup final against Celtic at Hampden Park at the start of the 1979–80 season in August. This competition wasn't regarded as being hugely important by most of the participating teams, but there is no such thing as a friendly football event where the Old Firm are concerned and this was no exception. Yet it was one of the quirks of the preliminaries to what materialised into a remarkable contest that, as Bobby Russell confirmed, John Greig wasn't unduly interested in this Cup, preferring to concentrate his attention and resources on loftier challenges:

"In the build-up to our match with Hibs, John instructed us not to score a goal and although he didn't set out to lose any game on purpose, it was made clear to us that this didn't figure large on his list of priorities, considering that he had the Championship and European action to worry about in the weeks after that. Anyway, we went out, and it was a pretty strange situation because there were still plenty of Rangers fans watching us and, as usual, they wanted us to win, no question about it. Several of our fringe players were involved in the fixture and it was one of them, Billy Urquhart, who scored what turned out to be the winning goal. Greig wasn't happy and I don't think Billy stayed at Ibrox for very long after that. [He left in 1980.] But that took us into the final and perhaps it proved everything happens for a reason because if we hadn't beaten Hibs, we wouldn't have been facing Celtic and Davie wouldn't have been able to do what he did."

As the denouement beckoned and the weather provided a compelling argument for the virtues of summer football, Cooper and his colleagues prepared for this resumption of Old Firm hostilities in atypical sunshine and balmy conditions, which presumably inspired the squad to work beyond their normal parameters, considering the fashion in which their collective excelled themselves. Sandy Jardine contributed a memorable goal, running the length of the pitch, with a string of Celtic personnel trailing in his wake, prior to finishing calmly by slotting the ball behind Peter Latchford. On any other day that shaft of inspiration would have been enough to delight the most demanding spectator, but as it transpired, Cooper surpassed his teammate's exploits by conjuring up a goal from the recesses of his imagination, which contained such sumptuous skill, vision and aesthetic beauty that even many Celtic supporters later described it as one of the most magical moments they had ever witnessed. In a wider context, this wasn't a World Cup qualifier or a high-profile international contest, so his heroics might not have carried the same resonance as Archie Gemmill's blink-and-you-missed-it balletic *entrechat* past the Dutch defence at the 1978 World Cup, or Jim Baxter's fabled piece of spontaneous keepie-uppie against the English at Wembley in 1967. But, judged by any reasonable stand-ards, Davie's instinctive act of derring-do contained all the requisite ingredients to thrill even those without an obsession with football, but who can recognise those rare instances in sport or life itself when everything good converges in the one moment to leave us with a priceless memory which, once glimpsed, creates an indelible mark.

The pictures testify to the brilliance and audacity of the execu-tion. They paint an image of Cooper in his pomp, a young man of twenty-three, possessed of perfect balance and the sweetest of left feet, latching on to an Alex MacDonald cross and calmly weighing up his options in a trice. At that juncture, his opponents had scant reason to be apprehensive over what Davie might be plotting, but suddenly, with the precise delicacy of a chess grandmaster destroy-ing his rival's ramparts as inevitably as the fall of the House of Usher, he had flicked the ball with inch-perfect dexterity up and over Roddie MacDonald, then, as the first stirrings of alarm were ignited among the Celtic defence, Cooper ghosted past Murdo MacLeod, continued his spectral advance beyond Tom McAdam and despite the panic-stricken stampede by his rivals, continued to weave a silky menace which was doubly breath-taking given that the ball hadn't touched the ground.

If that brought the audience to their feet, there was always the risk that the attack might fizzle out in anti-climactic fashion, but not a word of it. Instead, Davie repeated his previous trick to cruise past the challenge of Alan Sneddon and eventually, after waltzing majestically into space, fired an unstoppable shot past the blameless Latchford as the prelude to the whole arena becoming enveloped in a crescendo of acclamation and celebration.

Even from a distance, a few aspects of this wondrous solo recital stick in the mind. The first and most obvious is how many things had to go right throughout the performance – if any Celtic player had fouled Cooper, or managed the merest contact with the ball, the probability is that the attack would have been snuffed out – for it to progress to fruition. While the tabloids rhapsodised over the goal, Davie basked in warm glow, but he never took the adoration too seriously and regarded what he had done as a "once-in-a-lifetime" moment. Other, less talented players would have regaled audiences for the next twenty years with tales of their magnificence, embellishing their yarn as they moved into middle age, but, for better or worse, Davie was as modest once he returned to Hamilton as if he had just cracked in the winner in a schoolboy match. Of course, beating Celtic provided a warm glow, and he was able to enjoy that evening with Christine and his parents at their normal haunts. But it wasn't in his nature to dwell on these matters or believe any of the hype in the following day's newspapers, just as he would change the subject after a while if people started to ask him for autographs, or to discuss what made him tick.

Perhaps he was right in that assessment. He would certainly have been astonished to learn that Rangers supporters subsequently voted his Drybrough Cup final goal the greatest in the club's history and would probably have laughed it off with the riposte that he had got lucky with a few auspicious bounces of the ball. Yet it wasn't by chance or by accident that Davie was the catalyst for so many of these moments which can make the heart soar with their sheer exhilaration and spontaneity. From an early age, he had knuckled down to the philosophy that genius is an infinite capacity for taking pains and had worked relentlessly on being at ease in his vocation, whether dribbling, taking corners or free kicks, or sparking mayhem with his mazy incursions beyond those in his path. Such qualities can be taught, they can be refined and developed, but the best players invariably have something instinctive in their genes, helping them to excel on the football stage. Andy Roxburgh, the former Scotland coach and the Technical Director at UEFA, had watched Cooper enhance his skills when the duo were briefly in the same Clydebank squad and he was as enraptured by that marvellous goal as everybody else:

"I spend a lot of my time doing video analysis of Champions League matches and you soon get to appreciate those players who have a little bit extra in terms of quality and having time on the ball and being able to do things which most other people can't. Davie Cooper was one of those special individuals who could transform matches and turn ideas into reality and the goal he scored against Celtic in 1979 was top, top drawer. In fact, if a young Scot did that today, floating the ball over four or five defenders and leaving them for dead, before finding the net, people would be calling him the new Pelé or the new Maradona and they would be raving about him. Now, I'm not going to get carried away, because it can be silly to make comparisons between players from different eras, but Davie would have adapted to any setting, any time in football history, because he was born with perfect balance and he worked at his craft from when he was a small boy.

"Yet from the outset he was a mass of contradictions. I remember one night early on at Clydebank when he came into training and I said to him, 'Hi Davie, I've got a treat for you – we're being allowed to practise on the full-size pitch this evening.' I thought that he would be thrilled, because we normally had to make do with very basic facilities, but he looked a bit worried and then replied to me, 'I cannae play, Mr Roxburgh, I have to go home early to take my dog out for a walk.' Well, I was speechless for a few seconds, but that was just Davie being Davie. His life revolved around his family and nothing ever got in the way of being with those he held dear. He wasn't bothered about fame or fortune or the high life, even though he could have gone where he wanted with his gifts.

"In the end, I think he took the view that if he could play football for his favourite club, it was a privilege, an honour, and he counted himself one of the luckiest men in the world, because he knew how many others wanted to be in his shoes. Whether at Clydebank or when I was working with the Scotland Under-21s or the full national team in the 1980s, he was a joy to be around and I never understood the 'Moody Blue' tag, except in one sense. Namely, that he was like an artist: he had to get into the right mood to be at his best and if that meant shutting off any distractions, so be it. Early on, I did my best to persuade him to practise with his right foot, but he was similar to Ferenc Puskás – he could do things with one foot that most others could only dream about with two. "

The warmth of these words testifies to the affection with which Cooper was regarded throughout Scottish football and one of the most heartening features of writing this book lay in discovering that tribal loyalties were torn asunder when it came to fans from other clubs recalling their memories. Gary Burgess, an Aberdeen fan with no great affection for Rangers, recollected one afternoon at Pittodrie where Davie both scintillated his own supporters and scared the wits out of the opposition yet finished up gaining no tangible reward for his endeavours because of the profligacy of his strikers.

"He must have gone past the Aberdeen defence half a dozen times, shimmying one way and weaving the other and his ball control was fantastic, but every time he cut us apart, there was nobody to polish off the moves and it must have been incredibly frustrating," said Burgess. "We were going into that period where Rangers lost their ability to intimidate opponents, and we got used to taking them apart at Pittodrie. But Cooper was always a threat and, when you look back at it, it was remarkable that he should have been allowed to drift out of the picture at Ibrox, but most of us in the Beach End felt relieved about that."

Understandably, these sentiments weren't echoed by Rangers followers, who had to grow accustomed to their rivals indulging in *schadenfreude* as the glory years under Jock Wallace become a distant memory. Indeed, any expectations fostered by the 3–1 victory in the Drybrough Cup final were swiftly cast to the wind as Greig and his charges slumped from one crushing blow to another, en route to becoming embroiled in the sort of league campaign whose lack of achievement will doubtless astonish those people who grew up during the nine-in-a-row heroics of the 1990s. There were problems for the manager in almost every department, nor was his cause assisted by persevering with players who were past their sell-by date, and it added up to an embarrassing season when Rangers plummeted to fifth in the championship race, all of 11 points behind the winners, Aberdeen, who garnered seven from a potential eight points from their Glasgow opponents. Worse still, in some respects, for an organisation which had always prided itself on being able to travel anywhere without feeling any undue apprehension, Greig's squad gained only 10 points from eighteen away fixtures – a record of spluttering incompetence which was bettered by every other team in the division, except the two clubs who were relegated, Dundee and Hibernian.

There was further misery in the quest for silverware, with Aberdeen eliminating Rangers from the League Cup, then, just to rub salt in the wounds, Celtic beat their Old Firm rivals, courtesy of a deflected George McCluskey goal, on an afternoon at Hampden Park in 1980 which has gone down in infamy. Football became irrelevant amidst the violent pitch invasion at the end, which was the prelude to scenes of visceral hatred between the opposing fans, mounted police trying desperately to deal with a maelstrom of random alcohol-fuelled violence, and a riot which provoked commentator, Archie Macpherson, to declare, "It's like Paschendaele out there."

That might have been an over-the-top reaction to what he was witnessing, but here was proof, if it was required, that the bigotry and prejudice which had festered throughout the decades still cast a grievous blight on Scottish life. To his credit, Macpherson excoriated both sides for their collusion in the process, in terms which explained why the alleged mystique of the Old Firm remains a mystery to so many people outside Glasgow.

"The roots of the tribalism which produced the Scottish Cup final riot lie deeply embedded even yet," he wrote in 2005. "We still see the uncomfortable truth that the terraces mirror certain aspects of our society. We see the two sets of supporters travelling to the final from the pub in the Lanarkshire village of Glenboig, which I know well. It had two doors, one for Protestants, the other for Catholics, who drank on separate sides of the bar, but got on famously nevertheless. The tradition was upheld at a different level when the council from the same county, in 2004, spent an extra £600,000 to provide separate staffrooms for teachers of the respective faiths, without consultation. We still live in a two-door society. So is it any wonder that they still sing the songs of hatred?"

Back inside the dressing rooms at Hampden, even as the fights continued to rage outside, there were contrasting reactions from the players involved in the match. Murdo MacLeod said he was unaware of the scale of the incident, declaring, "We didn't find out about the trouble that erupted until later that night when we got back to the hotel. We were told [by SFA officials and the police] that we couldn't take the Cup onto the pitch, but I didn't really think about it and when we left the stadium, everything had quietened down."

His opposite number, Gordon Smith, was equally in the dark as to the extent of the violence and lawlessness which was partly fuelled by incipient religious animosity and partly a consequence of the alcohol which had been on sale at Hampden. "I was totally unaware of the fighting on the pitch afterwards," said Smith. "We were led up a back stair to collect our medals and I had my head down the whole time. Afterwards, a few of the lads remarked on a riot, but I had no idea what they were talking about."

Yet Cooper knew. Even as he had glanced backwards while leaving the auditorium, he noticed a few spectators on the pitch and wondered how serious the situation might become. Later in the evening, by the time he had returned to Hamilton his friends and colleagues were talking about the enormity of what had occurred and, not for the first or last time in his life, Davie shook his head and wondered why football could be the focus for so much bitterness and detestation when many of those involved in the brawls would probably have had difficulty spelling "Protestant" and "Catholic" correctly. This isn't intended to depict him as some sort of plaster saint. In the heat of Old Firm derby action, Cooper was as animated and exhilarated as anybody else by putting one over Celtic and there were instances where he crossed the line or revelled in the problems of his Glasgow opponents. But, all the same, he was capable of recognising that football was only a game and that, however painful the hurt of defeat, it was only a transient sensation. In which light, he was repulsed by the pictures he watched later from the Hampden war zone.

As he later told the *Record*: "I was haunted by what went on after that match. Haunted! The result didn't matter in the slightest. It was the sickening trouble at the end of the game which stuck in my mind, and I was pretty depressed as I headed home that evening. We had all been consoling each other in the bath when we learned just how bad things had become out on the pitch and when you have people assaulting one another and who are prepared to use violence on total strangers, there is no excuse, no provocation for that behaviour. It was a tragic end to the day, and there should be no place in football for the things that went on that day.

"The authorities had to take action and I'm glad they did [with the sale of alcohol prohibited at football stadia]. It didn't make any of the later Old Firm matches any less intense, because these are games which you always want to win, but there is usually enough at stake on the pitch for the supporters to have plenty to occupy their minds. In my opinion, nothing matches an Old Firm derby. You have big games between the Milan teams in Italy and similar meetings in Manchester, Liverpool, London and across the world, but the ingredient a Rangers-Celtic clash has which the others don't is, unfortunately, religion. I wish it wasn't like that. And when you look at what happened at Hampden in 1980, you can see how destructive the whole thing could be. I was glad to lock my door and be home in one piece that night. Not because we had lost, but because this was one of the days where football suddenly didn't seem very important."

That occasion was a portent of things to come for Rangers. Their board had taken strides to create a stadium of which any supporter could be proud, but the expense involved in that project, allied to Willie Waddell's refusal to alter his strict budgetary policies, meant that their facilities were in much better shape than their personnel. Within the space of a couple of seasons, the likes of such stalwart figures as Colin Jackson and Alex MacDonald had gone from A-listers to men B-witched, bothered and bewildered by the pace of the New Firm's revolution. Greig, for his part, was less a proud figurehead at the helm than a fellow up to his neck in quicksand. None of this boded well for Cooper, as he would have ample time to reflect upon during the wilderness years which followed.

6

OUT OF SIGHT, OUT OF MIND

The early 1980s were a traumatic period for many people in British society, whether they worked in traditional manufacturing industries or were graduating from university or college and pursuing jobs. As the dole queues lengthened and the Specials sang their lament to wasted youth in "Ghost Town", football didn't have its problems to seek either. Trouble and hooliganism at matches was rife and would continue to cast a blight over the sport in the build-up to the twin tragedies of Heysel and Hillsborough and, with hindsight, it was astonishing that decent soccer supporters – the majority – should have acquiesced in a situation where the Prime Minister, Margaret Thatcher, treated them with barely-concealed contempt, even as they paid millions of pounds in admission money for the dubious privilege of standing in urine-soaked terracing, impervious to the weather and the lack of quality in their team. Nowadays, with Paul Whitehouse having breathed flesh and blood into the fictitious Ron Manager and his constant paeans to the days of "Jumpers for Goalposts", some of us can remember embarking on trips to Broomfield, Easter Road, Tynecastle or Love Street in the late 1970s and early 1980s and grimace at how easily we were fleeced of our cash by club owners and directors who had no intention of reinvesting the proceeds any further than their own bank accounts.

In those days, the Old Firm remained a law unto themselves. Comedians made cracks about the alleged "vanishing turnstiles" at Parkhead, where the official crowd figure bore little relation to the extra thousands of supporters who were jam-packed or sardine-crushed into every corner of the stadium. At Rangers meanwhile, Thatcher, who was sufficiently reviled in large parts of Scotland that fans waved a collective red card at her when she subsequently turned up as a dignitary at a Scottish Cup final, was regarded in some quarters as somebody who would restore the "Great" to "Great Britain" and her "Iron Lady" sobriquet was viewed as a badge of honour by the diehard unionists. Neutrals might have gazed on the two organisations and wondered why they seemed so committed to furthering the Irish conflict, with sport as the conduit, on Caledonian soil. But at that juncture in the Old Firm's history, even as they came under attack on the pitch from Aberdeen and Dundee United, bolstered by ambitious young managers in the guise of Alex Ferguson and Jim McLean and were condemned for their systemic failure to address sectarianism off the field, neither club was prepared to grasp the nettle and face up to the need for a genuine change in their mindset. Instead, the extremist IRA and UDA/UVF merchandise was openly on sale at both stadiums whenever the gates were open for football. Just another Saturday for the men who balanced the books.

Davie Cooper had more pressing concerns as Rangers sought redemption in the build-up to the 1980–81 campaign, fresh from a season where the majority of their endeavours had withered on the vine and provoked mounting signs of disaffection from the support. The squad had been enhanced with the recruitment of Tom McAdam and Jim Bett, the latter from the Belgian club, Lokeren, and the return of Willie Johnston, but nonetheless, there was a sense of anxiety hanging over the camp, almost as if the Ibrox hierarchy could sense a changing of the guard without possessing the means to halt the process. It hardly helped that the management resorted to cosmetic change when root-and-branch renewal was required, yet it was perhaps an indication of how relations had soured into sullen silence between Greig and Cooper that when the twenty-four-year-old was offered the opportunity to move elsewhere, following an approach from the Brighton & Hove Albion manager, Alan Mullery, he should end up staying where he was while the peripatetic Gordon Smith headed to England for a record transfer fee of £440,000. We have already discussed how reluctant Cooper was to leave his roots, but there is pride in origin, and then there is stubborn obstinacy, and this course of action veered perilously close to the latter.

The negotiations were terse and to the point. Mullery, a larger-than-life character with a twinkle in his eye and a charismatic hinterland, wanted to purchase both Smith and Cooper but was informed by Greig that he was only prepared to sell one of the duo. Given how little subsequent use he found for Davie in his plans, it beggars belief that the Rangers boss wasn't ready to move him on if the price was right, and I have been told by two of the Ibrox squad at the time that Greig made it clear to Cooper that he would be well advised to contemplate expanding his horizons and – considering the money which was on the table – putting himself into the shop window with a switch to Brighton. However, whatever the validity of this advice, the argument cut no ice with Davie, who glanced at the map, calculated that he wouldn't be able to get home to Hamilton very often, and that meant he wasn't interested.

To some extent, one can comprehend why a proud Ibrox man wouldn't be overly delighted at the prospect of joining the likes of Brighton – which wasn't exactly Manchester United, Arsenal or Liverpool in the grand pantheon of English giants – but in this instance, Cooper's intransigence was baffling, particularly in light of what subsequently transpired. After all, if he had completed the transfer and shown his capabilities under Mullery, there would surely have been other, more enticing offers for him to consider in the years ahead. Whereas he knew that for as long as Greig was his gaffer in Glasgow, he would be spending more time keeping benches warm than plying his trade in the thick of competitive action.

Even from Smith's perspective, this was a curious state of affairs, as he told me. "I had a chat with Alan and he had been keeping tabs on both Davie and myself and I am convinced that he wanted to sign the pair of us. But sometimes you have to accept that these matters can get complicated and I learned soon afterwards that John was only ready to let one of us go. If I'm being honest, I think Alan might have got the worse of the deal, although I think I acquitted myself pretty well at Brighton [where he famously missed a sitter in the 1983 FA Cup final against Manchester United]. I don't believe that Davie had any regrets about not going, but it was always one of the 'What if . . . ?' questions which made me wonder what might have happened if Coop had gone to Brighton.

"There is no doubt that he had more than enough natural gifts and the right temperament to make a success of it in England and I am convinced he could have fitted in anywhere he wanted, but that was the end of my time at Ibrox, although I came back very briefly [on loan] in 1982. Rangers were having problems in that period, but you have to understand that Davie was living the dream and he loved the club, it was as simple as that."

Ultimately, though, the compromise suited neither party and, now that it was obvious that Cooper wouldn't be wooed away from Rangers, he had to accept that he was a peripheral figure in Greig's plans, which was easier said than done. Yet, if he had any aspirations towards converting his manager to his qualities, they yielded precious little reward in the next three seasons. On the contrary, his talent was used sparingly, both in the league championship, where he started less than half the games in the 1980–81 campaign, and even more sporadically in the Scottish Cup. For those who cherished thrilling football, regardless of club affiliation, this was a dreadful waste of one of the few genuine entertainers on the Scottish domestic circuit, but while Greig could be faulted for his dearth of flexibility, especially given the mediocre results attained by those players he *did* select, Cooper wasn't blameless either and as the months passed he fell into a slump exemplified by a lack of intensity at training and unwillingness to scrap for his place in the first team. It might be that he had concluded there was little merit in battering his head against a concrete wall, but that didn't excuse his attitude and Davie subsequently conceded that he should have battled harder rather than resort to the dumb insolence which typified the dialogue – or absence of it – between him and Greig.

Some of this was reminiscent of a playground bust-up between a pair of eleven-year-olds. On the one hand, Cooper started turning up a few minutes late for training, then, once he had got changed, he went through the motions, while refusing to make eye contact with his gaffer. It was childish and unbecoming of a well-paid professional, and he knew it. "I grew a bit sloppy and the more frustrated that I became, the less inclined I was to push myself as hard on the training pitch. Then, when I found myself on the bench, I don't think my attitude was all it might have been."

Occasionally – and more often than he cared to admit – he was in danger of falling out of love with football and Cooper became uncharacteristically prone to temper tantrums back at his home base, where the words "It's just not fair" were punctuated with a torrent of f-words of which even the martinet Jock Wallace would have been proud. Ultimately, this was a stalemate which couldn't have a happy ending. He and Greig were chalk and cheese, Cavalier and Roundhead, the young pretender against the old guard, and only one of them was cracking the whip.

Rangers, meanwhile, were off the pace and out of sorts and their championship foundered on a dreadful sequence of results in November and December where the fans made their displeasure known to the players and to Greig. This lack of achievement was all the more disappointing for the supporters because the Ibrox personnel had started the season in terrific shape, generating an unbeaten run stretching to fifteen matches, which featured a brace of Old Firm derby successes and a record-breaking 8–1 victory against Kilmarnock at Rugby Park. Cooper flitted in and out of first-team contention, orchestrating occasional pieces of brilliance along with some performances which were at best average, at worst completely anonymous, and that inconsistency typified his mood and reflected the reality that he was a player who needed to be sure he had the backing of his manager to weave his magic even if, inevitably, there were afternoons where his mojo wasn't working.

His side's barren spell in the run-up to Christmas put paid to their title aspirations and for most of the remainder of the season, they were chasing shadows, dressed in Celtic and Aberdeen colours. With no European football, as a consequence of their dismal form in the previous league battle, Rangers sought refuge in the Anglo-Scottish Cup, but instead suffered one of the most inauspicious events in their history when they were bundled out of the competition by lowly Chesterfield Town, whose players weren't even household names in their own living rooms. Nonetheless, they preyed on their opponents' diminishing confidence and vulnerability, gaining a 1–1 draw at Ibrox in the first leg, then trouncing the Scots 3–0 in the return match, an outcome which, predictably enough, provoked vitriol from the tabloids, who started to put serious pressure on Greig.

The consequence was that the manager, if anything, grew even more introspective and the weight of tradition hung heavily on his shoulders. He resorted to doing what many individuals do in these circumstances, slipping into his shell, depending on the men with whom he had chased Trebles, although it was evident they had lost their lustre with the passing of time, and generally ignoring everybody else. This was quite literally the case with Cooper, whose disenchantment with his treatment increased the more he found himself on the sidelines. It was an unhappy situation, but one which had been threatening to brew for the previous eighteen months, and Davie felt isolated, even unwanted at Rangers, even though he refused to take the easy option of demanding a transfer. The scale of his frustration, though, can be gauged by his explanation of how he would dread venturing to Ibrox on Wednesdays because he would regularly find out, from a second-hand source, that his services weren't required for the following weekend's fixture.

"It wasn't so much the fact that I was in and out of the team which bugged me as much as the way I discovered that I wasn't going to be playing in a particular match," said Cooper. "I would realise on the Wednesday or the Thursday, on any given week, that the writing was on the wall, because, at that point, John would stop speaking to me and simply walk past me in the corridor without a word. It was always the signal that I wasn't in his plans and wouldn't be picked and I know that other players experienced the same thing."

One of these, who requested anonymity, told me that the atmosphere in the dressing room was "dreadful", with cliques developing, between those who were Greig's favourites, those who were new to the club and couldn't quite believe what was happening, and those, such as Cooper, who were viewed with suspicion by the management.

"Jock Wallace was a hard man, but a fair man. He knew that Rangers Football Club was all that mattered, not how one guy got on with another, and although we used to sh** ourselves when Jock was on the warpath, he was never vindictive. If you screwed up, there would be hell to pay, but it was over in a few minutes and Jock realised that nobody deliberately went out to make mistakes. However, John Greig was a different character entirely. He was given the job too soon – I think even he would admit that these days – and it's difficult when you are one of the guys in the dressing room, having a laugh with the other lads, then suddenly, you are having to give orders to these same guys and impose discipline and talk tactics. John never got the balance right and although you can make excuses for him and say that his appointment was a mistake, and that the likes of Willie Waddell should have carried the can, he didn't really help himself either.

"The way he messed around with Davie Cooper summed it up. Given the problems Rangers had in 1980 and thereafter, Davie should have been one of the key players at Ibrox and yet he was marginalised, made to feel unwanted, and it did affect him. He tried to laugh it off, and told me once, 'That miserable bastard isn't going to get rid of me,' but it was a hopeless state of affairs and unbelievable when you think that Rangers were one of the biggest clubs in British football, yet this was amateurish beyond words.

"Every manager has to take responsibility for his actions and if John had gone up to Cooper and told him, 'Look, son, I don't think you can tackle and that makes you a liability, so I'm not picking you,' at least Davie would have known where he stood. But the way it was done was that Greig would get somebody else – and usually it was [coach] Joe Mason – to let Cooper know he wasn't playing and that just wasn't on. If you make a hard decision, you should be prepared to take the flak and the best managers all knew there would be times when they would be unpopular with guys in their squad, because you can't please everybody all the time. But John never seemed to appreciate that."

By the climax of the 1980–81 season, their relationship had drifted into stalemate, but, mercifully, that situation wasn't destined to carry on indefinitely. Celtic won the league, finishing all of 12 points in front of their third-placed Old Firm rivals, which for the Ibrox faithful constituted a fresh bout of failure and, in terms of short-term thrills or longer-term vision, there was a void at the heart of the club. Greig's team lacked spark and any semblance of aesthetic creativity and while the manager's efforts were scarcely boosted by a shortage of significant funds to invest in new blood, his selection for the 1981 Scottish Cup final against Dundee United was symptomatic of his tenure.

Cooper didn't even feature in the first meeting between the sides, consigned to the periphery, even as the clubs served up a dreich, extended yawn of a contest, which remained goalless, although Ian Redford was presented with a golden opportunity to settle the tie in Rangers' favour when his men were awarded a last-minute penalty but squandered the chance against his old employers. The grumbles from the fans at the death reflected the rising tide of antipathy towards Greig – but, in fairness, it should be noted that he retained his iconic status with many supporters, irrespective of his travails in the managerial hot seat – yet he was under pressure to deliver a higher quality of football and, at last, Cooper came in from the cold and provided ample evidence of his powers with a dazzling display in the replay.

It was as if he was releasing months of pent-up frustration in the space of ninety minutes and United were the unfortunate victims, caught in the midst of a hurricane. Time after time, he waltzed past their would-be tacklers, generated momentum for his teammates, cruised into space as if it was the easiest thing in the world and the Ibrox supporters were torn between marvelling at their man's master class and scratching their heads as to why Cooper was ranked lower in the pecking order than, for instance, Redford, a good, honest professional, without any pretensions to belonging in a higher category than that.

It was a rare afternoon to savour in the early 1980s and Cooper's skills ensured that there was a regular supply of openings and goals for his side. He scored one himself and was the catalyst for a couple of others, as John MacDonald secured a brace, with Russell adding to his tally amidst the 4–1 triumph, where Rangers shrugged off their general lethargy to remind observers of the fashion in which they had stacked up domestic trophies under Jock Wallace. Davie, true to type, celebrated quietly at the death – there were no recriminations, badge-kissing histrionics or intimations of resentment – and yet it was obvious to most people that his club required him more than he needed them.

Indeed, whatever misgivings Greig might have harboured about Cooper's work ethic, or perceived failure to track back if he lost the ball, they were rendered irrelevant by the desperate nature of the circumstances. One by one, the old guard were slipping into retirement – Alex MacDonald was the latest to bid adieu, sold on to Hearts for £30,000 after twelve years of yeoman service – and there was no sign of a new generation arriving en masse to mount a sustained challenge to Celtic and Aberdeen. In this light, Greig had little option but to bring Cooper back into the fold, and he became a first-team regular again in the 1981–82 campaign. Yet, no one individual could have transcended the morass into which the Ibrox ensemble had plummeted and so it proved, as their flirtation with the slough of despond led to a rising number of occasions where attendances dipped alarmingly, as brassed-off fans discovered other, more exciting pastimes to occupy their minds, whether in watching paint dry or going shopping on Saturday afternoons.

Those who remained loyal to the cause could have been forgiven for glancing wistfully at the dramatic contrast between Rangers in 1972 and 1982. A decade earlier, there had been a fabled European triumph in Barcelona; now, the fallen Ibrox giants were reduced to sustained mediocrity in Scotland, let alone entertaining any loftier ambitions. If one stepped outwith the Old Firm's queasily myopic perspective, it could be deduced that this enhanced level of competition in Scotland actually brought about an improvement in the fortunes of the national side, which started making a habit of reaching the finals of major tournaments. Yet such considerations have never mattered unduly to aficionados of Rangers and Celtic and the reality was that, during this period, Greig's stewardship of the side had reduced his club to a parody of how they were supposed to perform. Kick anything that moves? Check! Hoof the ball in the air at every possible opportunity? Check! Operate on perspiration and forget about such airy-fairy notions as inspiration? Check! These tactics might have sufficed had Rangers boasted a Baxter, McCoist and Laudrup up front, but sadly for John Greig, he didn't have access to a Tardis.

Instead, as Rangers sank further into the mire, their followers would have been entitled to believe they were stuck in some ghastly soccer variant of *Groundhog Day*. Or, to put it another way, like the previous twelve months, the 1981–82 season brought a paucity of reward, with Celtic once again marching to the championship title with a spanking twelve-point gap over their Glasgow rivals. Nowadays, such failure wouldn't be tolerated by the board, nor excused by the fans. However, even if behind the scenes, there were reports that the Ibrox directors recognised the scale of the malaise and were actively courting the likes of Alex Ferguson and Jim McLean, they had so many problems on and off the pitch that only a masochist would have been interested in taking on the job. As one pro-Rangers source – the Gersnet online site – summed up the situation: "It was around this time it became increasingly difficult to find any positives regarding Rangers and John Greig was becoming the focal point when fans discussed what was wrong. The simple truth was that we were just not good enough.

"Our European participation was halted by Dukla Prague, who totally outclassed us in Czechoslovakia [where the hosts won 3–0], although we regained some pride by winning the home leg 2–1 with goals from Jim Bett and John MacDonald. Then, in the domestic Cups, Rangers were losing 1–0 to Dundee United before a brilliantly-executed free kick by Davie Cooper drew us level [before Redford scored the winner with an equally stunning effort]. Rangers also reached the Scottish Cup final, where MacDonald gave us the lead, but after equalising, Aberdeen ran away with the game in extra time and eventually won 4–1. That marked the end of the careers of some of our stalwarts."

The tone of these remarks explains why many fans discovered alternative pursuits, rather than continually shelling out their cash on expensive season tickets. With the departure and/or retirement of such battle-weary luminaries as Tom Forsyth, Colin Jackson, Sandy Jardine and Alex Forsyth, the majority of Greig's lieutenants were no longer present to bolster him in the dressing room and the manager's job became an ever more thankless, precarious and isolated existence. Cooper found himself sucked into the malaise and despite conjuring up plenty of wondrous memories – one lifelong Rangers supporter, Scott Blair, told me how he had watched Davie scoring direct from corners on successive Saturdays, exhibiting a wicked ability to make the ball dance to his rhythm from set pieces – he was also pilloried by a section of the Ibrox crowd, who were plainly seeking scapegoats during this wilderness spell and found an easy target in Cooper, who was both infuriated by the cat-calls and indignant that he was being abused in this fashion. His indignation was sufficient for him to mention it later in a lengthy *Herald* interview:

"Throughout the basically lean years – by Rangers' standards – there was one thing which always irritated me. There were many occasions when the team was playing badly that I played well personally, yet that factor never seemed to be noticed. I was singled out by some fans who picked on me and seemed to blame me for the team's performance without ever really looking too closely at my own contribution. I was given quite a hard time and I have always felt that was a little unfair. The only justification which I can come up with is that for a while I was the only internationalist in the side and maybe for that reason I stuck out a bit. But, whatever, it was something that grieved me."

All the same, Cooper was sufficiently candid to recognise that his standards slipped in the midst of his side's myriad disappointments. As he told me almost a decade down the line, "I was out of sorts and I took it out on John, the longer that he was in charge of Rangers. It was unprofessional of me and I wish that I could have shown more application to the club because we needed all the help that we could get at the time and I suppose I didn't put in as big a shift as I could have for John. He offered me a second chance at Ibrox, but I just couldn't get it out of my head that he had given me a raw deal. I look back now and wish that I had realised that it wasn't personal; it was just that the two of us were different types of people. That didn't mean either of us was right or wrong."

However, even as Greig attempted, in what was to prove his last throw of the dice, to reinforce his squad with the recruitment of the likes of Craig Paterson, Sandy Clark and Robert Prytz, there were no stardust memories, nor sustained signs of a corner being turned.

By this stage, the manager was being hounded by the tabloids whose journalists scented blood, and leaks emanated from Ibrox on a regular basis, which made his life even more precarious. One such instance happened when Greig made an audacious move for the Scotland goalkeeper, Alan Rough, only for the bid to fall apart mysteriously, as the one-time Partick star later revealed when I worked on his autobiography:

"I was sitting at home one Friday, looking at the papers, when the phone rang. It was John Greig, who told me, 'Alan, I have been reading reports that you are poised to sign for Hibs and I want to find out if these stories are true.' I answered, 'Well, I have met [their chairman] Kenny Waugh and we have agreed a signing-on fee, but I haven't put pen to paper as yet.' John continued, 'Look, I want you to come to Ibrox, so can you sit on this until Monday? I will get together with my board and I am confident that I can persuade the directors to go for it. But please don't mention this to anybody else.'

"I was suddenly being chased by two of the biggest clubs in Scotland. But what I didn't appreciate at the time was that John was experiencing a crisis at Rangers – this was in the days when they were being surpassed by Alex Ferguson's Aberdeen and the crowds were drying up dramatically. Yet, it would still have been a good move for me and I felt like a struggling actor who has been stuck amongst the extras in *Coronation Street*, being offered leading roles by Steven Spielberg and George Lucas at the same time.

"However, when I woke up on the Sunday morning, the saga took a new twist when I picked up the *Sunday Mail* and the headline 'Rough for Rangers' was splashed all over the back page, in the kind of typeface normally reserved for assassinations and royal weddings. I guessed that I wouldn't be heading to Ibrox after all, because the Old Firm weren't in the habit of signing players via the media, and John had obviously been shafted by somebody in his own circle. To his credit, he rang me on the Monday, he sounded terrible, and said to me, 'Alan, I am very sorry at the way this has unfolded. Circumstances have conspired against me. I didn't mention this to the board, but now I look pretty stupid and the deal just isn't going to happen.' I had no doubts as to his sincerity and his tone was that of a fellow at the end of his tether. I wasn't a Rangers fan, but I would have been totally professional for them if I had walked through the gates at Ibrox, and would have been very happy to work for John because he was one of the most courageous, committed characters ever to represent his club and his country. But this incident showed me that he was under pressure and was in a very tough position."

Success remained elusive, and there were no magic formulae available to Greig. On the contrary, despite launching their 1982–83 campaign with a flourish, which saw Borussia Dortmund being eliminated from the UEFA Cup while Rangers stayed unbeaten throughout the course of their first eight league matches, they behaved as if they were always waiting for something to go amiss and the saturnine presence of Greig on the fringes meant that oblivion was never too far out of the players' eye line. At a stroke, both in European action and closer to home, misery kept gate-crashing the party: Cologne inflicted a demoralising 5–0 defeat on the Scots, and as their initial momentum stalled almost to a hearse-like pace, Rangers veered down a cul-de-sac of vulnerability and were nowhere to be seen in the race for the championship, eventually finishing a remarkable 18 points behind Dundee United, reduced to fourth place, in the title standings.

As if that wasn't depressing enough, Greig's personnel were pipped in the Scottish Cup final showdown by Aberdeen, who had swept to European Cup Winners' Cup glory against the might of Real Madrid only three days earlier in Gothenburg, and it was a measure of how substantially the balance in Scottish football had shifted that even in the aftermath of his side's 1–0 win, courtesy of an Eric Black goal, Alex Ferguson raged in public at his personnel after the match, describing their display as totally unacceptable – and this in a scenario where they had just beaten Rangers at Hampden Park.

Unsurprisingly, these factors offered naught for Cooper's comfort, and he derived scant consolation from the personal milestones which he posted throughout the season. These included him scoring his first hat-trick for Rangers – in a sectional League Cup tie against Kilmarnock – as well as orchestrating his first and only European goal in the victory over Dortmund. All that concerned him was that there were no trophies in the Ibrox cabinet again – Celtic collected the League Cup – and that the club were making no discernible progress. If anything, they were actually stuck in reverse gear and from this distance it appears unbelievable that Greig should have been permitted to carry on over a period of five seasons when the priority – winning the Championship – stretched further into the distance with every passing year.

Of course, the New Firm's hegemony, however temporary a phenomenon it proved, propelled another significant couple of factors into the mix, but the bottom line for both halves of the Old Firm is that they have to be pursuing honours and attaining silverware on a regular basis, and on that score, Rangers lurched from one problem to another between 1979 and 1983. If they had been serving up a feast of pretty football or a diet of attacking entertainment, that might just have provided some compensation for their acolytes, but too often the opposite was the case, with lumpen football and stodgy tactics combining to dampen the ardour of even the most blue-tinged supporter. Cooper was the main exception to the general shambles, and even he confessed that he should have been striving for greater consistency, so it isn't difficult to understand why there were mass cries for change at Ibrox in the summer of 1983.

And, thankfully for Davie, they brought him the chance to dazzle once more.

7

THE RE-BIRTH OF THE COOP

At the climax of one of the longest goodbyes in the history of Scottish football, John Greig finally resigned as Rangers manager at the end of September 1983. During his tenure, it was undeniable that the balance of power had shifted away from the Old Firm, and the Govan-based half of the Glasgow double act in particular, yet anybody who believed that the responsibility for their decline lay solely with Greig was living in a fool's paradise. Of course, he should have shown greater flexibility, and his treatment of Davie Cooper was hard to fathom, but the Ibrox directors were culpable as well in the malaise which had befallen their club and they remained in the shadows, largely avoiding any blame for the slump which had occurred on their watch. By comparison, Greig vacated his office in the autumn to the unfamiliar sound of booing from those who had once saluted him (and who would rediscover their affection for the man in the future). It was an undignified denouement to a saga of Forsyte proportions.

However, his exit hardly yielded immediate relief either for Rangers or Cooper. Instead, and demonstrating all the fleetness of movement of Mr Magoo in a minefield, the club swithered in public, dithered behind closed doors, hit a brick wall during one set of negotiations and were lulled into a false sense of security in another. Alex Ferguson was approached by his former employers, but the tough-as-teak Glaswegian declined the offer, principally on the grounds that he had witnessed at first hand the pernicious effects of sectarianism and considered it anathema that Rangers still adhered rigidly to the policy of not signing high-profile Catholic players. If ever there was a moment to embrace change and tear down the barricades, this was surely it – and one can only wonder what success the Stakhanovite motivator par excellence Ferguson might have achieved if he had been allowed a free rein at Ibrox – but the board dug in their heels and their intransigence may not only have contributed to them missing out on Fergie, but also dashed their hopes of luring Dundee United manager Jim McLean.

As it was, the latter figure spoke to the Rangers executives and during their initial meeting informed them that he intended to bring his deputy, Walter Smith, from Tannadice with him to Ibrox. The deal seemed cut and dried, but barely had the Scottish press started discussing how the new men could extricate the struggling club from the mire than McLean, who was normally such a prepossessing, firm-minded fellow, lapsed into procrastination. He sought Smith's opinion on the proposed switch from Dundee to Glasgow and the latter counselled him, "Let's go for it." He then decided to request additional time to weigh the matter over in his mind, and as one night passed into another and a swirl of obfuscation pervaded the business, it grew obvious that McLean was harbouring misgivings, which one former Rangers source told me principally revolved around his desire for the club to permit him to sign whoever he wished.

If that was truly the case – and there is little evidence to refute it – it offered fresh testimony that some of those in charge at Ibrox were still living in the 1950s and their judgement – or dearth of it – was costing their organisation dearly in the wider scheme of things. At the beginning of the following week, with one or two Rangers officials growing furious at how the affair was unravelling, McLean communicated forcefully to Smith that the pair were definitely going to Ibrox and that he had imparted that message to the Dundee

United chairman, Johnstone Grant. Yet it proved to be another false dawn. On Friday morning, a board meeting was convened at Tannadice at 10am, rather than the usual midday, and eventually a senior director, George Fox, announced to the players that McLean was staying where he was. Which was news that nobody was anticipating.

Ultimately, it was a horribly botched affair and the whole farrago represented a crushing disappointment for Smith, but nobody should have been particularly surprised at the manner in which things unfolded, given the maladministration which plagued Rangers in the early 1980s. What *was* ironic about the episode was that Rangers, briefly at least, finished up with Jim McLean's brother, Tommy, as temporary manager, even as the board sounded out other candidates for the vacant post. And that outcome provided relief to Cooper, who had learned enough about Jim's gruelling training regimes and warm-downs after matches to comprehend that he and the elder McLean's relationship might have resembled the Borgias on a bad night, whereas he had forged a rapport with Tommy, viewed him in a sympathetic light and admired his football brain and tactical acumen, which was taken for granted by too many other people in the game.

Indeed, with Greig out of the picture Cooper's mood brightened. In the bigger picture, there was little cause to be overly optimistic over the prospect of a renaissance at Ibrox, and those expecting a rally in the club's fortunes were gradually disabused of that notion during the next three seasons, as Rangers continued to flirt with ignominy like Frank McAvennie at Victoria's Nightclub. It wasn't for lack of application or desire, and when the board finally confirmed that Jock Wallace was returning to Govan, there was a sense that a corner had been turned, even if the road ahead was littered with obstacles. From Cooper's perspective, he was delighted to be back in tandem with a man who recognised his talents and knew how to motivate his troops. There is truth in the old adage that "You shouldn't go back" and Wallace discovered that Scottish football had changed significantly in his absence and the majority of the developments were to his detriment. But nonetheless, Davie offered a telling critique of how matters had altered and explained the improvement in his mood to a variety of newspapers at the time:

"There was a buzz around the place when we heard the news about Jock getting the job, because we loved the man, and although there were very few of the players remaining from when he had been in charge during the glory years of the 1970s, he had a bit of an aura about him. Sure, he might chew you out occasionally and anybody who started believing their own publicity was quickly put in their place, but he had two great things going for him. One was that he was so passionate about Rangers FC that it filtered down to the rest of the lads and even when results weren't going our way, the boys would have crawled over broken glass to have put a smile on Jock's face. The second was that he never ever criticised any of his players in public or slagged them off in the press. There must have been times where he felt like really letting rip, but he treated us all not just as footballers but as human beings and that didn't go unnoticed in the dressing room."

These sentiments cut to the heart of the qualities which defined Davie. By this juncture, he had developed into a cult hero among the majority of those Ibrox supporters, who were blessed with the ability to distinguish between a silk purse and a sow's ear. With the return of Wallace, there was a renewed sense of urgency, of doing the right thing by a manager he admired, and when the duo briefly convened at Ibrox for the first time since 1978, the first thing the elder man said to his confrere was, "Chin up, son. I know you think you have been badly treated, but I want you in my starting eleven."

The only other piece of advice was more in keeping with Wallace's mantra that he could tolerate defeat, but not if it happened as a consequence of lack of effort or commitment to the cause. On Greig's watch, Davie had started putting on weight: the frequent sojourns to the bookies' premises in Hamilton were more regularly accompanied by visits to the adjacent cafés for a snack here, a bacon sarnie there, and although he was never in any danger of resembling Mr Creosote, Wallace quickly detected the extra poundage and instructed Cooper to get back in trim within a month. It was a measure of the instinctive bond between the pair that the message was immediately heeded. It was also symptomatic of their relationship that the subject was never spoken about again. A nod, a quiet word in the ear, and a tacit appreciation of the Herculean task they faced – this was the mutual shorthand both men deployed to communicate with one another. There was no need for theatrical gestures or foul-mouthed rants when their challenges were so pressing.

And in this regard, it was noticeable that despite Wallace proving unable to reignite the spark which had previously brought Rangers glory in Europe and domestic Trebles at home, the supporters, for the most part, clung on to slivers of consolation where best they could find them. They had no love for the board, and there were evenings during that extended lean period in the 1980s where Lord Lucan and Shergar could have turned up at Ibrox and nobody would have noticed them because nobody was there, as the paltry attendance figures confirmed. But in the midst of this Stygian gloom, Rangers aficionados derived solace from the man in their midst who remained wedded to his origins and whose head wasn't turned by the trappings of fame or the so-called lure of nightclub liaisons and high-falutin' black-tie functions. He was no longer referred to as "Davie" and nobody in Govan had to call him "Mr Cooper" any more, as long as they didn't invade his privacy. Instead, after seven or eight years at the club, he was simply "Coop": the fellow who could make the stars shine on the dreariest night in Glasgow, the player who performed with such derring-do that most young lads wanted to be him and the majority of young ladies wanted to take him home to meet their parents.

In some ways, there wasn't so much difference between the Scot and the original "Coop", the Hollywood actor Gary Cooper, whose passing in 1961 elicited the sort of national grief in the United States which only occurs when somebody truly special dies. Alistair

Cooke, the chap whose trans-Atlantic missives illuminated the lives of so many of us who grew up in the 1960s, penned a tribute to the virtues which had embodied the star of such films as *High Noon*, *Mr Deeds Goes to Town* and *The Plainsman* and it painted a vivid picture of how Cooper's fame increased in inverse proportion to the amount of ego or posturing which he brought to his roles. Less was, indeed, more:

"What the world mourns is its lost innocence, a favourite fantasy of it fleshed out in the most durable and heroic of American myths: that of the taut but merciful plainsman, who dispenses justice with a worried conscience, a single syllable, a blurred reflex action to the hip, and who must face death in the afternoon as regularly as the matador, but on main street and for no pay.

"It is easy to forget now, as always with artists who have matured a recognisable style, that for at least the first dozen years of his film career, Gary Cooper was the lowbrow's comfort and the highbrow's butt. However, he lasted long enough, as all great talents do, to weather the four stages of the highbrow treatment: first, he was derided, then ignored, then accepted, then discovered. We had seen this happen many times before, and, looking back, one is always shocked to recognise the people it has happened to . . . But he filled an empty niche in the world pantheon of essential gods. He was Eisenhower's glowing, and glowingly false, picture of Wyatt Earp. He was one of Walt Whitman's troop of democratic knights, 'Bright-eyed as hawks with their swarthy complexions and their broad-rimmed hats, with loose arms slightly raised and swinging as they ride.'

"He represented every man's best secret image of himself: the honourable man slicing clean through the rolling world of morals and machines. He isolated and enlarged to six feet three an untainted strain of goodness in a very male specimen of the male of the species. He was notoriously known as the actor who couldn't act. Only the directors who handled him had daily proof that he was nobody but himself. Very soon, the box offices, from Tokyo to Carlisle,

Davie Cooper signs for Clydebank in 1974 after being
encouraged to join by club chairman Jack Steedman.

Davie Cooper in action for
Clydebank. He was part of the team
which won the Scottish Second
Division championship in 1976.

David signed for Rangers in 1977 for £100,000 and
formed a close bond with their manager, Jock Wallace.

Cooper scored a wonder goal against Celtic in the final of the Drybrough Cup 1979
– one of the greatest goals ever scored.

1981 Scottish Cup final replay Rangers v Dundee United (4-1) – Frank Kopel collides with the post after failing to stop Cooper's shot entering the Dundee United net.

©SNSPix

Davie Cooper and Ian Redford, proud trophy winners.

©Eric McCowat

Gruelling training in the sand dunes of Gullane – something Cooper utterly detested. He was all about the games.

©Eric McCowat

©Eric McCowat

John Greig and Cooper were never great friends, but they did make a great team.

©SNSPix

1985, playing for Scotland – Cooper scored the penalty which meant Scotland gained a draw with Wales in their World Cup qualifier…

©SNSPix

…however, the whole night was overshadowed by the death of Jock Stein.

©SNSPix

Cooper scored a wonder goal for Rangers against Ilves Tampere of
Finland in the 1986-87 UEFA Cup.

©SNSPix

Cooper stepped up to score the winning penalty (with Packie Bonner in goal)
in the 1986 League Cup final against Celtic.

Davie's scorching free kick in the final of the 1987 League Cup flew past Jim Leighton and was a memorable piece of genius from the Scot.

After years in the doldrums, the arrival of Graeme Souness at Rangers promted the arrival of plenty of silverware at Ibrox.

Davie Cooper was allowed to leave Rangers and join Motherwell for a paltry fee of £50,000.

©Eric McCowat

©Eric McCowat

Cooper was one of Motherwell's most influential performers in their famous 4-3 win over Dundee United in the Scottish Cup final 1991.

In 1994 Cooper went back to his roots and was treated like a hero by Clydebank.

©SNSPix

Cooper died in tragic circumstances in 1995 while working with
Charlie Nicholas on a kids' coaching programme at Cumbernauld.

Alex Ferguson and Graeme Souness were among
the mourners at Cooper's funeral.

The CIS Cup final in 2005 between
Rangers and Motherwell was officially
known as the "Davie Cooper final".

Rangers supporters unveil a banner in memory of Cooper.

confirmed this theory in hard cash. Then the intellectuals sat up and took notice. Then the Cooper legend took over."

Cooke also made reference to Gary's "Yup-No" tendency, and alluded to how he could be as garrulous with those he trusted as he was monosyllabic with those he didn't. Across the Pond, even as one Coop was slipping into the ether, another with similar qualities was emerging in a different sphere, but one which possessed artistic merit, for anybody prepared to revel in the cinematic images of the 1979 Drybrough Cup final goal, or the fashion in which Davie ran rings round the hapless Dundee United defenders as if he was on a single-handed mission to entertain his audience. Off-camera or off the pitch, these were old-fashioned, unworldly characters, who shunned the limelight with an almost heroic determination to cling to the foundations of their early life. They could charm their friends and were tolerant of their acquaintances, but their most obvious similarity was that they were most comfortable in front of an audience, on a film set or a pitch.

Certainly in Davie's case, there was plenty of evidence to suggest that away from his natural environment he couldn't really comprehend why so many thousands of people placed him on a pedestal, stuck his photograph on the back pages of the newspaper and sought him out for quotes, autographs, locks of hair and speech-making assignments. In his own mind, and those who cherished his talents, he was forever the Boy Next Door. Consider, for instance, the following recollection from Rangers fan, Ian Oliphant:

"It was a midweek game at the old 'Broomfield' in Airdrie and I must have been fifteen or sixteen years old. Davie was brilliant that night, although the game ended in a 2–2 draw. After the game, my mates and I went to a chip shop and came back to the bus station that was directly opposite the stadium and we were sitting on a bench opposite one of the many bus stances. It was quiet by this stage, but two stances down from us was Davie, just sitting there, alone, waiting on the Hamilton bus to take him home. It was so poignant, a man with so much talent quietly minding his own business and waiting for a bus. Can you imagine that now? But that was Davie for you: a humble superstar who was content to have a few quid in his pocket because he was playing for the club he loved."

By this stage, he was feted wherever he travelled in the West of Scotland, but unlike some other footballers of his generation who erected barriers to keep the public at bay or were downright obnoxious to those they viewed as the hoi polloi, Cooper felt an obligation to satisfy the demands of the supporters who queued patiently outside grounds, irrespective of the weather or the length of the line. Colin Wood was one of those youngsters who braved the elements in the early 1980s and cherishes the reward for his patience:

"He once came to my hometown, Kirkintilloch, to play in a charity match at Rob Roy Stadium, so I waited behind once the game had finished, to see Davie. I was twelve years old and when he came out of the changing room, I asked for his autograph and he replied, 'Anything for you, Smiler.' He then put his hand on my shoulder while he signed 'Davie Cooper' on my yellow and blue Scotland away top, which happened to have a tomato soup stain on it from my lunch! Anyway, to this day [early 2010], I have never washed that top and it proudly hangs on my garage wall with the stain still there. While it is there, I have always felt as if a part of Davie Cooper has been there with me as well."

Such a level of adoration might appear over the top in most other circumstances, but as they approached the midway point of the 1980s, Rangers were in the doldrums and straw-clutching was at least preferable to wrist-slitting. Considering the litany of prizes which had been achieved under Wallace in his first term at Ibrox, the fans were probably justified in expecting a resurgence when he picked up the reins again, but a quick glance over the resources at his disposal should have provided a sobering reminder that even the best coach cannot advance without petrol in the tank. In both the 1983–84 and 1984–85 campaigns, Rangers could finish no higher than fourth in the Championship race and for all the manager's coaxing, cajoling and occasional recourse to expletive-laden tirades, his anger was directed less at his squad than at the sustained failure of his employers to provide the requisite money with which Wallace might have created a new team, which was capable of vying for honours both domestically and in the European theatre.

Cooper, for his part, was too often a flickering light in a barren sky, and despite his efforts at sparking those around him, there was a plethora of evenings where the team ran on empty, ploughing on in a sea of apathy, as their followers temporarily deserted them. The Old Firm contests still contained their fair share of grisly tackles and sufficient nasty niggle to delight the diehards on both sides of the tribal divide, but Cooper wasn't as motivated as he had once been: it's one thing to be excited by these clashes as a raw twenty-one-year-old, another matter entirely to relish the sensation of stud marks up your back, after being scythed by a Celtic defender for the umpteenth time. Worse still, he felt anguish at the manner in which Wallace, the big proud sergeant-major, was reduced to raging at his team's deficiencies, despite maintaining the support of the dressing room. It wasn't that they didn't care. It was simply that man for man they weren't good enough.

Thankfully from an Ibrox perspective, Scottish football provides plenty of chances for redemption and one of these arrived in March 1984, when the Old Firm squared up in a League Cup final, which turned into a classic of the genre. Amidst this period of transition, Rangers had unearthed a bright young talent called Ally McCoist – heaven knows what has happened to him since! – and his intoxicating mixture of ebullience and cheeky banter offered a merry counterpoint to the blood-and-guts rhetoric of Wallace, who had only been back in the hot seat for six months and was determined to prove that he hadn't lost his reputation as a master motivator. "The Big Man's speech was one of the most passionate team talks he ever gave and the boys all looked round the dressing room at the end and nobody needed to say a word," Cooper said later. "If any of us had doubted what it meant to him to come back to his roots, he had spelled it out and the guys who hadn't known what Jock was all about soon got an idea of what he wanted."

Rangers, whose season had fizzled out elsewhere, duly proceeded to take out some of their pent-up frustrations on their Glasgow rivals and, fuelled by the ubiquitous menace of McCoist and the purposeful running of Cooper and Bobby Russell, seized the initiative in the early stages and threatened to overpower their opponents. In such an intimidating environment, one might have imagined that Ally's stomach would have been churning, but just as Ian Botham has always claimed that hangovers are a state of mind, so McCoist forcibly contended that nerves were for other people to worry about. Whoof, as Archie Macpherson might have shouted, and he had broken the deadlock with a penalty in the forty-fourth minute! Jings, as Arthur Montford would have countered, and he had doubled his tally just after the hour mark and established a position of supremacy for his team. Yet even with time running out these Celts weren't inclined to throw in the towel and gradually clawed their way back into the match. Brian McClair reduced the deficit in the sixty-seventh minute, then as both sides traded blows – sometimes literally! – the pendulum swung once more when McCoist conceded a penalty with an ill-judged tackle on Murdo MacLeod, all of ninety seconds into injury time, and Mark Reid, oblivious to the bedlam which had erupted around Hampden Park, slotted the ball past Peter McCloy.

It seemed that the momentum had switched to the Cup holders, but there was another twist in the tale, as described by the late Alex Cameron in the *Daily Record*: "Agatha Christie could not have scripted more thrills or improbabilities as the match unfolded, but Rangers threw Celtic out of Paradise with a hat-trick by Ally McCoist. They won dramatically, routed forecasting pundits, and left Celtic in a rage at what they perceived to be refereeing injustices. It was a display of nerve, determination and persistence by the winners, which was orchestrated over 120 minutes of hard, unclassical slogging by the superb Robert [Bobby] Russell. Rarely has one player done so much for so many in a controversial final, which, in the end, Rangers deserved to win.

"Referee Bob Valentine awarded three penalties – two to Rangers and one to Celtic. And rarely has Hampden seen such drama, mingled with the stubborn soccer mediocrity, which usually stems from a collision of the Old Firm. Eight players were cautioned and I cannot say that I agreed with every booking. They were Mark Reid, Jim Melrose and Roy Aitken of Celtic and Sandy Clark, Russell, John McClelland, Dave McPherson and McCoist of Rangers. It was Aitken's booking a minute from the end in an incident with McCoist which finally upset Celtic to such an extent that they were thoroughly and inexcusably unruly. A senior policeman had to step between protesting players and Mr Valentine as he waited by the touchline for the presentation ceremony and it was a shame that these scenes marred the end because, however aggrieved Celtic may have felt about the referee's handling, there was no excuse for such provocative behaviour.

"Earlier, in the first period of extra time, Valentine penalised Aitken a couple of steps inside the box for fouling McCoist. There was no doubt about the award, in my view. McCoist took the kick and lunged to his left – having previously gone the wrong way for the first spot award. He stopped the ball but couldn't hold on to it and McCoist followed up to score. And so the cup went from the Parkhead trophy room over to Ibrox."

Unsurprisingly, the celebrations were raucous in the Blue Room that evening. Yet, where once this sort of victory might have been the catalyst for a recovery in Rangers' fortunes, consistency still eluded them and their players and management remained perennially unsure whether they stood on the cusp of a windfall or a catastrophe. The consequence was that such triumphs as that secured by McCoist were interspersed with months where nothing continued to happen. To his credit, Wallace attempted to get his team playing more attacking football than had been the norm under John Greig, and his philosophy might have paid dividends if the club had boasted a better defence to augment the labours of such luminaries as Cooper, Russell and McCoist. But instead, they fielded men such as Ally Dawson, Tom McAdam and Craig Paterson, honest artisans whose commitment to the cause was never in question, but who were a class below the calibre of Rangers personnel with whom Wallace had enjoyed such rich pickings a decade earlier.

Given these constraints, the manager's task was as easy as steering the SS *Ibrox* between Scylla and Charybdis, and Cooper agonised over the sight of Wallace toiling – and generally failing – to keep the club on an even keel. It clearly pained Davie, because when we met nearly seven years later, he was still rhapsodising about the fellow. "Maybe Jock never quite got over the fact he was only the third choice for the job, behind Alex Ferguson and Jim McLean, because he seemed to have lost a wee bit of the spark which was there first time around, but I thought he did as well as anybody would have done in the circumstances. The bottom line was that the gaffer didn't have much money to spend and the newspapers kept going on about how there was a crisis at Rangers, week in, week out, and it got to everybody," said Cooper, who suffered problems with his own contract, which required protracted discussions behind closed doors, before the board (partially) relented on their stinginess.

"I felt very sorry for Jock – although you couldn't tell him that, because he would have hated anybody suggesting he was in trouble – but even if something was missing, and it was unacceptable that a club the size of Rangers went eight seasons without winning the league, he was a hero of mine. He gave everything he had to Rangers in both his spells as manager, and he did wonders for the club. And if he had a beef about anything which was going on behind the scenes, he fought the players' corners and shielded us from any problems. He was a big, big influence on me."

Nothing, though, could disguise the scale of the malaise which afflicted Rangers throughout the 1984–85 campaign. From time to time, they would fleetingly hint at a transformation, such as when they tackled Inter Milan at Ibrox in the UEFA Cup, trailing 3–0 from the first leg, and almost retrieved the situation with a coruscating 3–1 victory, with a brace of goals from Iain Ferguson and David Mitchell. They even secured a piece of silverware when Ferguson seized the winner in the League Cup final against Dundee United. But for the most part, poor results coincided with shrinking crowds, and in these days before the arrival of the two Davids, Holmes and Murray, and Graeme Souness, it was as if the footballing equivalent of a slow puncture had befallen Rangers. If you require evidence, what about the attendance for the home meeting with Dumbarton on 2 March 1985, which attracted a crowd of only 8,424? Or that for the next fixture against Dundee on 23 March, which pulled in 9,954 spectators? These were statistics that underlined the level of disenchantment with the club beyond any reasonable doubt.

Typically, it was left to the Old Firm battles to generate passion and ticket sales, along with salacious headlines, testifying to the visceral nature of these contests. One such meeting occurred towards the end of that barren '84–85 season, on 1 May, by which stage there was nothing for Wallace's troops to play for except pride: indeed, they had drifted so far out of the picture that Rangers limped in a record 21 points behind champions Aberdeen. But as habitually transpires in these scenarios, Rangers and Celtic flung themselves at each other, like two ageing heavyweights, operating from memory but still capable of landing blows if offered the opportunity. What *was* unusual was that Cooper, who normally managed to transcend the aggro, found himself in the thick of the trouble at Parkhead and lost his rag with Peter Grant as the game turned into a ticking time-bomb of insanity.

Nobody was there for the quality, or if they were, they were destined to be disappointed, but the action held the same ghastly fascination as a train wreck. Inside two minutes, Roy Aitken missed a penalty, whereupon the rancorous exchanges between Cooper and Grant saw the former exact revenge for an earlier tackle which he considered closer to GBH than a legitimate sporting challenge, and given the fact that Davie's retaliation came less than a minute after the original sin, he couldn't have any real complaints – nor did he – about being sent off. By that stage, Celtic led 1–0 and it seemed that Rangers were destined for another dispiriting defeat, especially when Ally Dawson suffered the same fate as Cooper and the Ibrox side were down to nine men.

Yet, even as the embarrassed duo sat in the dressing room awaiting their punishment, their blushes were partly spared when, somehow or other, Rangers created some pressure, equalised through a McCoist penalty and eventually secured an against-the-odds 1–1 draw. It might be asked why a team with the ability to dig themselves out of such holes was incapable of mounting a credible title bid. But this was the Old Firm and as Cooper explained, "There were nothing like these moments when you heard the Celtic crowd go quiet and you realised that if you could keep up the pressure, you would be able to hear your own fans, even though there were only a small number of them inside Parkhead. It was times like that which made everything worthwhile and put a smile on your face."

Sadly for Wallace, however, these heroics weren't materialising frequently enough for an extension of his tenure to remain as a viable option. Instead, as 1985 moved into 1986, there was the beginning of a revolution on and off the pitch at Rangers, which would change the history of the club in perpetuity. It wasn't before time, not least for Cooper, who was approaching thirty and entitled to wonder where his future lay in the bigger picture. He was still a favourite among the supporters, and the number of "assists" which he had laid on for the likes of McCoist and Iain Ferguson testified to his continuing penchant for influencing the outcome of important matches with a killer touch here, a rapier-like thrust there. But he had to be realistic and accept that his role was poised to change.

That prospect didn't faze him. Nothing much did and while he had demonstrated that he could succumb to the volatile character of an Old Firm slugfest, Davie also retained a sense of perspective about these matches, as supporter Charles Sharp told me:

"The best memory I have of Davie is one from a Celtic-supporting pal of mine. He was standing in the 'Jungle' during an Old Firm match and amidst all the abuse which was being aimed in Davie's direction, somebody threw a couple of oranges, which landed at his feet. Suddenly, the call came from the crowd, 'Hey, Cooper, you've dropped your balls!' Apparently, Davie stopped taking the shy and started laughing while turning and delivering a handclap gesture. In this day and age, it's nice to remember times when some people didn't take the huff over normal, everyday exchanges!"

8

TRIUMPH AND TRAGEDY WITH SCOTLAND

Some people were inspired by pulling on their country's jersey and listing to the chants of "Scotland the Brave" resonating through the terraces at the old Hampden Park. One thinks of such gnarled warriors as Billy Bremner, a snarling, cantankerous mass of emotions, who was never afraid to turn any piffling spat into a full-blown sporting Armageddon, even if his reputation suffered with the publication (and subsequent feature film release) of David Peace's splendid *The Damned United*, a book whose author's name was at odds with the maelstrom of turbulence contained within the pages.

There were others, of course. The toothless but defiantly unbowed Joe Jordan charging forward in the penalty box with a reckless disregard for his own health; the seething mass of bias which answered proudly to the name of Gordon McQueen; the indefatigable trickery and patriotism of the onliest Archie Gemmill, whose heroics in Argentina at the 1978 World Cup eventually provided a calamitous odyssey with a codicil of glory; and Kenny Dalglish, who, if he had been given a pound for every time a myopic member of the Tartan Army alleged that he never tried as hard for his country as he did for Celtic and Liverpool would be even wealthier than he is today. These men were warriors under a succession of managers and, with hindsight, they achieved significant amounts for their nation. They didn't collect any international trophies, but it certainly wasn't for lack of commitment, resilience, class and downright cussedness in the face of adversity.

Davie Cooper never fitted into this category, which perhaps explains why he only gained 22 caps, stretching between 1979 and 1990: a period of retrenchment and pursuit of credibility for the SFA's panjandrums, in the aftermath of the soccer equivalent of the Darien Scheme during the summer of '78. Others might have rattled claymores or shed tears during the pre-match anthems at Hampden Park, but Cooper adhered to the philosophy that his club took precedence, because they were paying his wages and if international recognition arrived as a by-product, it was a nice little bonus.

"He was always pretty cool and laid-back whenever he was involved in the Scotland squad, and although he obviously enjoyed these experiences, he never got as worked up as some of the boys in the team," recalls Alan Rough, the fifty-three-times-capped goalkeeper, who shared his compatriot's notion that football was never to be regarded as a matter of life and death. "After the debacle in Argentina, there was a lot of talk from the powers-that-be about how the Scots had to take the game more seriously, get involved in things like diet and nutrition, and strive to follow in the footsteps of the Europeans, but it was always going to be difficult to change the culture overnight." Especially, as one of Rough's counterparts observed, when the administrators maintained the same level of interest in fine cuisine, luxury hotels and junkets, masquerading as "fact-finding" exercises.

If that sounds cynical, it's meant to be. Cooper, for his part, had no illusions about the contrast between the perks which were available to the bureaucrats and the players, and although he was hardly one of the sport's more mercenary figures, as he demonstrated by showing loyalty to Rangers, he told one or two of his compatriots about his anger at the arrogance of the blazerati, who accompanied the squad on foreign adventures. From Davie's perspective, matters only improved once Jock Stein started wielding an axe through the excesses of the gravy-train brigade and told the men in charge at Park Gardens that their priorities had to be on the international team first, their youth development programme second, the fans third and their own desire for self-aggrandisement and freebies a distant fourth in the pecking order. Predictably, this didn't make him popular with the suits, but it earned the admiration of the players, including Cooper, whose affection and admiration for Stein straddled the Old Firm divide.

They couldn't have known it at the time, but their lives and deaths were to be inextricably linked in a shroud of tristesse. And, in other respects, both men were treated shabbily by the clubs for whom they would have crawled over broken glass. Indeed, if there is a recurring theme to Cooper's story, it lies in his former comrades expressing regrets over what might have been, while Stein, having guided Celtic to previously unprecedented achievements, was dumped by them as soon as he was (thought to be) past his expiry date. Neither case reflected well on the underlying prejudices which existed within the Scottish game. But sadly, these failings haven't vanished even in the twenty-first century.

"Davie was ahead of his time, he could do things which others couldn't, but people tended to focus on his weaknesses, not his strengths," says Rough. They did, and it was an antediluvian mindset which might have cost the Rangers man another 30 caps.

At the outset, of course, Davie was simply happy to be called into the Scotland Under-21s while he was still at Clydebank. He met up with and forged friendships with such diverse personalities as Roy Aitken, Willie Miller, George Burley and David Narey, and eventually made six appearances at this level – four when he was at Kilbowie and the last two once he had completed his move to Rangers. Even at this juncture, there were moments to savour and results to relish, including a 2–1 victory over Czechoslovakia at Tynecastle, where Cooper was kicked all over the park, but kept dusting himself down and returning to the fray, while the fans rose to acclaim a new star in the making.

It was a confidence-boosting induction to a higher standard of action, but we shouldn't forget that these matches took place between 1975 and 1977. Scottish football was enjoying a rare outbreak of unanimity where fans, pundits and players alike indulged in a mutual love-in, under the stewardship of Ally MacLeod, and there was plenty of Micawberish talk about the national team's prospects of bringing the World Cup back home from South America. In this climate, a youngster with Davie's gallus gifts could expect a warm reception and honeyed words from the media. Everything had changed by the time that he was selected for his senior debut against Peru in September 1979.

It was billed as a friendly, but given the embarrassment which the South Americans had doled out to their rivals only fifteen months earlier, the tussle bristled with an intensity which testified to the Scots' determination to set the record straight. Under Stein and blessed with a prodigious clutch of players, including Dalglish, Graeme Souness and John Wark, the hosts were a steelier proposition that the achy flaky men of MacLeod and the debutant made a decent impression, and should have marked the occasion with a goal, only to see his shot crash off the crossbar. He was substituted shortly afterwards, but although Davie felt a bit disappointed with his miss, Stein was generally supportive, as the dust settled on a 1–1 draw between the sides and the veteran manager showed sufficient faith in his new charge to select him again for the European Championship qualifying match against Austria the following month. It should have been the start of a glorious career. Instead, this presaged almost five years in the wilderness.

Quite why that should have been the case remains a mystery, although when one scans the starting eleven for the match in Glasgow – comprising Alan Rough, Sandy Jardine, Gordon McQueen, Kenny Burns, Iain Munro, Graeme Souness, John Wark, Archie Gemmill, Arthur Graham, Kenny Dalglish and John Robertson – it is easy to understand why the inexperienced Cooper had to settle for a berth among the substitutes. All the same, some of these individuals were nearing the end of the road, en route to alternative careers as bit-part players in the execrable Hollywood film *Escape to Victory* (Wark) and as the inspiration for future ballets composed in their honour (Gemmill). In that light, and particularly considering that Scotland's European campaign spluttered along from one damp squib to another, it beggared belief that, following his cameo role in the 1–1 draw with the Austrians – with Gemmill cancelling out Hans Krankl's earlier effort – Cooper was frozen out from 1979 to 1984. If Davie had looked out of his depth or had flung a few punches at an opponent or gone out on a bender in the aftermath, one might have fathomed why he wasn't deemed to be international-class material. But none of these things were applicable in the Rangers man's case. He was twenty-three, already capable of transforming matches with mercurial acts of hooraymanship and from any logical perspective, his best years were ahead of him. A long, long way ahead of him!

Perhaps he didn't wear his heart on his sleeve enough for the SFA's liking. He certainly spelled out his attitude to representing his country in rather pragmatic tones later: "I appreciate that most children and, for that matter, any amount of adults in Scotland, would give their right arms to wear the dark blue jersey. Don't get me wrong – I consider it an honour whenever I am picked, but it is never the end of the world for me if I am not included in the Scotland squad. It boils down to simple loyalties. Week in, week out, Rangers are paying my wages and looking after me, and my first responsibility is to them because they have signed me on a contract and we have shaken hands on the deal. Some people look forward to playing for Scotland and regard it as the biggest highlight of their careers and good luck to them if that is the way they feel. We all have different opinions about what is and isn't important in our lives and we have to do what we think is best. If I am picked for Scotland, that is great and I will do my best for my country the same as the other boys in the side. But if I am not, there is no point beating myself up about it. Maybe that sounds callous, and if it does, then I am sorry. But when I was growing up, there was only one team which I wanted to play for and that was Glasgow Rangers."

However, this stance was at odds with the enthusiasm which Cooper displayed as part of the Scotland Under-21s. Andy Roxburgh, who was coaching the youngsters during that period, told me that Davie had been a "joy to work with", had always "appreciated the chance to pick up lessons and tips from others in the ranks" and that his levels of application, skill and desire were "second to none" in what was one of the most distinguished groups ever produced by their country. More probably, as a former Rangers teammate of Cooper told me in confidence, he found himself between a rock and a hard place in his dealings with John Greig on the one side and Jock Stein on the other:

"If everything had been equal, Davie would definitely have been involved in the 1982 World Cup qualifying campaign because the Scots were struggling for wingers by the time we got to 1980 and he fitted the bill perfectly. The trouble was that the more Davie got p***ed off with Greig and the more John gave him the cold shoulder, the more it looked to people on the outside [like] Coop didn't care, that he thought he was a prima donna and that he could pick and choose his matches. It can't be a coincidence that within less than a year of Greig getting the heave, Davie was back in the frame at both Rangers and Scotland. But I don't blame Stein for that. His attitude must have been: 'well, if Cooper isn't getting a game for his club, it would be too risky to pick him for Scotland.' It should never have happened and the situation might have been avoided if Davie had moved to another club. But then we are back to square one, because he had no intention of going anywhere else. The whole thing was stupid, but it could all have been avoided if Greig had accepted that Davie had exceptional talent and had built his team around him. But he didn't and Rangers suffered, Scotland suffered and Cooper suffered."

In anybody's language, it was absurd that such a stalemate should have arisen, but the combination of intransigence, inflexibility and obstinacy meant that one of the most naturally gifted performers of his generation was employed only sporadically by his country, while Cooper's reaction to his travails was to climb on to the Burger King express and embark on a journey to Palookaville.

As far as Scotland was concerned, he was posted missing between September 1979 and February 1984. In which circumstances, it was perhaps predictable that when he *did* return to the ranks, in the Home International Championship against Wales, Cooper produced an excellent display, scored his maiden goal for his country – from the penalty spot – and was one of the stand-out individuals in their hard-fought 2–1 success, with the debutant Mo Johnston sealing victory for his team. At the end, there was the potential for fresh controversy when it emerged that Scotland's next fixture, against the Auld Enemy at Hampden on 26 May, coincided with a world tour which had been organised by Rangers, and Cooper briefly wondered whether he might have to choose between the two. But thankfully, following years of fatuous dog-in-the-manger gestures, the twin Jocks, Wallace and Stein – two gentlemen of the old school with an innate respect for the other – sat down together and reached an agreement which satisfied everybody. It was a compromise which simply would not have occurred under the old Ibrox regime.

It guaranteed, though, that Cooper would savour his first taste of grappling with the English and discover how the charged atmosphere could intimidate even the most sanguine of characters. Never normally bothered by pre-match butterflies, he was a-flutter with anticipation in the build-up – so much for all the protestations that Scotland duty figured low on his to-do list – but once he walked out onto the Hampden turf and heard the roar from more than 70,000 souls inside the stadium, the anthems passed in a blur and Cooper was equally quick to make his presence felt in the contest. It was a typically macho-laden affair, fought out against a nationalist backdrop, as sections of the Tartan Army used the occasion to fulminate against the policies of the increasingly unpopular (in Scotland, at any rate) Prime Minister Margaret Thatcher. Yet although Scotland took the lead with a goal from Mark McGhee and created several other chances thereafter, with Davie generating momentum on the wing and also benefiting from being an unknown quantity to the visitors, the English, as always, stuck to their tasks, refused to be cowed by the racket on the periphery and eventually gained parity with a terrific equaliser from Tony Woodcock, which reduced the stadium to stunned silence.

These were the afternoons when the elite could pit their wits against each other and, in Cooper's case, escape the monotony of scrabbling for minor league placings. He spoke afterwards of how he had heard about the depths of passion which habitually surrounded these matches, yet was still surprised at the ferocity of the decibel level as the Scots hunted down their traditional adversaries. "It wasn't like an Old Firm game, but there was still an incredible atmosphere in the ground and it made the hairs rise up on the back of my neck," he told reporters, swapping banter with one or two of the faces he recognised in the media throng, as if to demonstrate conclusively that the days of the "Moody Blue" had been consigned to history. From now on, even if he never accepted, and was right to do so, that the tabloids had no right to pry into his private life, he acknowledged that most journalists were only trying to do their jobs to the best of their ability and if that meant hunting him down for a quote now and then, he could live with the hassle.

Belatedly, these Scotland assignments became more regular occurrences. In September 1984 he was part of the ensemble which thrashed Yugoslavia 6–1 and featured amongst the scorers, in the company of Souness, Dalglish, Paul Sturrock, Mo Johnston and Charlie Nicholas: a roll call of talent in the one side which contrasts forlornly with the recent famine in Scottish football, where journeymen fling their teddies out the pram if not assured of automatic selection. That demolition was the prelude to the beginning of Scotland's World Cup qualifying campaign and Stein's personnel laid down the best possible marker in their opening brace of matches when they beat Iceland 3–0 and Spain 3–1, both in front of passionate crowds in Glasgow.

The first of these wins was an efficient performance from the hosts, with Cooper setting up the first of Paul McStay's two goals and Nicholas applying the coup de grâce. Stein, characteristically tight-lipped in front of the media – he knew better than anybody that these qualifying schedules were marathons, not sprints – expressed satisfaction with the manner of his side's success, but declared that the true test of where they stood would only be supplied with the visit of the fiery, unpredictable Spaniards to Scotland.

Yet, oblivious to his pleas for calmness, there was no preventing the Caledonian hyperbole machine from cranking into full throttle by the end of that splendid mid-November night, when the visitors were not just knocked out of their stride by a superb display from Stein's men, but were left deflated and discombobulated by the sheer efficacy and effervescence of their rivals. From the outset, the hosts boasted a creativity and cutting edge which hadn't been witnessed on too many occasions in the previous five or six years, and whether marvelling at the *joie de vivre* of Cooper or his confrere, Jim Bett or rejoicing in the dextrous finishing of the home strikers, this was a night where all the positive qualities inherent in Scottish football combined to delicious effect.

Even Cooper, rarely a fellow given to superlatives and certainly not when it came to assessing his own contribution in these encounters, was wreathed in smiles as he reflected on his compatriots' showing. "As it happened, I believe that Scotland produced their best performance of any I have been involved with in that game and we were brilliant that night," he enthused to the *Record*. "Everything just fell into place and with Jazzer [Bett] behind me, I reckon it was one of my own best performances as well. Every one of us was at the top of his form – Stevie Nicol was outstanding, Graeme Souness did brilliantly, Paul McStay was terrific – and it was really a privilege to be part of that side, as Mo Johnston scored twice and Kenny

Dalglish got the other in a style that only he can. [The Butcher of Bilbao himself,] Andoni Goicoechea, got them a consolation goal, but it really was no more than that, and the 74,000-plus crowd went home that evening well pleased with life.

"Jock Stein was delighted too with the way that we had played. He never made a habit of displaying his emotions too publicly, but the players knew when he was pleased and, most definitely, when he wasn't. That night, he had a quiet smile of satisfaction on his face and we all knew that we had done the business for the boss and for Scotland."

With maximum points accrued from their opening two matches, this should have provided the requisite spark for the Scots to progress towards the World Cup without an excess of scares. Ha! One of the vital qualities required by every Scottish sports fan is the ability to celebrate the triumphs, because the only sure thing is that any flirtations with comfort and joy will soon be followed by an Icarus-style crashing back to earth. In which circumstances, Stein's early caution was entirely justified by subsequent events as we moved into 1985 and his charges steeled themselves for the return meeting with Spain in Seville.

The manager, as meticulous as ever in his preparations and fine-tuning, watched the Hampden demolition a number of times and decided that Davie should play from the start when the sides met again. His reasoning was straightforward, as he explained to the *Record*: "Cooper has a reputation in Spain because of his perform-ance at Hampden three months ago. He knows the importance of playing well and has shown a new sense of responsibility in a Scotland jersey, and I have faith in him. There is no doubt that [Spanish manager] Miguel Muñoz was surprised at what he saw Cooper do in Glasgow, because there aren't many wingers with his quality around nowadays." Coming from Stein, this was the equiv-alent of granting Davie the freedom of Glasgow, and even his refer-ence to the Rangers man's growing maturity testified to the fashion in which he and Jock Wallace, the same chaps who had guided their clubs to trophies galore in the 1960s and 1970s, were adult enough to work in harness for the good of their country. Behind the scenes, they maintained regular contact with each other, marked the other's card on who was hitting form and who was hitting the nightclubs to excess, and there was something paternal about the manner in which these redoubtable characters did their work.

Sadly however, their wealth of knowledge counted for little once the Spaniards began their revenge mission in their homeland. They had already upped the ante by switching the venue away from Madrid to the imposing Sanchez Pizjuan Stadium, one of those intimidating arenas where the banks of home fans seemed to stretch up forever into the sky and where the Tartan Army was drowned out by a partisan, rather scary wall of sound which engulfed the Scots as they sought to continue their winning ways.

Yet as the first half progressed, there was little reason for the visitors to be apprehensive. They marshalled their defence well, resisted any attempt to be knocked out of their stride and went in at the interval more concerned about the bedlam which was happening off the pitch than any threat from the Spanish team on it. Stein counselled his men to maintain their rhythm and try to engineer a chance or two when the game resumed, but he wasn't unduly concerned at the prospect of his men returning home with a draw. Indeed, that outcome would have placed them firmly in the driving seat. Yet, as transpired so often amidst these fraught European battles, the hosts exerted a rising tide of pressure as the tension mounted and suddenly, Paco Clos, the Barcelona striker, conjured up the goal which was sufficient to extinguish the Scots' aspirations. It wasn't especially deserved on the run of play, but how often have we heard these hard-luck stories in the past?

Still, there was no need to panic just yet. In the cold light of day, Stein probably wouldn't have expected any more than an even share of the spoils with Spain. What nobody could have anticipated was the utter awfulness of the Scots in their next fixture, at home to Wales, where the hosts seemed to have forgotten all the virtues which had brought them success over Muñoz's squad. Poise, precision, penetration . . . just three of the words starting with "P" which were conspicuous by their absence, as the likes of Souness, a world-class performer at his best, but a mixture of Flashman and Mr Hyde at his worst, entered into a kicking match with Peter Nicholas, which transformed a World Cup qualifier into something more akin to a pub match between two villages with centuries of mutual loathing.

In the end, as the hosts struggled for cohesion or even a couple of passes strung together in the right direction, the supporters grew restive and their mood darkened when Ian Rush seized the only goal to put Scotland in danger of missing out on a trip to the World Cup for the first time since 1970. It was a shocking display, a "disgrace" according to the next day's newspapers, and there was understandable anxiety over the way the group was unfolding. But such was the cut-throat competitiveness of the participants that nobody was particularly surprised when the Welsh trounced Spain 3–0 in Wrexham, then the Scots – minus Cooper, who had sustained a knee injury which ruled him out of the England match as well – orchestrated a precious last-gasp victory over Iceland in Reykjavik, courtesy of a goal from Jim Bett, allied to a magnificent save by Jim Leighton, who blocked Teitur Thordarson's penalty: the two incidents which, although nobody could have known it at the time, made all the difference between success and failure as the qualification campaign advanced towards its climax.

Basically, everything now boiled down to the outcome of the all-British clash between the Scots and Welsh in Cardiff on 10 September 1985, one of those unforgettable dates which encompassed all manner of conflicting emotions as triumph and tragedy collided with a sickening thud. The tension in the days leading up to the match was of such a rare intensity that few observers took much notice of how Jock Stein seemed unusually out of sorts, slouching around the team hotel in Bristol with a ghastly pallor on his face. Cooper thought that he might have picked up a virus, while others suspected that, finally, the Big Man was beginning to feel his age, and Alan Rough, who didn't expect to feature in the proceedings, told me, "Whereas Jock normally loved his food, a few of us spotted that he would only nibble at his plate without really eating anything, and he just didn't seem right. He was surviving on morsels and his brow seemed constantly furrowed."

As the countdown commenced, in the twenty-four hours before kick-off, Cooper was told by Stein that he would be on the substitutes' bench and the manager, as honest as always, advised Davie that he was unlikely to feature at all. "Don't take it personally, but this won't be a night for silky football, we just need to grind out a win," was the gist of his message. Rough, for his part, was only in the squad as cover for Leighton, and he and Stein held a brief conversation on the eve of the game. "I had staved three of my fingers while playing for Hibs against Celtic on the previous Saturday, and in bygone years, this might have led to him blowing a gasket or sending me home," recalls the goalkeeper. "However, in this instance, Jock simply looked at me with a weary, care-worn expression and remarked, 'It's okay, you won't be needed.' Suddenly, from being a masterful and commanding presence, this famous son of the Lanarkshire coalfields who could demand loyalty and inspire fear amongst the most battle-hardened veterans, looked tired and grey."

Yet on an evening when all the old certainties were scattered to the wind, Cooper and Rough, who turned up as peripheral figures, found themselves being thrust onto centre stage. In one sense, it spared them the anxiety which had begun to envelop the rest of the squad and, from Davie's vantage point, there were no hassles, no problems on his horizon as he walked off the team bus and marched into the changing room, oblivious to the pandemonium which always surrounds an invasion of any city by the Tartan Army.

Why should he have been worried? Whatever materialised, Cooper couldn't be blamed: the situation was out of his hands and it was up to the eleven Scots on the field to steer their country to the World Cup – or at least the prospect of a play-off. And yet, within a few minutes of the commencement of hostilities, it was clear that Mike England's men were properly fired up for the challenge, driven forward by the classy menace of Mark Hughes, who must have derived added confidence from the sight of some early jitters among the Scottish defence, and Leighton in particular looked vulnerable. It was therefore no surprise when the dangerous Hughes pushed his team ahead with a tremendous goal and he and Rush created sufficient chances for the match to have been over by the interval.

At the break, there were chaotic scenes and angry exchanges between people such as Stein and Alex Ferguson, and the gasket-blowing filtered through everybody in the Scotland camp. "When I entered the dressing room, there were teacups splattering off the walls and Jock and Alex were cursing and screaming at each other in the toilet area," recalls Rough, who suddenly found himself being told to get stripped for action in the second period. 'You never told me that Jim wore f***ing contact lenses,' bellowed Stein. 'That's because I never f***ing knew it myself,' retorted Ferguson, and the veins on the temples of both men were bulging. It was a scary scene."

Outside, once a semblance of order was restored – but only a semblance – Cooper was instructed to do some warm-ups. Rough, meanwhile, was approached by Stein and the latter man simply said, "You're f***ing on!" Plans were being torn up on the hoof and new strategies and tactics unearthed as the Scots strove to weather the storm. For a while the outlook remained gloomy, and Rough had to pull off a smart save to thwart Mickey Thomas, but eventually the tide began to turn, although the hosts were still a goal to the good. After seventy minutes, Ferguson told Cooper to carry out a couple of runs up and down the track, in preparation for making his entrance. Then, with a quarter of an hour left, Jock approached him and said, "Go out and play wide on the left. Go at them and try to get behind them as often as possible." It was the last throw of the dice for Scotland. It was also the last time Cooper would hear the sound of Jock Stein's voice.

He replaced Gordon Strachan, and blessed with the gifts to take advantage of any side, let alone one which was visibly tiring, Davie reignited the optimism among the fans on the terraces, first by nut-megging Joey Jones, then by delivering a couple of telling passes as the Welsh retreated ever deeper. The clock was against Scotland, but suddenly, as David Speedie tried to dink the ball over Dave Phillips and only succeeded in playing it against the Welshman's hand, the Dutch referee, Jan Keizer, pointed to the penalty spot. In an instant, tens of thousands of eyes were focused on Cooper, who, together with Strachan, was one of their team's designated penalty takers, and even as the Scots in the crowd dared to dream of Mexico again, Roy Aitken marched up to Davie with the ball in his hands, passed it over to his erstwhile Old Firm opponent and said, "Get on with it!"

It was a daunting proposition for the faint of heart, but this was where Cooper thrived. He claimed later that he wasn't bothered by the booing of the Welsh supporters and, as usual when presented with a spot kick, backed himself to convert the opportunity.

"I just wish I had a pound for every time somebody has asked me how I felt at that moment. It's not easy to describe. I wasn't espe-cially nervous despite the bedlam going on all around me, what with the Scots fans going wild with delight and their Welsh counter-parts simply going wild," said Cooper, who was pitted against Neville Southall. "My initial thought was that here we were, just a few minutes away from making an inglorious exit from the World Cup, and I had a chance to salvage it all. It was all I could think of and it was only much later when I was sitting with a cup of tea that it really hit me. Then, and only then, I started shaking at the notion, 'What would have happened if I had missed it?' Imagine being labelled forever as the man who lost Scotland the chance to go to Mexico."

Mercifully, Cooper retained his composure and was the calmest man in the auditorium. He had been through these routines so often that he was *au fait* with the drill and was confident enough in his own abilities to believe that even somebody of Southall's pedigree shouldn't be able to save a penalty if it was struck correctly. He steadied himself, then ignored a spot of gamesmanship from the keeper and made good contact with the ball. For a nanosecond, he gazed in horror as the bold Neville dived the right way and did his utmost to resist the shot, but although he was close – hands-in-mouth close – the ball found its target. Goal! 1–1! And vast swathes of Cardiff rose up in acclaim. Cooper, for so long in the wilderness, was now hogging the limelight.

There was no way the Welsh could recover from that blow, but the draw meant that Spain would qualify automatically for the World Cup, while the Scots had to lock horns with Australia in a two-leg play-off tussle. Yet even as Davie converted the penalty and basked in the acclaim of his teammates and the adulation of the fans, he noticed that, whereas Alex Ferguson was on his feet celebrating, Stein was wedged in his seat. Initially, Cooper dismissed this as another illustration of Jock's pragmatism and level-headedness, but soon enough, it was clear there was a problem, a serious problem.

At the final whistle, at exactly the time when the Scots should have been able to unleash their pent-up emotions and enjoy the moment, they instead found themselves being ushered to the dressing room by Ferguson, who told them that Stein had collapsed. He didn't have any more information at that juncture, but the look on his face told the likes of Cooper that there was no prospect of this being a minor scare. On the contrary, as the squad assembled en masse, the majority of them numb and unable to comprehend what was happening, with journalists seeking out interviews and flashbulbs popping in their faces, there was an eerie silence, the stillness of young men whose hearts and heads were being torn in different directions. Eventually, after a period lasting only nine or ten minutes, but which seemed like an eternity to those who were there, the SFA president, David Will, came into the room, with tears in his eyes, and communicated the message that nobody wanted to hear. "We've lost the manager. Jock has passed away."

The next hour was one of the worst of Davie's life. Nothing which had occurred earlier seemed to have any relevance and, for many in the Scotland ranks, it was as if their best friend or their father had died. Long ago, in a different decade, while Stein had steered Celtic to title after title, Cooper had grown sick of his achievements, but that was purely in the tribal milieu which surrounds those connected with the Old Firm. On the wider stage, the players had grown to love the Scotland manager and they would have done anything to have spared him this kind of demise.

Within that dressing room, big hard individuals, the sort of men who would have regarded crying in public as a sign of weakness in any other setting, shed tears openly. Alex Ferguson, a fellow hewn from Govan grit, was distraught, and yet it was somehow typical of this multi-faceted character that while everybody else fell to pieces, he retained enough composure to talk to the players about the qualities which had made Jock great and which they should remember now that he was gone. Cooper later described Ferguson's behaviour as "remarkable in the circumstances", but he and the rest of the Scots were grateful for the manner in which he took charge, organised their return to the bus and thence on to the airport. There cannot have been many occasions in the history of sport when a team which has just achieved its objective has been reduced to such inconsolable depths, but that journey from the stadium was one of the worst of these young men's lives.

On the road, Ferguson sought to break the players up into different groups, to try and ensure that those who had known Stein better than the rest were not isolated in their grief, but it was a night where sadness trumped any notion of group therapy. Jimmy Steele, the Celtic masseur and long-term confrere of the former Celtic boss, was inconsolable and Ferguson asked Davie and Paul McStay to look after Steele, a man who, in the normal run of things, was their Mr Fix-it, always there with a crack and a smile and the latest news from the tabloids. But in the hours after Jock's death, there was nothing to joke about, and although Cooper and

McStay did their best for him, they knew that it probably wasn't good enough.

In essence, football had been put in its place. For many days afterwards, there was a realisation that it really wasn't that important, allied to a nagging misgiving that Stein hadn't been accorded his true worth while he was alive, which perhaps accounted for the lavish scale and lachrymose nature of the valedictions which appeared in the Fourth Estate. The fans, for their part, behaved as impeccably as one might have anticipated in the circumstances – even if a cynic might have asked why it required a tragedy for them to pull together in a common cause – and Scotland and Wales were united in their mourning and their appreciation that a giant among men, a genuine hero of the sport, had been snatched away. Indeed, Mike England spoke emotionally, passionately and with unstinting decency about his sadness at what had occurred and looked as balefully at the Welsh journalists who asked him to talk about the Scotland penalty as Stein himself had done when a myopic hack asked him whether he was disappointed at Celtic conceding a late goal in the 1971 New Year match which precipitated the Ibrox Disaster.

Eventually, as the days passed, Cooper reached three conclusions about the events which had come close to overwhelming him in Cardiff. The first was that Stein would not have wished his players to walk around with their shoulders hunched, forlorn at the gaffer's demise. With his mining roots and his proud belief in community, he would have urged them to carry on with their lives and make him proud. This led on to the second thing: the knowledge that the best means of honouring the Big Man's memory was for the Scots to complete the job which they had started in Wales and book their passage to the World Cup in Mexico with the kind of football which would have enthused him. And thirdly, and poignantly when one considers how his own story finished, Davie resolved that he would no longer allow himself to get bogged down in petty contract disputes with his employers, but live his life to the full.

As Stein had told him on a number of occasions, he had a talent, a rare talent for bringing a warm smile to the faces of those on the stands, on the terraces and in the pubs which screened Scottish football matches. It was a message which he had occasionally forgotten about while involved in his protracted stand-off with John Greig, but that wouldn't happen again if he could help it. This didn't mean that Davie wouldn't continue to enjoy a good moan when the mood took him – as somebody who was becoming a senior player at Ibrox, he was entitled to air his grievances – but, henceforth, he would never forget how fortunate he was to be a professional footballer and always recall the debt he owed to two people called Jock, Stein and Wallace.

In that light, it was scarcely surprising that Scotland unusually experienced few scares while tackling the Australians under the stewardship of the redoubtable Ferguson. There was no need for tub-thumping speeches prior to the first match at Hampden: every man in the ranks was committed to carving out victory for Stein and the job was achieved with the minimum of fuss. They had to be patient and a number of decent chances were squandered throughout a goalless first half, but the hosts turned the screw in the second period and Cooper broke the deadlock with a marvellous, unstoppable free kick in the fifty-eighth minute. Immediately, a massive tidal wave of emotion swelled through the ground and, even as it reached a crescendo, Frank McAvennie added a second and if it wasn't quite job done, the Australians must have wondered about the wake they had gate-crashed as the salutes to Stein reverberated from every corner of the arena for the final half hour and continued while the supporters waited for a fresh opportunity to pay due homage.

In the aftermath, Ferguson refused to be overly confident and instructed his charges to assume nothing in advance of the second game. He knew that his Oz-based counterpart, Frank Arok, would be trusting that the pasty-faced Scots came a cropper in the sweltering heat of Melbourne and counselled his men to take copious amounts of sun cream with them for the assignation on 4 December.

As it transpired, there were plenty of diversions off the pitch, with Cooper managing to visit his mother's brother and his wife and children, while Ferguson also decamped for a tryst with relatives, leaving Walter Smith in charge for part of the mission.

In the midst of their preparations, David Speedie was booked to appear on BBC's *Grandstand* programme, to lend an insider's perspective to their preview of the play-off fixture, but nobody had warned Speedie before he decided to sample a drink, or eight, following a round of golf in 100 degrees where he had passed out with sun stroke. The show was anchored by the former Scotland goalkeeper, Bob Wilson, who was no doubt hoping to conduct a fairly bland, light-hearted interview, but instead found himself in the midst of an X-rated exchange when Speedie responded to being asked, "Hi there, David, how are you enjoying yourself in Australia?" with the words "Och, f***ing nae problem, big man, how's yourself?" The plug was promptly pulled and the usual nonsense trotted about "problems with the satellite", but the real source of bother was the eleven-hour time difference, which meant that this – ahem – chat happened at close to midnight in Melbourne. Thankfully, although Smith and Ferguson were not amused about the incident, it wasn't part of some wider malaise within the squad.

On the contrary, and a world removed from how other Scots have struggled in these scenarios, the players were determined to do a professional job, free of self-inflicted wounds or needless mishaps, and irrespective of those in the press who jested that they were between Arok and a hard place, they knuckled down with an admirable display of collective responsibility. The Australians tried hard, as one would have expected, but they were bigger on perspiration than inspiration, and with Jim Leighton producing a couple of smart saves, the game eventually petered out in a goalless stalemate. At the end, the Scots avoided any excessive triumphalism, partly because the heat was truly as stifling as they had feared, but also in recognition of the fact that they shouldn't be doing cartwheels over getting the better of opponents such as Australia. The acid test would arrive the following summer when they bumped into some genuine soccer powers.

Indeed, as far as Cooper was concerned, there was nothing to celebrate, beyond being relieved at ensuring qualification. "We were pretty awful, and the conditions meant that we had to play at a walking pace for long periods of the match, so with the Aussies running around making life difficult, the best thing you can say about the match was that it wasn't a classic," said Cooper. "All that mattered to us really was the result, and even if it wasn't the sort of performance of which we could be happy, we had done it, we had got to the World Cup, and that was a great feeling.

"When we returned to the team hotel, there were a few supporters who had flown over from Scotland – they always travelled to cheer us on, whatever the cost and the inconvenience – and I got talking to some of them and they told us that they had already booked their holidays to Mexico, even before the game. With fans like that, who are happy to fly to the ends of the earth to cheer you on, you can't go far wrong, and when the players and management met up for a meal that night, the overall attitude was that we owed it to these people not to let our standards slip. But the most overriding thought among all the squad as we pondered on the possibilities for Mexico was simple and straightforward . . . we had done it for Jock Stein."

9

ON THE SANTA FE TRAIL

By the time that Davie Cooper turned thirty in February 1986, he was starting to appreciate that, for all his vaunted achievements and resplendent contributions across Scottish football, he was part of a Rangers side which was going nowhere slowly. It had been eight years since the Ibrox club had last enjoyed League title success – the only currency which satisfies Old Firm supporters – and Cooper was entitled to be frustrated at the general lack of direction or even ambition which defined the dog days of Jock Wallace's second spell at the club, where he had masterminded so much success in the 1970s.

He had nothing like a similar impact upon his return and the reality was that the bold Jock's recourse to old-fashioned training regimes and forging a siege mentality around his dressing room grew increasingly anachronistic as the 1980s rolled on. Cooper could sympathise with his gaffer's plight, but he knew that reaching thirty in football terms was the equivalent of hitting fifty in any other vocation of life: there might still be plenty left in the tank and it should be too early for anybody to be put out to pasture, but the suspicions began to heighten that a player's best days were behind them. By this stage, Davie had long since made it clear to any would-be suitors outwith Scotland that he wasn't of a peripatetic persuasion and, for better or worse, he had made his bed with Rangers, settled down to married life with Christine in Motherwell and had grown wearily accustomed to hearing his mates in Hamilton complain about the down-turn in the club's fortunes.

Privately, he told some of his closer comrades that change was in the air, and within the Ibrox enclave even a section of more conservative elements were waking up to the fact that the twenty-first century was approaching and that it might be a good thing if they got round to moving into the twentieth. It was, essentially, a battle for the organisation's soul between those who bought into all the old Orange-and-Unionist affiliations and believed that hell would freeze over before a high-profile Catholic pulled on a Rangers jersey, and those with a (slightly) more progressive and pragmatic approach to the club's problems.

Of the latter, there were many as the 1985–86 campaign reached its climax. Week in, week out, a squad comprised of largely modest players was struggling to average a point a game and was gradually slipping further into mediocrity. At the summit of the table, Celtic eventually edged past Hearts, with the latter infamously committing hari-kari at Dens Park on the closing afternoon of their title surge. Then, next in the standings came Dundee United and Aberdeen, with Rangers a rather pitiful fifth, having amassed a paltry 35 points from thirty-six matches, and only finishing in front of Dundee on goal difference. There was no case for the defence, nor that much to be said for the strikers either, and Wallace could not have been surprised when his tenure was brought to a conclusion in April, as David Holmes decided to emulate his political counterparts in Europe and seek a revolution in the way that Rangers conducted themselves on and off the pitch.

What *was* surprising was the speed with which the changes were made after such a long period of dithering and dilatory behaviour from the board. The catalyst was the Old Firm match of 22 March, a typically controversial, inflammatory contest, where torrential rain in Glasgow failed to dampen the warmth of the hostility between the combatants at Ibrox. Cooper found himself amongst the substitutes: this, reckoned Wallace, was not an affair for silky artistry or aesthetic beauty, but a time for Rangers to proclaim their defiance with lusty renditions of "The Sash" and for his team to remember their roots and rely on industry over invention. Mo Johnston sent the visitors in front after twenty-one minutes and Brian McClair soon doubled their advantage, but in a match with more twists and turns than a Raymond Chandler novel, Celtic suffered a double blow, first when Willie McStay was sent off for a foul on Ted McMinn after thirty-three minutes and Cammy Fraser immediately reduced Rangers' deficit.

It was a bruising, grisly encounter, and with Cooper replacing McMinn, the balance ebbed and flowed thereafter with a juddering intensity which could never have been mistaken for the "beautiful game". Tommy Burns restored his side's two-goal cushion shortly into the second half, but the Ibrox men responded with a ferocious barrage, which yielded three goals for Ally McCoist, Robert Fleck and Fraser's second of the day. Even then, with a numerical advantage and as their supporters dutifully whipped up a maelstrom of sound and fury, it summed up Rangers' deficiencies that Murdo MacLeod managed to secure a seventieth-minute equaliser, as the tussle finished in a 4–4 draw. Bafflingly in the circumstances, Wallace reacted as if this result was a triumph, leading his players in a run-through of their tribal anthems and making it clear these derbies were his No.1 priority and that sealed his fate.

There was no longer any doubt that this obsession with meeting and beating Celtic, and with constantly working themselves into a lather of loathing for their Glasgow rivals, was limiting Rangers' horizons. Holmes, a smart fellow with no particular axes to grind or knees to jerk, was only on the board to represent the business interests of the then-owner of the club Lawrence Marlborough, who was based in the United States, but he knew that change had to happen and the sooner the better. None of this should have been surprising to football insiders, but the Aye-Been mentality which pervades much of Scottish sport was prevalent among the Govan supporters at that point in their history. The board knew their side was crap, they knew that their fans knew their side was crap, but at least they were crap in red, white and blue and could remember the words of the anthems. Holmes saw this clearly and deduced it was time for an injection of new blood:

"Lawrence Marlborough was a tax exile, so we had to have the whole Lawrence Group meeting in Paris and that, of course, included Rangers Football Club, which was losing money hand over fist, with the stadium only quarter-filled every week. I spelled out what needed to be done, which certainly did not go down well with the Rangers chairman, John Paton, who was present. But I was given the reins as the new chief executive and after coming to terms with a few of the directors for their removal and meeting Jock Wallace in a car park in Strathclyde Country Park and coming to an amicable agreement with him about his removal, I decided that I had to project this club to a wider world. One man was in my mind – Graeme Souness, who was known throughout Europe. We needed somebody who could project the club's image internationally and who would be widely known throughout the game. I contacted him through the good offices of [the late sports] journalist Ken Gallacher and promised him an exclusive on the story if it happened. I think in doing that I incurred the enmity of other colleagues of his who were in the same business. But it did happen and my whole life was then turned upside down."

Souness's recruitment was certainly not without risks. At Liverpool, he had shown a mixture of sublime skill and a combative streak which occasionally boiled over in tackles which were closer to muggings. Untried in the managerial sphere, he wore his volatility like a badge of honour, insisted that he only would sign players, irrespective of race or religion, who he felt could steer the club forward and declared within a few days of being appointed that the Ibrox mindset had to change from the mentality where beating Celtic was considered the be-all. In the latter respect, Souness quickly discovered that nobody, not even a fellow with his radical instincts and revivalist fervour, could erase decades of history, hostility and ingrained prejudice in the space of a few months, or even a few years, and one of the most conspicuous aspects of his reign was how some of the players he signed – including the England duo Terry Butcher and Graham Roberts, and Oldham-born Andy Goram – were amongst those whose conversion to the Rangers tradition meant that they detested Celtic with a passion bordering on the psychotic.

The only thing that could be declared with absolute conviction was that Rangers were transformed dramatically when Wallace departed and Souness set to work. Even as the former was staging an emotional press conference at the Grosvenor Hotel in Glasgow, the latter prepared himself for a whistle-stop tour of Ibrox before returning to Sampdoria and it must have been obvious from the instant he clapped eyes on some of his players that they were destined for the exit door, before you could say P45. Davie was at home, relaxing in the bath, when Christine heard that Souness was the new Rangers manager, and when she shouted upstairs to pass on the news, his first reaction was dismay, allied to the apprehension that at thirty he might be deemed to be surplus to requirements.

This was always a feature of Cooper's split personality. Some days he could swagger and strut in the knowledge that he possessed the gifts to justify his confidence; on other occasions he would question his ability, worry that he wouldn't measure to the standards expected by his employers and beat himself up unnecessarily. Perhaps players in his mould are more prone to these conflicting emotions than those with less talent but a greater degree of consistency. Yet, whatever the reason, Davie required constant reassurance from those around him, even after everything that he had achieved in the game. In the heat of battle, when he didn't have time to fret about such matters, he could be serene, cool as you please, and even arrogant in dismissing the attentions of lesser opponents, without straying into disrespect. But, whereas the majority of Rangers fans responded to the news of Souness's appointment with a mixture of elation and relief that this marked the start of a glittering new era, Cooper was worried he would end on the scrapheap, as he subsequently revealed in an interview with the *Sunday Express*:

"I was pessimistic and concerned during those first few days. That might sound a strange thing to say when you consider the euphoria which greeted the announcement, but I was at a stage where I had to think about myself and look at the bigger picture. We hadn't been performing well for the previous few years and I knew that Graeme would want to make big changes because he was ambitious to get the club back to the top in Scotland and the newspapers had reports that he was going to sign a load of big-name superstars. So, of course, I was worried about him swinging the axe. We had also heard that he was a fitness fanatic and took training very seriously, which was another thing to be concerned about, because although I always tried my best at the sessions, I wasn't one of life's grafters and I had seen enough of Graeme for Liverpool and Scotland to be aware of the high standards he set for himself and which he expected everybody else to follow.

"I wasn't the only guy who was thinking along these lines. Most of us who had been at Rangers for more than five years realised that the club's results in that time had been totally unacceptable and that the new man would have a shake-up. The biggest problem was the defence, because for us to score four goals against Celtic and only get a draw was a disgrace, especially when they were down to ten men for the last hour. So the mood in the dressing room was edgy, with a lot of boys anxious about their futures and whether they still had one at Rangers. We knew that this all came with the territory of being professional footballers and earning our living from kicking a ball around, but it was a step into the unknown for everybody and that included Graeme himself."

Those first few weeks of the Souness reign passed in a giddy whirl. Cooper was in a more positive mood after meeting his international confrere and being told to prepare himself to be a pivotal player the following season. Both men were tiptoeing in the dark at that juncture and the newcomer admitted that he would require time to find his feet and acquaint himself with the ways of Scottish football, but he proved that he was in a hurry by installing Walter Smith as his assistant and instructing his charges to get ready for the challenge of big-time European football again. There wasn't an alternative, as Souness stated at the outset, and although he was in a slightly strange position, jetting to and from Italy on a regular basis, as well as conducting transfer business wherever he happened to be staying, even whilst he was steeling himself for that summer's World Cup – which saw Scotland drawn in the so-called "Group of Death" against Germany, Denmark and Uruguay – nobody could ever have accused this chap of being a shrinking violet. In his domain, there was only one way and that was his way. If anybody disagreed with that philosophy, they could hit the highway. For the moment at least, following seasons of torpor and stagnation, his shoot-from-the-hip approach made him an instant hero with a Rangers support which had craved the arrival of somebody who would shake things up and restore some of the glitz which had surrounded the team in the 1970s.

Smith's appointment was another shrewd move. What he didn't know about the game in his homeland could have been inscribed on the back of a postage stamp and he and Davie forged an immediate rapport. They hit it off on the practice pitches, to the extent that Cooper actually started enjoying these sessions, and Smith reciprocated by coaxing and cajoling his Rangers colleague into an extra few minutes working on his set pieces here, another couple of laps there. There was continual gossip in Glasgow about Souness's grand plans at Ibrox and one can imagine a succession of agents gleefully phoning the tabloids on a daily basis, touting the services of another of their clapped-out clients, but with English clubs banned from European competition following the Heysel atrocity, suddenly the more extravagant rumours didn't seem that far-fetched.

149

The bottom line was that Souness, a bona fide football A-list figure, had hitched his star to the Rangers wagon. From that moment, as Smith asserted later, almost anything appeared possible, where there had been despair, discontent and deserted stands only a few months earlier. "He was the catalyst for change. He turned the dream into a reality. He brought it alive. Without him, it wouldn't have happened," said the willing lieutenant as the likes of Chris Woods and Terry Butcher were ushered through the Ibrox portals. "He knew these players; they knew him. And they all recognised that if Graeme Souness was going to continue his career in Scotland, it was worthwhile joining him."

Prior to the commencement of his tempestuous tenure at Rangers, there was the little matter of the World Cup to deal with for Cooper and Souness. In the build-up, the SFA eschewed the poor preparation which had marred their personnel's previous appearances on the global stage, while there was none of the hyperbole which had presaged the fiasco-strewn trail of Ally's Tartan Army. But there is a fine line between going over the top and waiting for accidents to happen and, whatever the reason(s), this particular Cup sojourn failed to provide an abundance of cheer.

On the face of it, the Scots should have been in with a decent opportunity of progressing out of their group for the first time. There was nobody with the potency of a Brazil or Argentina in their section, and with Alex Ferguson at the helm, his players committed to doing their utmost to make Jock Stein proud and a redoubtable work ethic in the ranks, it shouldn't have been beyond their grasp to make a serious impression in the tournament. The party comprised: Jim Leighton, Alan Rough, Andy Goram, Richard Gough, Willie Miller, Alex McLeish, Maurice Malpas, David Narey, Arthur Albiston, Gordon Strachan, Graeme Souness, Jim Bett, Paul McStay, Roy Aitken, Steve Nicol, Steve Archibald, Frank McAvennie, Charlie Nicholas, Graeme Sharp, Paul Sturrock, Eamonn Bannon and, of course, Cooper. Maybe it wasn't as individually gifted as the 1978 ensemble, but there was solidity in the defence, flair in the midfield and plenty of goals up front – on paper at least. With hindsight, one or two omissions were surprising. What about Alan Hansen? And David Speedie? (Although he had hardly endeared himself to the management with his drunken *Grandstand* interview the previous December.) Mo Johnston must have wondered why he hadn't gained a trip to Mexico and even the young Ally McCoist might have brought his youthful brio and joke-laden *joie de vivre* to the squad. But none of these were back-page-scandal material. And even then, few queried Ferguson's *modus operandi*.

All the same, it was a low-key summer interspersed by a series of squally showers, involving Souness and Ferguson, who spent much of their time arguing over concerns which to outsiders seemed relatively trivial. As head of the players' committee, the new Rangers boss became embroiled in a number of heated exchanges with his more senior compatriot, and there were disputes over such matters as the number of overseas phone calls which the players were allowed to make. This impacted on Cooper as much as anybody, because, as usual, he couldn't bear to be away from home, but he had grown more pragmatic as the years had passed. He wondered about the spats between these two men he admired, but reached the conclusion that Ferguson felt uncomfortable in the role because, essentially, he had inherited a squad from Stein, which included one or two players he wouldn't have touched with a barge pole. Souness, for his part, was gearing up for the hot seat at Ibrox and didn't want to betray any sign of weakness in front of his peers.

It was a theory that had the benefit of recognising that the now-knighted Sir Alex has always fared best by nurturing young players and moulding them into a team over a sustained period. And he has never made any secret of his pride in his working-class addiction to Old Labour values and suspicion of those who party too heartily. In which light, one can imagine his response to the arrival of Rod Stewart at the Scotland HQ during the build-up in Los Angeles, and the ostentatious fashion in which six of the squad – Souness,

151

McAvennie, Johnston, Archibald, Rough and Sharp – embarked on a chauffeur-driven limousine ride to a restaurant on Sunset Boulevard, where they spent most of the evening in the company of Stewart getting noisily out of their faces.

In the weeks leading up to the World Cup, Ferguson spoke to every player and virtually nothing was left to chance. Playing at altitude inevitably caused problems, and the Scots knew that they would be performing in stifling heat and would be at risk of serious dehydration unless they drank enough liquid, none of it alcoholic. But, as Cooper told me later, there was something about the whole campaign which smacked of going through the motions, of tensions simmering beneath the surface and of the manager and captain pulling in different directions.

There was, for instance, a bounce game against Northern Ireland in Albuquerque, where Ferguson and his counterpart, Billy Bingham, devised a three-part structure, which allowed every player to get a run out at some stage or another. The Scots were leading 6–4 until the closing moments when their opponents were handed a brace of late penalties, at which point Rough, to his chagrin, was instructed to dive in the opposite direction from the ball. Cynics might retort that he could have done this without recourse to team orders, but the exercise ended in a 6–6 draw which provoked criticism from some quarters – and within the party itself – that this was no way to plan for three strength-sapping fixtures in sweltering heat in the space of a week.

On a more personal note, Cooper recognised amidst these knock-about affairs that his participation in the World Cup would be limited. He enjoyed being in the company of international-class players, and got on wonderfully well with his mate, Jim "Jazzer" Bett, but there was always a streak of melancholia lurking not too far beneath the surface:

"When you are a wee laddie from Hamilton or Clydebank, you dream about being involved in tournaments like the World Cup. And even as a child when I was playing in the park by myself, I would come up with scenarios where I was scoring the winning goal in the final against Germany, or Brazil, or England. When I was struggling to get a regular game at Rangers in the early 1980s, I wondered if that chance had gone forever, so I was just delighted to be part of the whole thing in Mexico and when I looked around me and saw all the Scottish fans who had spent thousands of pounds to be there, waving their flags and asking for autographs, it sometimes brought a lump to my throat.

"But unlike some of the boys, I knew that I was going to the World Cup probably, at best, as a substitute. There is still a place in modern-day football for wingers, but there is also a time and I was realistic enough to know that my role might well be confined to the bench and a late run if things weren't running Scotland's way in any of the matches. Nobody told me as much, but you didn't have to be a genius to suspect it. And although I would dearly have liked to have been proved wrong, it turned out exactly as I anticipated. I didn't see forty-five minutes – not even half a game – of action while I was in Mexico."

It was as if even the brightest members of the footballing Brains Trust didn't quite know how to harness Davie's talents and utilise them to their best advantage. Some might wonder whether Ferguson, a man who has never tolerated anything less than 100 per cent from his charges, harboured reservations over Cooper's ability to prosper in a World Cup setting, yet, as Sir Alex told me at his Carrington base whilst taking time off from steering his injury-ravaged Manchester United squad through some choppy waters, he had been a long-time admirer of his compatriot, not least because his Aberdeen personnel had been on the receiving end of the Rangers man's tricks in the preceding years:

"Davie was a beautifully cultured footballer, a pure footballer, somebody who, with his wonderful left foot, usually looked a bit silkier than anybody else around him on the pitch. I first saw him in an Under-18 Juvenile cup final at [Falkirk's old] Brockville Stadium – Andy Gray and Dave Narey were also playing in the match – and straight away you could tell he was a player. Maybe he didn't have blinding pace, but he could beat an opponent with skill, his control was exemplary, and he made difficult things look easy. A lot of Scots went down to England in the 1970s and 1980s, but Davie was happy at Rangers and you can't criticise a boy for showing loyalty to the club he supported.

"He never wanted to up sticks and move his tent around every two or three years and I have a lot of respect for people such as him, who loved football and wasn't that worried about anything else. Perhaps he could have played somewhere else than on the wing – though he was excellent in that position. I think he could have been used just behind the strikers, and he scored some wonderful goals during his career. The one against Dundee United in the [Scottish Cup] final replay sticks in my mind because not too many players could have orchestrated that goal, but he made it look straightforward. I was fortunate to work with him at the 1986 World Cup finals and you couldn't fault his professionalism or his attitude and, on a personal level, he was a lovely lad, very down-to-earth and obviously in love with football. He just wanted to play and didn't let anything else get in the way."

Perhaps that was part of the problem in Mexico. Other less reserved and more voluble individuals would probably have marched into Ferguson's office and demanded the chance to prove their worth. The likes of Souness, Gordon Strachan and Steve Archibald were certainly disinclined to hide their light under a bushel and weren't afraid of stating their case bluntly, regardless of any teapot treatment they might receive in response, but Cooper simply disliked conflict and the macho posturing which often pervaded these dressing room spats. Sadly, from his perspective, it saw him consigned to the periphery as the Scots reached their base at Villa Arqueológica in Teotihuacuan and prepared to open their campaign against the Danes, who had achieved some excellent results in their qualifying group and possessed sufficient menace to pose problems for anybody.

Indeed, many of their number went on to lift the European Championship title in 1992 and there was no disputing the efficacy of such individuals as Michael Laudrup, Jesper Olsen, Søren Lerby, Frank Arnesen and Jan Mølby, whose achievements at club and international level spoke volumes for their ability. Nonetheless, a personality such as Cooper boasted the qualities to trouble these warriors, and even though it is always easy to be wise with the benefit of hindsight, Scotland's decision to plump for industry over inspiration seemed puzzling, especially in temperatures which called for economy of movement and a preference for the rapier over the blunderbuss.

As a consequence, the match developed into a pattern which has become horribly predictable to those of us who have followed Scotland on the global stage in the last thirty years. Namely that although they battled courageously, rarely allowed their Danish rivals to crank up any momentum and created one or two fine chances, they eventually conceded the only goal of the game in the fifty-eighth minute when Preben Elkjær-Larsen gained the break of the ball in a tussle with Willie Miller, and that was enough for the Scandinavians to force victory.

This was scarcely a disgrace, nor did the media view the outcome as any great surprise. But once again the sliver of magic, the soupçon of elusiveness which might have been supplied by Cooper, was left unused on the side of the pitch. Granted, as he sat stoically surveying the proceedings, even Davie reflected on how difficult the conditions were for the Scots – many of whose number lost half a stone in weight throughout the contest and were flagging by the climax – and there was no guarantee that he would have derived any joy against a sturdy, battle-hardened Danish defence. But the fact was that given the heat, the altitude and the requirement to avoid having to chase your tail for any significant lengths of time, these were tussles where retaining possession and making passes count were absolutely crucial and Davie was surely better equipped to excel in these circumstances than a number of those who gained selection ahead of him.

Understandably, the pressure intensified ahead of the next match, with the always powerful West Germans, although it was a measure of the desultory fashion in which the event progressed during these early stages that Cooper, never the happiest of travellers, found time to ask himself how on earth the Mexicans had been awarded the World Cup again, only sixteen years after first hosting the planet's premier tournament. Whilst staying at the Villa Arqueológica – a place the squad dubbed Colditz – there was just one telephone in their hotel and it only accepted incoming calls – in 1986!

Outside, as he walked around the nearby villages, Davie was struck by the abject poverty of these places, where dead horses lay in the streets, where children begged the players for money and many of the residents looked in their fifties or sixties when they were twenty years younger, such had been their struggle to eke out a living for a pittance. "If I ever started feeling sorry for myself, then meeting the locals was enough to remind me that I was one of the luckiest men alive," he declared later in the pages of the *Daily Record*. "Many of these folk had nothing, and after we had all gone home, they would still have nothing. Some of us, on the other hand, were complaining because we didn't have fridges in our room, as if it was the end of the world. It just seemed obvious to me that Mexico had bigger problems to worry about that spending millions of pounds on building football stadiums and when we went to Querétaro [the venue for the Germany match], we drove past a shanty town where children looked like skeletons. You don't forget these things."

In the build-up to the next game, at least Cooper found himself included among the substitutes, and that allowed him to contemplate making his World Cup entrance at some stage in the contest. Never at ease in the role of spectator, he shifted around in his seat uncomfortably as the game kicked off, but the whole squad's spirits were lifted by the pugnacious manner in which Ferguson's men took the fight to their opponents, and they duly seized the lead when Strachan latched on to Aitken's service and finished adroitly in the eighteenth minute, temporarily provoking screams of partisan support from those Tartan Army infantry who still kept the faith.

Gradually, though, the Germans weathered the storm, not with electrifying football, but through stringing passes together, making their opponents run harder than them and waiting for opportunities to arrive. They were helped by the fact that Rudi Völler had equalised almost immediately, prior to surviving another Scottish surge, but the danger in these scenarios is that the more clinical team gets the job done, without recourse to style or glitz, and there was something inevitable about the manner in which Klaus Allofs pushed his team ahead in the fiftieth minute.

If that hardly reflected the run of play, so what! The reality was that the Scots had hurled themselves into a brick wall and virtually burned themselves out by the time that Cooper was introduced to the fray as a substitute for Eamonn Bannon in the seventy-fourth minute. Yet as so often happens in these chronicles, history could have been very different. The writer Gordon Williams coined the phrase "Scots? Wee boys looking for fairy tales" in the mid-1970s and there was invariably that sense of hushed expectancy, of fingers and everything else being crossed, while the national football team was seeking to retrieve an apparently lost cause. Usually, maddeningly, they would unearth a spark of hope, a fresh reason to believe, only for the optimism to be extinguished again, mostly through self-inflicted wounds.

In this case Cooper, immediately elusive and posing problems for a German rearguard which was itself displaying signs of fatigue, slipped past his would-be markers and created an opening for Richard Gough, and a few million people held their breaths. But just as swiftly, the opportunity was squandered and despite the usual frantic finale from the Caledonian contingent, they had lost 2–1 and their World Cup aspirations hung by a thread. It wasn't Davie's fault. On the contrary, even as he trudged off at the finish, feeling as if he had been sprinting in a sauna for ninety minutes, several of the Germans expressed surprise that "the Cooper man" hadn't been involved from the outset. That episode could have served as a microcosm of his international career; glimpses of class, interspersed with longer periods of mildly irritated inactivity. In one sense, he was delighted that he had provided some contribution, but it had been too little, too late to seriously worry Germany and he had a decent idea he would be back on the bench.

To his credit, though, and as Sir Alex Ferguson stressed in our conversation, Cooper's attitude was first class. He sweated for his country without a word of dissent, remained 100 per cent committed to the cause and refused to let his ego intervene in the bigger picture. Yet behind the scenes, even as the recriminations started following the Scots' second defeat, there was definite discord in the camp, and despite the fact that Scotland could still qualify for the next stages if they beat Uruguay in their final match, the schism between Ferguson and Souness was made plain when the latter, who had captained the side against Denmark and Germany, was peremptorily dropped and didn't even feature among the substitutes. The conspiracy theorists had a field day, even if the majority of the players in the squad appeared as surprised at the news as the supporters. Even now, most of them are reluctant to discuss the matter, but Alan Rough, who had sat through the World Cup with a knowing detachment – he was only there as Scotland's third-choice keeper – was typically forthright in offering his opinion of what had materialised:

"A number of issues had caused disagreements between Alex and Graeme and they just didn't seem to get on during the trip to Mexico. But then, they were a contrasting couple. You had Ferguson, the Govan shop steward, whose normal response to footballers demanding perks was similar to [TV detective] Jim Taggart being informed about another murder in Partick; and Souness, the Edinburgh-born property-owning capitalist with a penchant for personal grooming and a belief that players were part of the entertainment industry and deserved to earn as much money as any Hollywood film star.

"But all the same, we were astonished when we heard that Graeme wasn't in the team to face Uruguay, because despite some talk about dehydration having affected some of the guys who had played against Germany, nobody had been forced to resort to the oxygen canisters which were stored in the dressing room, and there were five days between the two matches [The Germany game was on 8 June, the Uruguay tussle on the 13th]. Moreover, Souness was one of the fittest members in the Scotland camp. He always prided himself on his stamina and taking care of himself on and off the pitch, and it was hard to avoid the suspicion that his omission was due to a personality clash."

Cooper had other issues to occupy his attention. In the days leading up to the Uruguay clash – with the latter being the operative word, considering the cynical philosophy adopted by the South Americans – he spoke regularly to Christine, back in Motherwell, and she told him that the tabloids were speculating that Davie would be on from the start for the showdown. It made sense, given that both he and Jim Bett had fresh legs and their direct approach was likely to harass the Uruguayans, but as rumour and gossip enveloped the squad, nobody could be sure of anything.

Eventually, Ferguson, who must have thought that massaging the egos of Eric Cantona and Roy Keane was a breeze after this ordeal, confirmed his selection and Cooper once again was on the bench. It hurt him a bit, persuaded him never to believe anything that he read in the papers, and he went to bed that night with a hollow feeling, allied to recurring pangs of homesickness. The squad had been on their peregrinations for over a month and, in Cooper's terms, this was equivalent to a Homeric odyssey away from his nearest and dearest. Basically, he thought his World Cup was over, and even as he consoled Bett, was in a dark mood himself. But these flirtations with the blues never lasted long. At least, as he reminded himself, he was in contention on the bench. Bett, in contrast, was out of the picture altogether.

Usually, when the Scots are embroiled in these World Cup missions, the nation pretty much grinds to a halt. On this occasion, I watched the match at the Dreadnought Hotel in Bathgate with a couple of sporting buddies, Peter McKenzie and Terry Clark, the former a Celtic aficionado, the latter a Rangers diehard. In normal circumstances, they were affable fellows who could be relied upon to deliver dry-as-Nevada drolleries on every subject under the sun, but all that changed as soon as they began watching Scotland, regardless of the sport, involved in international action. This was no exception, and even before the game commenced, both were bemoaning Ferguson's selections, McKenzie because Mo Johnston hadn't been picked in the squad and Clark, who reckoned – not without reason – that Cooper was one of the few world-class players at the manager's disposal, so it hardly made a lot of sense to leave him languishing on the bench.

Both were valid opinions, and the feeling amongst us all in advance was that Scotland would discover some way of failing to qualify; it was in the genes, a natural disposition to snatch defeat from the jaws of victory and there had been too many instances of heroic/botched failure in the past for it simply to be regarded as an aberration. Yet, no sooner had the contest began and Uruguay's José Batista had been deservedly sent off for a wretched challenge on Gordon Strachan – the one Scot who unequivocally enhanced his reputation in Mexico – than our optimism rose appreciably. Surely, being reduced to ten men inside fifty-four seconds would allow Ferguson's personnel to secure control of the proceedings and impose their authority on the South Americans. Typically, this premise assumed that Scotland would reproduce the form they had displayed in the first half against Germany. But as it transpired, they were strangely pedestrian, lacking in effervescence, and soon enough my two comrades were slumped in dejection, even as they discussed the newspaper reports, which hinted at friction behind the scenes in the Scotland camp.

"Their whole body language looks flat, it's almost as if they don't believe they can win," said Clark midway through the first half, while McKenzie, a chap whose language when off-duty would have amazed the children he taught at the nearby primary school, waxed indignant about the lack of penetration of his compatriots. "Why Ferguson didn't pick Souness is beyond me. If he's not injured, it is f***ing crazy. He wouldn't have taken any crap from this shower of dirty bastards and he would have made sure the boys were really up for this match," he raged as the interval arrived with Uruguay happy to defend their ramparts and kick anything that moved in a blue jersey.

"I mean, Willie Miller as f***ing captain! Arthur Albiston? Give me a f***ing break! Graeme Sharp! Jesus Christ, he shouldn't even have been in the squad, let alone picked for this match . . ."

And so it continued, even as those around us started expressing similar words of disapproval. One old lad at the end of the bar, who was drinking stout and whisky, earned purrs of approval when he piped up on the hour mark – while nothing significant continued to happen on the pitch, "You know, at least in 1978 we went out with a bang and we showed the world that we could play football, although we left it too late. The Dutch were proper footballers, much better than this dirty South American shower, but we had a swagger which was too much for them. It was great to watch that game and it put a smile on our faces." (Pause for dramatic effect.) "But this is just shite."

It was an astute, if uncouth, summing up of the tedious fare on display. But it also reflected how quickly Scotland supporters can lose patience with their personnel. On my right, Clark was growing increasingly incandescent at the sterility and timorous approach of his countrymen and kept piping, minute after minute: "Where's Cooper? Where's [Charlie] Nicholas? Where's f***ing anybody? Ferguson has got to make changes because these guys could play all day and not score."

Eventually, with the tussle drifting into stalemate, fresh blood was introduced, with both of the aforementioned players brought on for the ineffectual Steve Nicol and Paul Sturrock, but with only twenty minutes left the pattern and tempo of the match were beyond repair. Later, as he assessed the match, Cooper's typically frank opinion chimed with the sentiments which had been aired in the Dreadnought:

"They weren't going to concede anything that day, and the early sending off just made them even more determined to be negative because they only needed the draw," said Davie to the media in Mexico with trademark candour and refusal to proffer excuses. "We were poor. I can't put my finger on what was wrong, but I wasn't surprised that we got some stick from our fans, because we didn't do the business, we didn't create any clear-cut chances and we should have been capable of putting them under more pressure than we did. It was pretty dreadful, to be honest, and I am not going to make any excuses for how we performed. We can't blame anybody but ourselves, and the people I feel sorry for are the supporters who spent good money and their holidays coming over here to cheer us on. They deserved better than we gave them."

Cooper could have asked why he gained so little time on the pitch, but his candour was refreshing. Questions remained, though, as Alan Rough pointed out to me. "I have never fathomed why there was so little fuss over our elimination from the World Cup in 1986. We collected one paltry point against Uruguay's ten men and were largely unimpressive, without much fuss being made about it, whereas 1978 was viewed a national disaster. We were portrayed as laughing stocks and our failure subsequently proved the subject of endless post-mortems and breast-beating. Under Ally MacLeod we had confidence in ourselves and there was a tangible sense of ambition in the ranks. We also stuffed Holland, who just happened to be one of the best sides on the planet. But just eight years later, an ignominious campaign was shrugged off with murmurs of 'So what!'"

Perhaps it had something to do with the lowering of expectations which had occurred in the wake of the Argentina debacle and the self-inflicted wounds of 1982 where the Scots would surely have qualified for the later stages of the tournament if Willie Miller and Alan Hansen had managed to avoid colliding with each other and gifting the Russians a goal.

From Davie's perspective, the Mexican trip simply highlighted his opinion that the Scots lacked sufficient international-class performers to be anything more than bit-part players on the global stage. There was undeniably a grain of truth in that contention, but all the same, nothing adequately explained the Scots' dearth of urgency during that final clash with Uruguayans, who might have won a world kicking competition but were a shadow of the side which had lifted the Jules Rimet trophy earlier in their history.

Still, Davie had enjoyed his foreign sojourn, despite any lurking frustrations. He had also been impressed in his conversations with Souness about the scale of the latter's plans for Rangers and how he was determined to transform them into a genuine force on the European circuit again. Even as the squad spent a few weeks with their families, re-charging their batteries and escaping from the limelight, the touch paper was being lit at Ibrox. Life for everybody connected with the club would never be the same again.

10

BACK ON THE TROPHY-WINNING BEAT

Love him or loathe him, Graeme Souness's arrival in Scottish football could never have been described as boring. Whether arguing with journalists, accusing one of the heinous crime of being a "little socialist", falling out with tea ladies or wading into trouble and strife with officialdom, the former Liverpool star was proof positive that machismo and metrosexuality can live together in the same body. It might have been true that Souness was a ticking time bomb of histrionics and grand gestures, and that falling out with him was akin to picnicking on Vesuvius, but the reality is that Rangers badly required somebody with his drive, passion and occasional nastiness to rouse them out of their moribund state and, whatever flak he copped on his journey in Glasgow, he dealt with it in much the same visceral manner that he deployed to halt opponents in their tracks.

During the first few weeks of his reign at Ibrox, Souness put the fear of death into the squad he inherited and spelled out the message that they would have to shape up or ship out, that fifth position in the league was no place for a club of Rangers' magnitude and that he wasn't simply striving for domestic domination, but coveted success on the European stage as well. If he was a holy terror when his hackles rose, Souness was also smart enough to appreciate he had to be selective in picking his targets and although he initially proclaimed that he would be comfortable with losing every match

against Celtic if his club still won the championship, he was sufficiently sensible to change that stance once he and his early recruits,
Chris Woods, Terry Butcher and Trevor Steven, were thrust into the
ritual loathing which pervades an Old Firm derby. If anything, men
such as Butcher, the big, proud Englishman who admitted that he
wasn't cognisant with sectarianism and religious bigotry prior to
joining Rangers, became even more caught up in the tribal hostility
and traditional baggage which accompanied these matches.

Once he had returned to training following his World Cup diver-
sion, Davie Cooper worked as hard as anybody at Ibrox to prove
that he was lean, mean and desperate to orchestrate a transformation in Rangers' fortunes. He and Souness were like Tennent's lager
and Moet, but their differences weren't so great as their joint determination to resuscitate an organisation which had fallen into disre-
pair. Davie was quiet where Graeme was strident, as uncomfortable
with celebrity as his manager revelled in the spotlight, and where
Cooper was a parochial boy, Souness was the world traveller, with
a cosmopolitan attitude to life within and outside football. He was
also ruthless when he needed to be, and as the 1986–87 season
hoved into view, a number of players, amongst them Derek
Johnstone, Dave McKinnon, Billy Davies and Andy Bruce, were
told that there was no place for them in the manager's plans.
Meanwhile, he attempted to sign Richard Gough from Dundee
United and although the initial approach was unsuccessful, the tabloids were packed with stories of those who were allegedly being
courted by Rangers.

If Souness was the man with the vision, his assistant, Walter
Smith, was the beating heart with – please excuse the mixed meta-
phor – his finger on the pulse. An assiduous individual with a relish
for the hard slog and the ability to make every person in the squad
feel that they were integral to his schemes, Smith coped with sailing
through choppy waters on many occasions, and even as Souness
attracted a plethora of headlines both positive and negative, his
senior partner was toiling effectively behind the scenes. The

relationship worked because they knew their lines, mastered their parts and ventured on stage with a theatrical flourish when the new campaign eventually commenced.

Perhaps it was inevitable, given the hype in the build-up to his reign, that Souness seemed to have the word "controversial" appended to his name for most of those early weeks. Yet nobody could have envisaged the scale of his rage, nor the maelstrom which erupted when he took his team to Easter Road for a match which has now entered the annals, though not for the right reasons.

Quite understandably, Hibs weren't ready to cede an inch to their opponents, and as a string of ferocious challenges provoked fury on the sidelines, Souness quite simply lost his head and perpetrated an awful, eye-watering tackle on the home centre forward, George McCluskey. He was immediately red-carded, and the pictures of him walking off the pitch seem to show him smiling as if he was proud of his actions, although I have been told that he was actually embarrassed by what he had done. At any rate, his original sin prompted a mass brawl involving all the players except Alan Rough, who had already been booked, and the referee, Mike Delaney, was faced with an impossible situation, which nearly spiralled out of control and subsequently saw both clubs punished by the SFA.

Cooper, who had been granted an extra week's holiday by his gaffer on his return from Mexico, wasn't involved that afternoon, as Rangers slumped to a 2–1 defeat, but he admitted that he would probably have joined in the affray if he had been playing and the whole affair left a sour taste in the mouth, even before we consider what happened to Souness later that night.

"After the match, Graeme was a nightmare. We all went out in Edinburgh that evening to drown our sorrows, but he almost finished up in a fight in a bar," recalled Terry Butcher. "A guy was trying to be smart and clever, and I tried to placate him, but Graeme got fed up with his attitude and told him to f*** off. It was time to catch a taxi back to the Norton House Hotel, and some sort of sanity, before something worse happened to cloud a pretty bad day."

Cooper, for his part, was baffled by the resentment which hung over the squad that night. "It was as if we had lost a Cup final and players were walking around with long faces and there was all this talk about how the press would have a field day, as if that was important," said Davie. "Of course, it was not an ideal way to begin the season, but going to Leith was always a tough assignment and some of our boys went a bit over the top. It was as if they had bought into the excitement which had greeted the signing of the new boys and couldn't believe they had lost. But these things take time. We had a new manger, a lot of new players, guys who had never played in Scotland before, and it was the start of August. I just laughed it off as one of those things."

However, for fans fed so long on a diet of dross these initial teething troubles proved understandably irksome. Nor did their mood improve throughout the next two matches as Rangers continued to struggle to string together anything resembling a complete performance. They were grateful to the increasingly prolific Ally McCoist for pouching the winner against Falkirk, but although Cooper sat out this game, he was in the starting line-up for the next fixture, at home to Dundee United, and for most of the game the hosts were in the ascendancy, producing some free-flowing, thrilling football, which gained approbation from the crowd. The trouble was that, despite McCoist netting another brace of goals which sent Rangers 2–0 in front, the Tannadice men refused to be cowed and they rallied from their early difficulties to capitalise on some nervy defending from the hosts.

By the end, the visitors emerged with a 3–2 success, an outcome which had appeared impossible to forecast after forty-five minutes, but if the silence from the stands was unnerving, Souness soon started wading into Cooper and his colleagues once the team were back in the dressing room. It was an explosive outburst from the manager, an apoplectic stream of consciousness which laid bare the manager's annoyance at what he regarded as amateurish mistakes by people who should have known better. He warned them that he hadn't journeyed to Scotland to become associated with mediocrity and that, by God, if the players thought they could simply drift away into the night and enjoy a bevvy with their friends, they better find another club with lower ambitions. In this mood, Souness was a frightening figure – one of the players told me: "He went nuts. And if any of us had tried to butt in, I think he would have lamped us!" – but his diatribe had the requisite effect. After three matches, the Ibrox men had accrued only two points. But from that moment on, there was a transformation in their fortunes and nobody was more instrumental to the process than Davie, who suddenly clicked into a sublime gear.

Nobody, least of all himself, could explain what lay behind these periods when he sparked into life. But there again, genius often can't be rationalised; we should just be appreciative when the phenomenon arises, and certainly the Rangers following were grateful to Cooper for leading them out of the wilderness on the pitch, while Souness continued his role as the puppet master in the background. The latter remained a hard man to please and expressed dissatisfaction with a number of issues, not least the Ibrox side's tendency to take their feet off the gas when in control of games. Occasionally, this led to flirtations with embarrassment, such as when the high rollers were taken to penalties by East Fife in the Skol Cup, and it was one of the features of the season that Rangers could be terrific one day, such as when they destroyed Ilves Tampere in the UEFA Cup, and perform like a pub team on others, including their humiliation at the hands of Hamilton Academical in the Scottish Cup.

This inconsistency enraged and exasperated Souness in equal measure, but while there were still too many afternoons where the Blue Train was in danger of crashing off the buffers, Cooper's feats of trickery, ability to concoct opportunities out of nothing, and ball control in the thick of battle were already impressing the newcomers to Glasgow. "He was one of the best I ever played with," opined Butcher. "He was special," agreed Souness. "Coop could have featured in any team you care to name. He was a magnificent footballer," declared Walter Smith, whose contribution to his colleague's late flowering shouldn't be underestimated.

The upshot was that Davie began to wield an ever-increasing influence on his team. He was outstanding as Rangers triumphed in the first Old Firm derby of the campaign, a 1–0 success with Ian Durrant breaking the deadlock, and the margin of victory could have been much greater, considering how Cooper bamboozled the Celtic rearguard, as the prelude to his intelligent reverse pass to his confrere. He was in prime form again when they trounced Ilves Tampere 4–0, with Robert Fleck scoring a hat-trick before McCoist applied the coup de grâce. Then he dazzled his Dundee opponents into submission in the Skol Cup quarter-final, scored from a distance of all of two feet in the next fixture against Motherwell and was generally a ubiquitous livewire of invention. Rangers couldn't equal his prodigious exploits – they slipped to a 2–0 defeat in the return match against the Scandinavians and lost at Dens Park on domestic duty – as if to remind anybody with pound signs in their eyes that they were very much a work in progress, a club in transition, and that even Souness, a one-man wrecking ball of complacency and convention, couldn't transform them into Liverpool however much he tried.

Cooper, by his own admission, was unable to reach Olympian heights of excellence in every outing. It would have been a miracle had he done so. Yet for every sobering experience, such as that away trip to Finland where he was substituted before – and only just before – he took revenge on an opponent who had kicked him up in the air all night, there were other, sweeter occasions where everything he touched turned to gold and the equation was pretty straightforward throughout the campaign – if Cooper shone, so did Rangers. They were impressive in sweeping past Dundee United, 2–1 in the semi-finals of the Skol Cup, and masterly in disposing of the challenge of Aberdeen, 2–0 at Pittodrie, an outcome which was doubly savoured by Souness, because the papers at the time were hinting at a breakdown in the relationship between him and Alex

Ferguson. (Some people alleged to me this was because the latter had been approached about taking over from Rangers when Jock Wallace departed Ibrox, only to discover that while the old board were pursuing his services, David Holmes had gone directly to Souness. It's an intriguing theory, although there was no verification forthcoming from the relevant parties.)

Yet whatever the provenance of the bad blood, Souness celebrated in the aftermath of beating the Dons as if Rangers had lifted the European Cup. It was the start of a heady spell for his men, who embarked on a significant charge up the League table with a string of victories, in addition to recording some positive results in the UEFA Cup, where they disposed of the threat of Portuguese opponents Boavista, with the clinching goal arriving from Derek Ferguson, who latched on to Cooper's inch-perfect pass in the seventieth minute of the away leg, to ensure that Rangers had advanced to the third round of the event.

One might have imagined that Cooper enjoyed these kind of high-profile contests more than the usual run-of-the-mill fare in his homeland, but Davie was a proper craftsman and he later told me that he made little or no distinction between how he prepared and the pride he derived from an away meeting with St Johnstone or Hamilton and a major European occasion at Ibrox. Basically, all that mattered was that it was football:

"You hear some people talk about 'getting themselves up' for matches, but I have never understood what they were talking about. Every time I was involved in a game, I didn't need to 'get up' for it, I was determined to give the team everything I had. Of course, there were some days and nights where I didn't play very well, where things didn't go my way or the opposition were simply better, but I never stopped trying. Why would you? If you are lucky enough to be a professional footballer, you owe it to yourself to do the best you can and if you walk off at the end and it hasn't been enough, well, that happens to everybody in their career. You just have to pick yourself up, get over the disappointment and do your best to make sure that there is a different outcome the next time. Most of the best players I have worked with have shared that approach. The alternative to playing and winning or losing is not playing at all and I never wanted to be stuck on the subs' bench or watching from the crowd. So, basically, even if things haven't always gone in my favour, I can honestly say there hasn't been a time when I 'wasn't up' for a game."

As if to illustrate this mindset, Cooper singled out one of the less prominent results in Rangers' season – a 5–1 demolition of Falkirk at Brockville – as one of the relatively few matches in his career where he felt completely satisfied with his performance. He was certainly too much of a handful for his opponents, whose regular failure to close Cooper down was ruthlessly exposed by the thirty-year-old. There was one mesmerising foray which allowed McCoist to tap in at close range, another scintillating incursion which forced the harassed Falkirk defence into conceding a penalty, which Davie finally converted after he and Robert Fleck, who had already scored a brace of goals, argued over who should take the spot kick, with Souness intervening in favour of the older man. And then, just to prove that he was more interested in helping his team than pursuing personal glory, Cooper's wiles sparked another move, which eventually led to Fleck sealing his hat-trick and the travelling supporters were ecstatic at the climax. In these circumstances, when everything clicked, he was an imperious presence in the Ibrox cause.

Throughout the years he had often suffered, in common with Kenny Dalglish, from possessing rather too much vision, to the extent that he would despatch a glorious thirty-metre or forty-metre pass, only to be let down by teammates without the prescience to capitalise on his efforts. But now, suddenly, Davie found himself surrounded by excellent, international-class players – Graham Roberts soon joined the likes of Butcher and Woods in the Rangers ranks – and it provided the impetus and galvanising force to motivate him into the best form of his life. Both he and Souness benefited from their alliance and acknowledged the other's qualities as Rangers prepared for the Skol Cup final against Celtic at Hampden.

No Old Firm tussle was ever deemed irrelevant, and especially not when one mused on the paucity of trophies which had required polishing at Rangers in the preceding five years. But even in the midst of the usual media hoop-la, and as Souness and his squad prepared for the denouement together in Troon, it was made clear by the manager that he didn't rank this tussle as being pivotal to his priorities.

Cooper, for his part, recognised that his boss was far more concerned with collecting championship titles and cementing European qualification than with pre-Christmas finals. But still, it was a measure of how relaxed the players were feeling that Davie found time in the build-up to visit a local woman called Isa Anderson, who had been following Coop's career from the outset and had offered him encouragement and succour in a string of engaging letters from when he had been a teenager at Clydebank. These had touched the player, so, with the permission of Souness, he hired a taxi at the hotel, handed Isa's address to the driver and shortly afterwards knocked on her door, prompting a wondrous response from the old lady, prior to her inviting him inside for the inevitable cup of tea and fondant fancies.

It was a feature of Davie's personality that he never forgot about the fans, whatever their age, background or gender, and that explains why there are so many touching vignettes from his meetings with supporters at Clydebank, Rangers and, latterly, Motherwell, scattered throughout his journey from teenage wannabe to international star. Essentially, his personality never changed as his profile heightened and the nexus between the wealthy footballer and the often lowly supporters who wrote to him was never broken.

As for the Skol Cup final on 27 October, it was a characteristically testy encounter without ever threatening to develop into a classic of the genre. Durrant, a fledgling talent with no trace of nerves, amidst these high-octane jousts, pushed his side in front, only for Brian McClair to respond with a magnificent equaliser which rightly earned praise from several of the Ibrox personnel, including Davie, who described it as the highlight of the match. Perhaps he could afford to be magnanimous, because he was the man who scored the winner from the penalty spot after the referee, Davie Syme, adjudged that Roy Aitken had impeded Butcher inside the box. From a distance, it looked a case of six of one and half a dozen of the other, but Davie had more pressing matters to worry about. He calmed himself, did his best to block out the bedlam which had erupted within Hampden Park and quietly, inconspicuously, trotted towards the ball and completed the job with the minimum of fuss. All those nights spent practising these situations under the street lamps in Hamilton had done their job and he was an oasis of calm in a madhouse.

Later, when he was asked during a post-match interview if he thought he was going to score, he replied succinctly, "Aye, of course I did." If it sounded arrogant, it wasn't meant to be; instead, Cooper was simply offering an honest answer to what was a pretty dumb inquiry in the first place. He was a highly paid professional, amply rewarded for what he did and taking penalties was his bread and butter. It might not have made for scintillating copy, but none of the Rangers supporters packed into the stadium were remotely worried on that score. All that concerned them was that Souness, within a few months of pitching up in Glasgow, had steered the club to silverware. They listened to him afterwards and were impressed, not merely because he made it clear that Skol was pretty small beer in his vision for Ibrox, but because there was a steely edge to the manager's description of how his team had progressed. Never one to be caught up in the hype where it was unmerited, he praised Cooper and Durrant for their efforts, applauded the work ethic of his team and strolled away purposefully from the microphones. It was a wonderful exhibition of how to let actions speak louder than a thousand words.

Bolstered by that success, Rangers kept upping the ante and the momentum, and by the end of the year, they were on the march towards fresh honours, even if nobody at Ibrox was so stupid as to take anything for granted. They had defeated Celtic in their two most recent meetings, accumulated a potent sequence of results in the championship race and served notice to their New Firm rivals that the Gers were back in the groove. In Europe, their victories over Ilves Tampere and Boavista had earned them a third-round tussle with Borussia Moenchengladbach in late November and early December, and while Souness and Walter Smith recognised that they required more quality to pose a genuine threat at this level, the old qualities associated with Rangers – a never-say-die mentality, defensive solidity and the ability to wear down opponents by the sheer force of their will – had reappeared, following the dismal years under John Greig and Jock Wallace. The question now was whether they could progress further against the challenge of the Germans.

On the plus side, there was little to choose between two fiercely committed collectives, and with a soupcon of added poise in the first leg at Ibrox, the Scots might have amassed an unassailable advantage. McCoist broke the deadlock, following a superbly crafted build-up, and Rangers then carved out a string of decent chances, which were either squandered or foiled through last-ditch defending. In these circumstances, where one side has all the possession and territory for a significant period, there is invariably the danger that they will be laid low with a sucker punch, and so it transpired when Uwe Rahn latched on to Andre Winkhold's cross and headed past Woods in the thirtieth minute. It was against the run of play and a maddening goal to concede, the more so because it would be the last time Woods was beaten for more than 1,000 minutes of competitive action, but unfortunately for Rangers, the damage had been done. They huffed, they puffed and the likes of McCoist and Durrant came close, but the match finished 1–1. It was by no means an irretrievable situation and the German club had done little to suggest they were world-beaters, but the quiet sense of deflation at the climax told its own story. The fans had been happy for half the game, but their heroes had run out of steam at the end.

If this was merely another case of honourable Scottish defeat, it wouldn't be so bad, but our sporting collectives frequently seem unable to settle for valiant failure without flinging a sliver of shame into the mix. When Souness and his cohorts travelled to Germany, they did so with the confidence derived from an increasing dominance at home, where Woods was proving as much of an obstacle to strikers as Rahul Dravid became to bowlers in the cricketing sphere at the start of the twenty-first century. There was plenty of evidence to indicate they could force a victory abroad, but in the event, McCoist struck the bar, Butcher was denied what seemed to be a blatant penalty, and even as the Borussia fans at the Bokelborg Stadium grew increasingly apprehensive, Rangers decided to fling them the soccer equivalent of a few Valium tablets when Stuart Munro was sent off following a clash with Winkhold.

That was bad enough, but worse lay in store when Cooper was booked for comments allegedly made to the referee, Alex Ponnet, as he was poised to take a free kick in the eighty-seventh minute, and it was only after a few seconds of confusion that the official remembered Davie had already been cautioned and yellow turned to red as Rangers' dreams turned to dust. It was a messy conclusion to what had been a battling performance from the Scots, but confusion reigned at the finish, with Mr Ponnet claiming that Davie had called him a "dirty German", a crime which landed him with a three-match European ban, although the whole affair made little sense.

When the squad arrived home in Glasgow, Cooper vehemently denied that he had insulted the referee and, as he argued, why would he have called Ponnet – a Belgian, by the way – any kind of German when he knew that the match officials were always neutral on these European assignments? It would have been nice if Hercule Poirot could have used his little grey cells to investigate the matter, but the bottom line was that Rangers could only draw 0–0 and thus were eliminated on the away goals ruling. The worst way to exit.

Yet, there was at least satisfaction from the club's momentum in the heat of domestic battle. Woods, a gimlet-eyed keeper with a brilliant capacity for close-range shot-stopping and an ability to anticipate mistakes from those around him, began shattering all manner of records with a series of shut-outs and, as Cooper knew, the key to Rangers regaining their competitive edge lay in their ability to thwart and frustrate opponents. If that happened, they could rely on players such as McCoist, Fleck and Durrant to create goals at the other end of the pitch. In these circumstances, Rangers started to claw away at Celtic's advantage in the championship race, and gradually, inexorably, reeled in their old rivals with a level of commitment and urgency which was a far cry from the cloud of inertia which had hung over Ibrox for most of the previous decade.

There were routine victories over Falkirk and Hamilton, then, in the midst of the Christmas and New Year period, Souness and his charges maintained their winning sequence with important victories against Dundee United and most crucially, Celtic, with McCoist and Fleck basking in the role of tormentors and nagging away at opponents like the toothache, while Woods continued to defy anything flung in his direction. It added up to a potent brew and suddenly, as if to epitomise the surge in interest which had surrounded the New Rangers Army – the critics claimed that these people were fair-weather fans, but why on earth should supporters shell out cash to watch crap? – tickets for their bigger fixtures began to resemble gold dust on the streets of Govan.

On and on it rolled, with successes over Motherwell in the thick of a blizzard, as the prelude to wins against Clydebank and Hamilton, and even if the latter contest highlighted the volcanic nature of several of the Ibrox stalwarts, with Graham Roberts and Durrant both red-carded, they thrived on the unstinting work ethic and capacity to persevere until the last kick of every match, as demanded by their manager. These runs can't last forever, and when Rangers entertained Aberdeen in their next match, they eventually had to be content with a goalless draw. For as long as Woods was indomitable, his side were out of the woods and in the clear. But, unfortunately, but maybe not too surprisingly, given the roller-coaster campaign on which they had embarked, the sequence came to a grinding halt a few days later when Rangers were ambushed, in embarrassing style, by Hamilton, in the Scottish Cup.

It was one of those afternoons when the story filtered across the country like wildfire, and even in the days before twenty-four-hour rolling news channels and instant access to results and goal updates, the outcome sparked a giant swell of *schadenfreude* throughout Scotland. Within Ibrox, there had been little sign of the ignominy which loomed when 35,000 fans rose to acclaim Woods with a standing ovation when he broke the British record for minutes without losing a goal during the first half of the Cup spat with the Accies.

Yet these tussles – as they should – always carry the possibility of accidental heroes emerging with an unexpected piece of derring-do which allows them to enjoy transient fame, and it was Adrian Sprott who sparked a small forest's worth of headlines when he seized the only goal of the game, even as his opponents were scratching their heads, blaming one another, and asking, "What the hell!" In the dressing room afterwards, once the players had endured the wrath of their fans, Souness raged at them like Christian Bale on a bender, forcibly reminding them that the "disgrace" of this result would haunt them, and their children, and their children's children. Well, perhaps he didn't go quite that far, but Cooper, who had experienced one of his quieter afternoons in a Rangers jersey, wasn't spared, nor was anybody else in the ranks.

In the longer term, the defeat was fairly irrelevant to his or his side's ambitions – the league was the prize which mattered – but Souness didn't miss his target. Jimmy Nicholl picked that post-match tirade as his scariest moment in the game in the *Sunday Times'* "Best and Worst" feature in 2009, and Davie endured the most flak, because as a Hamilton-born lad, he suddenly found himself bumping into strangers throughout the West of Scotland. Coincidence? Aye, right.

What was unfortunate was that Cooper reacted – unusually in his case – to the vitriol which followed this Cup upset with a strongly-worded attack on the so-called negative tactics employed by Hamilton. "They weren't interested in playing football, they weren't bothered about putting on a show for the fans and if everybody played like that, people would stop turning up to watch," was the thrust of his argument, in which he suggested that he hadn't recovered properly from his mauling at the hands of Souness.

A few years later, he returned to the theme, asserting his opinion that there were too many "hammer throwers" masquerading as footballers in Scotland; that these people were hampering the development of the game; and, tellingly, he singled out Hamilton for special opprobrium. It wasn't typical of the man to resort to these kind of excuses, and he must have known that the obvious retort was, "Teams have to use whatever means they have at their disposal to try and halt the opposition. Hamilton walked into the lion's den against a team who hadn't lost for months and whose goalkeeper was nigh impregnable. What were they supposed to do – meekly accept their fate or crank their defence into gear and await an opportunity on the break?" None of this was rocket science, and Davie didn't exactly make a habit of complaining about opponents, but Souness had got under his skin. From now on, Rangers would be happy to win ugly, and they turned it into an art form.

As for Souness, he regained his composure fairly swiftly. In common with other tempestuous characters in the sporting sphere – one thinks of John McEnroe and Dennis Lillee – he possessed the capacity to leave those on the receiving end of his tantrums feeling as if they had been verbally whipped to within an inch of their lives, without letting his outbursts affect him to the same extent. He, in contrast, strode away to devise his schemes for the next few matches and, suitably chastened, his team stepped up their title charge with emphatic victories over Hearts and St Mirren, both of whom had no answer to the menace of McCoist and Fleck, who found the net six times in these fixtures, as if they were atoning for their prodigality against Hamilton. Consequently, any recollection of the Cup humiliation was soon filed away on the back burner: from this juncture, Rangers' bandwagon was rolling in the right direction, and even if the Ibrox faithful fretted occasionally during the countdown to the championship and there were eerie afternoons where you could have heard a pin drop within the cauldron of the stadium, the livewires, the McCoists and Nicholls, combined with hard nuts, men such as Butcher and Roberts, and conspired with the tricksters, Cooper and Durrant, to ensure that there were no serious slip-ups at the Glasgow club as they hunted their prey.

The points and plaudits stacked up accordingly and Rangers even found time in their hectic schedule to participate in a friendly against Bordeaux, which they won 3–2, before drawing with Hibs, beating Falkirk and gaining revenge over Accies with a comfortable 2–0 success, during which the hapless Sprott found himself the butt of as many barbs and abuse as he had revelled in his iconic status a few week previously. If Rangers felt under any pressure, their experienced squad kept it well hidden.

As the weeks elapsed and their objective grew ever more tangible, a sprinkling of fatalistic fans might still have feared the worst, but Ibrox was a fortress again, and the team managed to maintain their streak on the road as well, putting in a couple of terrific displays in the same week on Tayside, to douse the flame of both Dundee clubs, 4–0 at Dens Park and 1–0 at Tannadice. The latter outcome was especially pleasing for Walter Smith, whose decision to join Souness at Ibrox had been amply justified by events, and the more that he got to know Cooper, the better the banter was between the two. Davie always made a joke of his contention that "Wattie", a journeyman performer during his own career, couldn't really play football, but if you peered beneath the macho carapace, there was a genuine affection, respect and mutual passion for Rangers in their attitude towards their vocations. They egged each other on, and although their salty exchanges wouldn't have impressed the principal of a finishing school, they sparked off one another and rose to the challenge together.

The trouble was that, by this stage, Cooper had realised that the little niggles, the petty annoyances of training-ground injuries which he used to shake off in a day or two, now required a week or even a fortnight to heal. In an environment where there wasn't a conveyor belt of talent whizzing in and out of Ibrox, this wouldn't have been such a problem, but the all-seeing Souness started noticing that one of his senior professionals was missing games because of damage to his body. This wasn't important with regards to the friendly against Bordeaux, but Davie sustained a nasty shoulder injury in March, which forced his withdrawal, first against Motherwell, and then, of far more import, during his team's disappointing 3–1 loss to Celtic, in an outcome which offered a glimmer of hope to the Hoops that they might still retrieve the deficit. In the event, he recovered sufficiently quickly to feature again as Rangers turned the screw once more, with back-to-back wins over Dundee, Clydebank and Hearts, and the job was nearly completed. Souness, though, recognised that he would need cover for Cooper, and while it wasn't a matter of urgency, the wheels for finding his replacement began to roll.

Yet for the moment, Davie was in his element. After so many fallow seasons and distress signals from the boardroom, here was a Mayday he couldn't wait to embrace. He and his Rangers colleagues travelled to Aberdeen on 1 May, bolstered by the knowledge that they could wrap up the title that weekend, but only if they won at Pittodrie and Celtic didn't beat Falkirk at Parkhead. It was asking an awful lot of the gods to intervene and conjure up such a dramatic finale, but the Ibrox men knew they had the insurance policy of a home game against St Mirren in reserve, and their Old Firm rivals were tacitly resigned to losing their crown, but for the sort of twist which would have been regarded as excessive in *Roy of the Rovers*.

(Albeit one that they had achieved at the climax of the champion-ship twelve months earlier.) This was the scenario which Souness had craved from the moment he accepted the manager's job and the raging bull went out and did what might have been expected of him in the circumstances. He got sent off. Again.

From anybody's perspective, it was an astonishing breach in dis-cipline, one which might have cost his club dearly, but thankfully for those many Rangers aficionados who had ventured to the Granite City, their heroes stood firm, gained a point, with Cooper providing the cross from which Terry Butcher secured a 1–1 draw, and were finally permitted to crack open the champagne when the news arrived from Glasgow that Celtic had lost. For a few moments, their officials checked and double-checked the information, but it was true, it was wonderfully, irresistibly true for Cooper and his colleagues.

At the final whistle, thousands of fans mingled with the Ibrox personnel, security took a holiday, the players struggled to reach the sanctuary of the dressing room and Davie even took a whack in the face from an over-boisterous Rangers fan – or so he convinced himself. Within hours, the pain had subsided, as the celebrations commenced in earnest and Souness embraced every member of his squad, even as the players basked in the adulation of the crowds outside Pittodrie and, much later that evening, Ibrox.

"I enjoyed almost every minute of it," said Davie. "We had a fantastic team sprit and the boys really wanted to get the job done for the club. Personal glory didn't come into it and a lot of that was down to Graeme and Walter making it clear there were no favour-ites in the squad and that they valued the contributions of all the boys. It made up, it really did, for the years of pain and heartache, when there were years of nothing but disappointment, and you could see what it meant to the supporters. They came dressed as Teddy Bears, as Santa Claus [in May!] when we played St Mirren at Ibrox in our last game, and the atmosphere was brilliant, even before we won the match 1–0. At the end, we were able to wave to our families and it was a pretty emotional time, because you don't realise how tired you are until you have sat down and realised that the season has finished."

Once the dust had settled, Davie pondered on the new direction and zeal which Souness had brought to his employers. It was principally that factor, allied to the immense contributions of such inspired English recruits as Butcher, Woods and Roberts, which had allowed the home-grown Scots in his and McCoist's mould to transcend past campaigns and scale fresh peaks of consistency and occasional ruthlessness. On the debit side, there had been far too many sendings-off, with the manager one of the biggest culprits, while the suspicion lingered that Souness had all the calmness of a boiling kettle and that his temper might pose him greater travails when honours weren't flooding in his route.

But in this summer of 1987, Rangers were the best in Scotland and their ambitions didn't stop there. Cooper revelled in the moment, soaked it in, and was at his ebullient best among his friends when he returned to Lanarkshire. He wasn't to know that even as he lapped up the praise he was in the process of being written out of his role at Ibrox.

11

A SLOW TRACK TO THE EXIT DOOR

It is amazing how many leading sporting personalities persuade themselves at the apotheosis of their careers that they will bow out on their own terms and in the right milieu, only to change their stance as retirement beckons. I can recall interviewing the snooker maestro Steve Davis back in 1990, and he was absolutely insistent that he would never allow himself to be reduced to also-ran status or contemplate suffering routine defeats at the hands of opponents he once dominated. But more than twenty years down the line, the Englishman was still grinding away on the circuit, striving to qualify for major tournaments and putting himself through the protracted torment of crashing out of major events in the early stages, and being duly embarrassed by youngsters who aren't even old enough to remember how good the nuggety Londoner used to be. His former rival, Stephen Hendry, found himself in a similar position before finally retiring at The Crucible in 2012. Why do it? Why risk the humiliation and the incontrovertible proof that your powers are declining? Or could it simply be true that the nearer the exit door looms, the more these committed individuals realise that it isn't just a part of their life. It *is* their life.

Three years earlier, even as he basked in the warm glow of Rangers' title-winning exploits, Davie Cooper also convinced himself that he would bow out as soon as he was no longer deemed good enough to command a regular starting berth at Ibrox. It hardly seemed to occur to him that circumstances change, that relationships falter or break down completely, or that given the unsentimental approach adopted by Graeme Souness towards moulding a team which was capable of vying for honours on the European stage he might not have any choice in where and when he pursued the next chapter of his football career.

Instead, Davie declared bullishly in his 1987 autobiography *True Blue*, "I will know better than most when the time comes for me to pack it in, and when that happens, I will make a clean break from the game. I don't intend to let myself go into the reserves at Ibrox or drift down the leagues to let lesser players have a kick at me. When I finish, I want to be a Rangers first-team player." Doubtless, he was genuine in this assertion. As genuine as Lance Armstrong was when he vowed "No More Tours" of duty or Michael Schumacher abruptly packed in Formula One! But if that was Cooper's wish in the summer of 1987, he soon had to accept the unpalatable truth that he was destined for bit parts rather than starring roles in any future Ibrox productions.

That might sound harsh, but the reality was that Souness had no room for manoeuvre and no time for massaging egos or injury-prone individuals in his grand scheme. Instead, his was the pragmatic ethos of those who organise Royal Variety Performances. To wit, that if you assemble enough talent on the same stage, the odds are that at least one or two pearls will revel in the spotlight. As Archie Macpherson, the writer and broadcaster, wrote in his coruscating book *Flower of Scotland*, there were positive and negative repercussions for Rangers from their dalliance with the firebrand Souness.

"Butcher and Woods came for less than £1.3m. Jimmy Nicholl came for £70,000 and Graham Roberts signed for £450,000. Combined with other less prominent signings, he spent £2.275m in his first season – breathtakingly huge for the Scottish game at the time. Richard Gough then became Scotland's first £1m signing when he returned from Spurs. Defender Gary Stevens also came for £1m and Kevin Drinkell and Mel Sterland for £500,000 each. Trevor Steven also popped up for £1.5m and Souness also picked up, relatively cheaply, men who made useful contributions such as Trevor Francis and Ray Wilkins. It is calculated, in all, that he spent £15.5m on signings during his management of Rangers. His philosophy was to buy and discard, not develop and nurture. If you could not hack it immediately, you went. Of the thirty-seven players he bought, seventeen were moved on after varying periods. Richard Gough once said, 'Sometimes you wondered who would be in the dressing room when you arrived for training [at Ibrox] in the morning.'

"So, the criticism of a lack of judgement can be levelled at Souness for the merry-go-round he created. But there is also another way of looking at it. After years of languishing in a trough of mediocrity, Rangers wanted instant success. A ghostly-looking Ibrox on match days was intolerable, given the potential the club had. Any businessman would have come to that conclusion. So, when you marry the impulsive nature of the man to the impetus of the quick fix and the tolerance of a mounting debt, underwritten by the market value which was placed on the stadium, you get the revolving door to success."

It was an astute reading of the situation, but none of this offered any comfort to Davie Cooper as he strove to retain a central place in Rangers' long-term plans at the outset of the 1987–88 season. If he had been less mercurial and less inclined to try out ploys at which other more prosaic players would have balked, he might have sealed a regular position for another year or two. Yet such was the state of flux which spiralled around Souness that nobody could be really assured of their berth from one week to another.

In this febrile environment, Cooper really needed to sit down and discuss his future with his manager, but that might have prompted recriminations and rancour between the two men and, just as he had done throughout his earlier career, Davie shied away from that prospect, not least because he was worried that his age would count against him. He was thirty-one, and although he eschewed the self-destructive lifestyle of many of his peers, he began picking up knocks which regularly required treatment, even as a variety of newcomers threatened to wrest the No.7 jersey from his grasp. To be fair to Souness, he couldn't afford to be a prisoner of the past: in his world, all that mattered was the next challenge, the next fixture on the schedules, and pursuing the next victory. But it gradually led to an impasse between the respective parties, a scenario which was occasionally reminiscent of the breakdown in communications between John Greig and Cooper. In some ways, the latter was his own worst enemy, but only if loyalty is viewed as a fault.

The most frustrating aspect of it all was that Davie was still capable of gasp-inducing exploits. But unfortunately Rangers, during the next twelve months, were piloted on a labyrinthine path to nowhere in particular. In Europe, they made an auspicious start to their European Cup endeavours with an excellent 2–1 aggregate victory against high quality opponents in Dynamo Kiev, which hinted that Souness' exhortations might be bearing fruit, even if, as usual, the success was accompanied by controversy. The Scots – such as they were – produced a tenacious and committed display in front of 100,000 supporters at the Republic Stadium and although they conceded a late goal when Alexei Mikhailichenko converted a seventy-second-minute penalty, it was a result which reminded the older members of the Ibrox support of the virtues of old-fashioned obduracy and up-and-at-'em belligerence.

In that first leg, Derek Ferguson wore the No.7 jersey and couldn't be faulted for his effort. On reflection, it might not have been the ideal platform for Davie, who was suspended in any case, following his ordering-off against Borussia the previous year, and Souness was entitled in that early stage of the season to tinker with his options and work out which formation he required for specific matches, given the fact that he was plotting a war on four different fronts at home and abroad. In the short term, it reaped dividends, albeit not without Souness narrowing the touchlines at short notice for the return leg in a bid to negate the width and pace of Kiev's skilful wingers, Vasily Rats and Oleg Blokhin.

Some observers questioned the sporting nature of this ploy; others denounced it as patent gamesmanship or downright cheating, yet it should be borne in mind that it did not contravene the existing UEFA regulations and, in any case, Rangers had suffered enough slings and arrows of outrageous fortune during these Continental forays to feel that none of their rivals were entitled to lay claim to the moral high ground. The stratagem clearly unsettled the Russians, who were on the back foot when the action resumed in Glasgow, and a glaring mistake from their keeper, Victor Chanev, gifted the lead to Souness' men, who had Trevor Francis operating effectively on the wing, whilst the likes of new recruit, Marc Falco, McCoist and Durrant, reacted positively to the orchestral thrum which was generated by a voluble home support. Falco broke the deadlock in the twenty-fifth minute, and as the decibel level rose with every attack from the Ibrox men, Kiev looked chicken.

Obviously, given the fraught nature of the tussle, they were well in contention at 1–1 and an away goal might have sparked panic in the home ranks. But, as it was, Souness and his troops cranked up their exertions with sufficient intensity that the Russians were undone when a Francis cross was headed on by Falco to McCoist and the latter guided the ball into the corner of the net. Watching from the sidelines, Cooper must have felt a swirl of conflicting emotions rushing through him at that juncture. As a Rangers follower, he was clearly delighted at the swashbuckling manner in which his team had discomfited and discombobulated their opponents, but Francis had sparkled amidst the tumult, showing the form which had convinced Souness to sign up his former Sampdoria colleague, and in the manager's terms, he wanted leaders on the pitch, men who understood his objectives and were not afraid to voice their opinions within his earshot. The bold Trevor fitted the bill in that regard, and whereas Davie had gained the sobriquet "Albert Tatlock" from his manager because he could always be relied upon to find fault with some aspect of Rangers' training regimes, this wasn't the same as possessing the capacity to display positive leadership skills on the pitch in the heat of these big European occasions.

It wouldn't do to overstate the marginalisation of Cooper in the 1987–88 campaign. On the contrary, he made forty-three appearances, a tally which was surpassed only by Graham Roberts, Woods, McCoist and Durrant. Yet several of these were from the bench, and others were on apparently humdrum domestic assignments in midweek. In most of the fixtures which were of primary concern to Souness, he was a peripheral figure, and yet it was hardly as if Rangers were on some all-conquering streak during that period. On the contrary, they tasted fresh Scottish Cup misery at the hands of Dunfermline, were eliminated from Europe by the powerful Steaua Bucharest and the defence of their championship proved a horribly half-baked affair with Celtic powering to the title – in their centenary year – with an efficiency and control which meant that the majority of the headlines surrounding Rangers revolved around controversy and lurid publicity.

The worst of these – the 2–2 draw in the second Old Firm match of the season after the Hoops had won the first of the derbies – actually finished up at Glasgow Sheriff Court, with four players, Butcher, Woods and Roberts of Rangers and McAvennie of Celtic, facing charges, following their behaviour during a fractious encounter which some people unaccountably found funny.

Given that England's clubs were still banned from European competition, these affairs caught the attention of the London-centric media and the trial date – on 12 April 1988 – turned into a feeding frenzy, with the tabloids striving to outdo one another in the quest for headlines after the fashion of "Goldilocks and the Three Bears". Eventually, at the end of a story which was manna from heaven for the Fourth Estate, with evidence presented about crowd incitement and the referee's report being discussed at length, even as journalists wrung their hands in mock disgust about these so-called "role models" letting down Scotland's toddlers – I am exaggerating, but only just – McAvennie was found not guilty, the case against Roberts was not proven, Butcher was pronounced guilty and fined £250 and Woods shared his fate and faced a £500 imposition. It was a distasteful business, the more so because Rangers appeared to be out of control at this juncture, but their results on the pitch whilst this drama was unfolding were awful.

As for Cooper, he told at least one of his mates in Hamilton, "It's crap. We should be trying to beat Celtic by playing better football, not by kicking lumps out of them." But as the tensions boiled over increasingly on Souness' watch, his was one of the few rational voices at the club.

Indeed, it's instructive to examine three key matches in the course of that season, a trio whose divergent outcomes epitomised what happened when Davie was allowed a licence to thrill and when he was either incapacitated or ignored altogether. The first occurred on 25 October when Rangers tackled Aberdeen in the League Cup final at Hampden Park. These major events always quickened Davie's pulse; he relished the chance to dazzle in front of a huge audience and more than 70,000 spectators congregated to witness a thrilling encounter, which also featured one of the most stunning free kicks in the history of Scottish football when Cooper's unstoppable strike flew past the stock-still Jim Leighton to push the Ibrox men in front. It was an astonishing effort, one which prompted an initial collective intake of breath, as the prelude to the supporters hailing the goal with the raptures which it deserved. Scott Blair, a lifelong Rangers fan, was amongst the throng and the memory of that special set piece will stay with him forever:

"Davie had the ability to make things happen and to attempt things which wouldn't have entered other players' heads. That free kick against Aberdeen belongs in that category because it was a long way out and he was up against the Scotland goalkeeper at the time. But it didn't matter. He worked hard on these set pieces in training and you could see the benefits of his practice behind the scenes. He thought that he could beat anybody with that left foot of his, and he was right. One of the things about that goal was as soon as he had struck the ball he knew where it was heading – there was nothing fluky about it – and I can remember us looking around at one another and going: 'Jeez, did you see that!' It was fantastic. Later on, Leighton claimed he had almost got his hand to it. Davie's response was great. He said, in deadpan style, 'Aye . . . on the way back oot!'"

It was a marvellous vignette in a match littered with quality. Both teams attacked and counter-attacked and there was no respite from the ebb and flow, with Durrant and Fleck also finding the net for their club, while Davie's old mucker, Jim Bett, Willie Falconer and John Hewitt, replied in kind for the Dons as the game finished 3–3. Penalties were required and Rangers derived confidence from Cooper's poise in these pressurised situations, sticking one spot kick after another beyond the despairing Leighton. Woods, meanwhile, had greater success and Souness' ensemble eventually ran out 5–3 winners to seal another trophy and earn Cooper his seventh winner's medal in the process.

It was in so many ways an antidote to the noxious bile which proliferated for much of the rest of the season on and off the pitch, and even now many high-profile figures speak with something approaching reverence about *that* free kick. Terry Butcher, never one to dish out cheap compliments, declared recently that, in his opinion, Cooper's delivery of set pieces was superior to that of David Beckham. As for Andy Roxburgh, the former Scotland coach and now the technical director at UEFA, he told me that it was simply another illustration of how Davie could make the stars light up:

"It wasn't just the technical ability, but the wonderful balance which he displayed in timing his shot and hitting it with such sweet precision that it went from A to B in a few tenths of a second," said Roxburgh. "I once compiled a tape of his best moments and set it to the music of the Queen song 'A Kind of Magic' and the music fitted his exploits perfectly. Perhaps we took him a bit for granted because of how often he did these things, because if that goal had been scored by a Brazilian, we would have been raving about it."

Unfortunately, from an Ibrox perspective, that was as good as life got in the campaign. Thereafter, they exited the Scottish Cup quickly and were on the receiving end of three defeats and a draw in the season's quartet of Old Firm contests. The third of these, on 3 January 1988, carried a special resonance for Cooper because only a few days earlier Souness had signed the Aston Villa winger Mark Walters for £550,000. It was a smart piece of business for Rangers, because the Birmingham-born twenty-three-year-old had already made a favourable impression in England – and the man with the middle name "Everton" would later return there, to Liverpool, for £1.25m – but, to Cooper, the news felt as if another obstacle was being placed in his path and whilst he had all the requisite skills to weave past defenders, there was nothing he could do about beating the clock.

Worse was to come when the Old Firm match commenced at Parkhead and Celtic's well-deserved 2–0 victory pushed them firmly in command of the Scottish Championship, even as their traditional rivals slipped off the pace. The outcome was depressing enough for Davie, but his dark mood was heightened by being forced off after just twenty-eight minutes and being replaced by Trevor Francis. The hosts' goals came from McAvennie, the Jack-the-Lad blessed with a genuine talent, in the forty-fourth and eighty-second minutes and the *Sunday Times* wasted no time in portraying the result as a slap in the face to Souness' policy of spend, spend, spend: "The match will give Rangers much to ponder. If they were the team of 1987, they are not the team of the moment, in spite of a spate of extraordinary purchases," wrote Bob Ferrier. "The latest of these, Walters, made little impression on the match. Neither, strangely, did Souness, in what may be his final playing season.

"He clearly has a vision of Rangers as a dominant club, not only in Scotland, but in Europe. In buying players, he has become as acquisitive as Robert Maxwell and, as a manager, has taken an auto-cratic grip on the club. If you can't buy success, you can buy good players, the basis of success. That seems to be the Souness creed."

If it was harsh to compare any soccer boss with the late, unlamented, pension-stealing Captain Bob, these words addressed a central problem in his whole strategy, namely that it was one thing to splash the cash on expensive recruits, but there are only eleven places in a starting line-up and Souness wasn't much further forward in getting the composite parts to gel. Mr Cantankerous would later complain, "How can I win a European trophy with eleven Jocks?", but there were precious few instances when his sides were even close to having a Caledonian monopoly.

Indeed, by the time that we consider Exhibit C in that '87–88 schedule – which was the final Old Firm clash at Ibrox on 20 March – there were only six Scots in the ranks, as the hosts slumped to another debilitating 2–1 defeat, despite the inclusion of Woods, Roberts, Walters, Wilkins and Jan Bartram, with Butcher only out of the picture because he was recovering from a broken leg. It was one of those afternoons where the home side dominated the midfield, yet the visitors discovered the penetration to do what really counted, with Paul McStay and Andy Walker scoring on either side of Jan Bartram's equaliser.

By this stage, Davie had reached thirty-two and as he sat on the sidelines, the notion that he could preserve his first-team spot for another year, let alone two or three seasons, was starting to sound like pie in the sky. Off the pitch, he was growing increasingly frus-trated at the chopping and changing which had happened to Rangers throughout a thoroughly disjointed period and it affected him away from football. Where once he would be able to unwind with his wife and family back in Lanarkshire, his marriage was dis-integrating, a situation which was hardly helped by tabloids repeat-edly intruding into his private life. Suffice to say that Davie's twin passions were family and football and he was struggling with both of them.

Yet if he harboured any regrets, he remained in thrall to his boyhood heroes. He recognised that he might have to reconsider his future plans if he desired to keep playing, and while there was no formal confirmation that he was inching towards the exit door, the news that he had been granted a testimonial in the summer of 1988 told its own story.

One prominent former Rangers player told me, off the record, that he couldn't believe the "ridiculous" manner in which his former colleague was discarded and castigated Souness for his intransigence (not that he employed that word), but there seems to be some misapprehension over that final season for Cooper. Yes, he would have wished to have made more than thirty-three appearances – one for every year of his life by the time he finished at Ibrox – but that scarcely amounted to being air-brushed out of what turned into a triumphant last hurrah for Davie. His only source of disappointment was the fact that Graeme and the two Davids, Holmes and Murray, hadn't ridden to the rescue sooner:

"I suppose that a wee part of me wishes that Rangers could have achieved more success earlier in my career, because it was like a breath of fresh air when Graeme arrived and it was fantastic to be there at a time when people such as Terry Butcher and Chris Woods signed on the dotted line. How could I not be thrilled to be in the same dressing room as those kind of quality players? And when you look at what Rangers achieved in the next three years, it showed that Graeme was absolutely right to bring in new blood and aim high, because Rangers had been a sleeping giant for too long and he really woke them up. Maybe it is true that these good and exciting times came a little bit too late for me to really produce my best form for Graeme, but I definitely gave it my best shot."

None of the 43,000 supporters who flocked to Ibrox on 9 August 1988 for Cooper's testimonial match against Girondins de Bordeaux was inclined to criticise his contribution to the cause in the preceding eleven years, which, for the most part, had been book-ended by success, but with a significant filling of failure in the middle. These travails could be not be laid at Davie's door, and whatever his own reservations about his role in the ongoing Souness drama, any fair-minded assessment of Cooper's spell at Rangers would conclude that he had been one of their few beacons of light in the darkness; he had ignited a variety of stirring performances from those in his midst and had electrified those spectators who turned up, in dwindling numbers at Ibrox, principally to find out whether they might be served up another act of prodigious prestidigitation. Nor were the faithful disappointed when he flicked the switch again on a Tuesday night in Glasgow, as Rangers unveiled some thrilling football during their 3–2 victory with the goals coming from Butcher, Drinkell and the ubiquitous McCoist. The only thing missing in the script was a rip-snorting net-buster from the star of the show, but he was overcome by emotion at the reception he gained, which, according to lifelong fan Ian Paterson, was entirely heart-felt:

"There were lumps in our throats when he ran out on to the field. You could see that it wasn't really his thing to make a big song and dance about it and he told one of my mates later that he had no idea that he was going to receive this treatment. He was just a fan, a Rangers man through and through, and yet he looked so fit and so comfortable on the ball against Bordeaux that it seemed incredible that he would be leaving Ibrox any time soon. But he knew the score.

"There was a bit of a tear in his eye when he signed a few autographs after the match had finished and one of my pals asked him if he was leaving. He just smiled and said, 'I would never leave if it was up to me, because this is the club that I have supported since I was his height,' and he pointed to my mate Rab's three-year-old son, who had a programme and was looking for Davie's signature. He got it, of course – Davie was class when it came to things like that and he was really at home with kids and people who loved football and were only in it for the football. That was what endeared him to so many people. We all knew – we read the papers in these days – that he could have headed off to any of a dozen clubs in

England if he had wanted to. But he stayed with us through the rough times and we all loved him for that."

Some of these farewells were a bit premature. Mark Walters might have made forty-eight appearances for Rangers in the 1988–89 campaign, but Davie was involved in some important matches, helped his team regain their League Championship title and bowed out in the Scottish Cup final against Celtic at Hampden Park. He himself had vowed that he wasn't prepared to languish in the reserves, depriving younger players of opportunities to flourish, so he couldn't complain – nor did he – when Souness used him sparingly, but effectively at the highest level. There were instances during these last few months when he might have raged against the dying of the light, but even though he didn't feature in the League final against Aberdeen – a repeat of the previous year's denouement, which saw a brace of McCoist goals and another from Ian Ferguson secure a 3–2 victory – Davie's response was that he had ample medals in his collection. He yearned for one last crack at Celtic and that opportunity duly arrived, though Cooper had to be content with a place on the substitutes' bench for the climactic Old Firm game of another season.

In many respects, it was a momentous afternoon. For starters, even as Celtic celebrated a fraught 1–0 win, courtesy of a Joe Miller goal which began with a Roy Aitken throw-in – despite the fact that Aitken himself had put the ball out of play – this marked the end of trophy-clutching revelries around Parkhead for all of six years. There again, amidst the partying, their supporters cheered the news that their former hero, Mo Johnston, would be rejoining the club the following season. Of course, it never happened, and the Nantes striker instead hitched his star to the wagon being driven by Souness and David Murray as they continued their revolution of Scottish football.

In the midst of these tumultuous events, Cooper's exit from the all-pervading Old Firm spotlight was a low-key affair, once he was introduced as a replacement for Mel Sterland, a player who, with the minimum of respect, wasn't fit to lace Davie's boots. But there were no last twists, no lip-smacking hints of his former glories as the match slipped away from Rangers and a few waves at the climax were as emotional as matters got. By now, the only question lay in where he would be plying his trade upon waving adieu to Ibrox, but Cooper was determined that he wouldn't leave Govan under a cloud or with recriminations.

There were hints from some quarters that he was being pushed out against his will and that he was keen to become more involved in the youth set-up at Rangers, but the truth seems to be that he still believed he had the requisite motivation and skills to do a decent job for another organisation in his country's premier division. If Souness didn't possess the nous to comprehend that Davie, even in his thirties, boasted qualities which remained of value to any genuine football enthusiast, that was his loss. Cooper might have felt regret over the desultory fashion in which he had been treated and colleagues related how he couldn't quite believe he was being escorted out the exit door at Ibrox, but he knew the old gifts hadn't vanished and that he could still do somebody a turn. As for those conspiracy theorists who have linked the arrival of Johnston at Ibrox with the departure of Davie, they have probably spent too much time watching the *X-Files*.

I spoke to enough people, both on and off the record, to be sure that Cooper would never have allowed any sectarian considerations to dictate his career choices – he was a child of the 1960s, not the 1690s – and there is not a shred of evidence that it did. On the contrary, he simply appreciated that he was surplus to requirements in the Souness milieu, but privately reckoned that he might still retain the ability to shine elsewhere.

He was right in that assessment. In fact, he was so correct that there wasn't simply a new flowering of his talents across Scotland, but another call to international duty as well. That summer, he worked hard, met up with some of his former Clydebank team-mates, participated in a number of charity tournaments on

Wednesday afternoons, and several of his acquaintance noticed a renewed glint in his eye, almost as if a burden had been lifted off his shoulders. On his regular trips to the bookies in Hamilton, he said "Hello" to the punters who nodded in his direction, but when they attempted to find out what his plans were, or whether he felt disillusioned by the manner of his departure from Ibrox, he smiled enigmatically, collected his winnings or tore up his betting slips and kept his own counsel. It was only later on in his life that he would acknowledge the scale of the wrench when he spoke to the *Sunday Times* in a wide-ranging interview:

"When you spend as long as I did at Rangers, you can't help but make friendships, and I know that I can pick up the phone and speak to Ally [McCoist] or Walter [Smith] or any of the other lads in the squad and these people are part of my life. I went through good times and bad times, wonderful experiences and painful days with these boys and these are things that you never forget. Some of my best mates left before I did – Jazzer [Jim Bett] went to Aberdeen, Gordon [Smith] moved back to England and Bobby Russell moved on to Motherwell. So it wasn't the end of the world when I left Rangers. It had to happen, sooner or later, and I was glad that I was able to go out with them winning the league and getting to a Cup final. Better that a hundred times than to be playing in front of 200 people in a reserve game and suddenly realise that you are an old has-been."

Only somebody with Davie's innate modesty could have dreamt up such a bleak future for himself. In the real world, he was in demand and ready to rumble again. Those who had imagined he would fade quietly out the picture were in for a rude awakening.

12

THE BOY DONE WELL!

Sometimes the listener hears statements on the radio which force one to sit up in disbelief, reduce one to helpless convulsions of laughter or leave one's jaw hitting the floor. One recalls an entertainment boffin declaring, without a trace of self-awareness, when discussing the creation of a new theme park in Florida: "This isn't some Mickey Mouse company, after all – this is Walt Disney!" Or the astronomy expert trying (and failing) not to talk down to his audience while discussing the NASA space shuttle with the assertion: "Let's face it, sending a man to the moon isn't rocket science."

I was on my way to a cricket match in 1989 when a sports broadcaster relayed the news that Davie Cooper had signed for Motherwell from Rangers for a fee of £50,000. It was one of those snippets of information which required several seconds to digest, but then, as the ramifications filtered through my mind, I remember thinking three things. Firstly, what a bargain this was for the Fir Park club and what an incredible piece of transfer business this had been from Tommy McLean. Secondly, what on earth were Rangers doing, releasing an individual who had performed for them in such stalwart fashion for an absolute pittance? And thirdly – and, with hindsight, completely without foundation – how would a man such as Cooper respond to life on the provincial circuit? Was this another case of a man winding down towards retirement with a few years of going through the motions before he finally hung up his boots? It had happened with other individuals. But those latter comments most certainly did not apply to Cooper.

On the contrary, Motherwell offered redemption and release for the thirty-three-year-old in a way which would never have occurred if he had festered in the Rangers reserves. Suddenly, he was back in his beloved Lanarkshire, he was a stone's throw from his home, and where he had been latterly frozen out by the ticking time-bomb of volatility, Souness, he now found himself back in harness with his former manager, McLean, one of those redoubtable characters who was in the process of establishing an excellent blend of youth and experienced personnel, without making a huge song and dance about it.

The pair had forged a natural rapport during their spell at Rangers. They had played in the same team, experienced highs and lows on a regular basis, and when John Greig had departed under a cloud in 1983, McLean had stepped into the breach on a temporary basis with such a sense of purpose and refusal to be deflated by the club's litany of woes that Cooper was genuinely impressed with his managerial and motivational powers. In that sense, it was perhaps not wholly surprising that they were reunited as the decade reached its conclusion, but nonetheless, a section of the Motherwell fans wondered whether Davie could possibly recapture the brilliance of his golden years. They were entitled to be sceptical, considering the cheapness of the sale, but as it transpired, Davie had a new spring in his step from the moment he welded forces with the Steelmen.

Tom Boyd was one of those who benefited most from Cooper's arrival. As a talented twenty-three-year-old, he might have been a decade younger than his new teammate, but the fellow who subsequently amassed 72 caps for Scotland and enjoyed a glittering club career at Celtic was galvanised by the trickery of his confrere and they sparked off each other, with sufficient brio and bonnie panache, that it was as if they were old friends, not master and pupil. In these circumstances, it was hardly surprising that, as Boyd told me, he has never forgotten the empathy which developed among that special band of brothers:

"When Davie walked through the door at Fir Park, it was a real coup for us, because we all knew that the man had a huge amount of talent and here he was, coming to what he might have regarded as a run-of-the-mill organisation. But straight from the outset, his attitude was first rate and he was never anything less than whole-hearted in his attitude. He talked to every member of the squad and he told us that he wanted to make a genuine impression at Motherwell, and he and Tommy McLean both did a terrific job over the next few years. It was as if Davie found a new lease of life from escaping the Old Firm spotlight and I was pleased as punch that I had the opportunity to play with him, because you could see at close quarters just how much class he had at his disposal.

"You can't argue with the transformation which happened at the club during that period. Mind you, the move was good for Davie as well, because it meant that he could use his qualities of ball control, vision, ability from set pieces and technical mastery to benefit those around about him, and the younger guys in the team were able to latch on to his service and use their pace to good effect. It was an ideal combination and it provided Tommy with lots of options and there were days where Motherwell played some really, really good football. In fact, even though Davie couldn't have guessed it, the supporters and rival teams quickly noticed how he had the old spring in his step and he made such an impact that Scotland came calling again. I learned an awful lot from him and, of course, the Scottish Cup run in 1991 was one of those unforgettable experiences where everything comes together for a small club and nobody talks about the Old Firm for a while. Some folk might have imagined that he was running down the clock when he left Rangers, but he proved a lot of people wrong and it was great to be a part of it."

For those diehards at Fir Park who had dutifully kept the faith and embarked on the less-than-magical mystery tour of duty around the lower-league hinterland of Caledonia, this was a period to savour, a time when the side's star was in the ascendancy, and no matter the opposition, they could be confident that their team would be as competitive and as steely as the roots from which their club had originated. Throughout this spell, Motherwell thrived on the industry of such indefatigable customers as Boyd, Phil O'Donnell and Billy Davies, while Cooper and his former colleague Bobby Russell regained their mojo, linking and generating menace for any opponents, be it the Old Firm or their counterparts in Edinburgh, Dundee and Aberdeen. Given that Souness, bolstered by the fresh investment of David Murray, was on the verge of gaining a stranglehold over the rest of the Scottish game, there was never any genuine prospect of McLean's charges winning the league championship – although they subsequently came far closer than most observers predicted – but their acolytes were as thrilled by the metamorphosis, as recounted by lifelong fan, Graham Barnstaple of the Fir Park Corner website:

"Like many other Motherwell supporters, I was initially sceptical about the reasons for Davie's move to Fir Park and thought that he had maybe come to see out his days and would not be the type of player to help us out of the lower half of the Premier League. Well, I was proved totally wrong as the man did everything in his power to help us finish in our best league position for many a year – sixth – at the end of season '89–90.

"During the whole season, we saw that his contribution was immense, whether making chances for Nick Cusack, or bringing Tommy Boyd to the fore with his passing on the left wing, and Davie gave his all to the cause." These opinions were shared by Barnstaple's colleague John Wilson, who revelled in the opportunity to swagger in the spotlight:

"I wondered if Tommy McLean was just giving his pal a last hurrah, but I soon changed my mind on that score. It was obvious that Davie cared about the team's performance and he made up for his lack of pace with pure skill," said Wilson. "His on-field understanding with Bobby Russell was nothing short of telepathic, and at times, the pair of them produced wonderful exchanges in and around the opposition box and left defences utterly bamboozled. Tom Boyd and Phil O'Donnell owed much of their success later in their careers to the tutoring and lessons which they learned from the elder statesman."

By this stage, Davie knew exactly what he could and couldn't do in the heat of battle. His approach to training, which had once veered between agnostic and lackadaisical, was also transformed. If it was an unexpected late blooming, nobody was complaining from Fir Park to Park Gardens, as the SFA monitored Cooper's level of performances.

Back in early 1987 it had appeared that Cooper's international career was at an end, following his participation in a 2–0 loss at the hands of Brazil in the Rous Cup, but suddenly, in the build-up to the World Cup qualifying match against Norway at Hampden on 15 November 1989, he was recalled to the fold by Andy Roxburgh, who had been sufficiently impressed with his former Clydebank colleague's displays to ignore those who paid closer attention to birth certificates than ball control. Cooper was as surprised as anybody by this development – "I thought they had pensioned me off," he remarked to the *News of the World* – but Roxburgh had no inhibitions about the move and told me that one of his regrets was that Cooper wasn't fit enough to take part in the 1990 World Cup.

That opinion was echoed by Craig Brown and also by Sir Alex Ferguson, who told me that Cooper's behaviour on these international assignments never veered away from the enthusiastic. Other players raged and sulked at being left on the bench or being omitted from certain squads as a consequence of fluctuations in form, but Davie was just delighted to be involved. On his reprise to the Scotland fold, he demonstrated that the days of the "Moody Blue" were long gone, to the extent that one of the journalists who interviewed him the week before the Norwegian clash told me had felt sorry about his treatment of the player in the past.

"We mistook his shyness for arrogance, we never understood in these early days that Davie was simply intense about his football, but if he had been a bit more like a Souness, a McCoist or an Alan Hansen, he might have gained another 20 or 30 caps," said my tabloid source. "Sometimes I wonder if we crack him up these days because of how he died so young, but then I go back to watching the footage and you can't argue with it. He was a bloody marvel and he was so happy to be back in the picture that a few of us were a bit embarrassed by how wrong we had been."

Other, more knowledgeable observers had reached this conclusion much sooner. Ruud Gullit, a sublimely gifted performer on the European stage, rhapsodised about the Scot, and Sergei Baltacha, when asked to name his most dangerous opponent, replied, "Davie Cooper for Motherwell."

Privately, it must have been disconcerting for the player himself to find himself in the midst of history being re-written, but even if his performance during the 1–1 draw with the Norwegians was at first a bit tentative, by his own exalted standards, others who watched him went away from the match biting their tongues.

"It was a weird experience reading the match programme and seeing Davie Cooper's name next to Motherwell in the Scotland line-up," said lifelong Rangers fan, Gordon Strang. "Those of us who had followed his career always thought that he got a bum rap from the Ibrox managers – Jock Wallace was the only one who really understood what made Davie tick – and I wonder what was going through Souness's mind when he heard that the player he had flogged for fifty grand three months earlier was back in the Scotland set-up. He would probably try and tell you that he had given Davie the rocket up the backside he needed to find his best form again. But that was nonsense. The fact was that he and the guys before him never knew how to get the best out of the man."

By the early part of 1990, Motherwell were a joy to behold when things clicked. There was one evening match against a stuffy Hibernian line-up, where Cooper could have been carrying a baton, such was the imperious style with which he controlled the tempo and orchestrated the flow of those around him. His economy of movement was only equalled by the accuracy of his long-range passing, allied to his dextrous ability to ghost past opponents as if they weren't there, and the only shame was that some of his younger teammates were unable to capitalise on the concert he was conducting. Yet if this was a less rarefied setting than what Davie had grown used to at Ibrox, there was no sense of "Look at me!", no self-aggrandising attempts to admire his own handiwork and, unlike a Barry Ferguson, for instance, he never sought to deflect blame elsewhere with angry gestures or exaggerated finger-pointing if, occasionally, one of his passes strayed off the radar. His only source of wrath was aimed at rival defenders who resorted to brute force to halt his progress, and Cooper was never shy of letting referees know what they should do with these fellows. But, in most respects, he was loving the whole Motherwell vibe.

A few weeks later, I met Davie in Motherwell, and our conversation amply confirmed that he was flourishing from being handed the responsibility of nurturing a grassroots organisation, even as he declared that he felt "re-energised" from being surrounded by players in the foothills of their careers. He refused to discuss the background to his departure from Rangers, insisting that he "understood" their desire to invest in fresh legs, but no other subject was deemed off limits, including Mo Johnston's controversial signing for Souness as the first high-profile Catholic recruit to the Ibrox cause. In Cooper's eyes, this had been a "brave" decision by his former Scotland colleague, because Davie recognised how deeply the Old Firm tribal divisions separated friends and communities, come the clubs' regular derby-day meetings, across Lanarkshire, Ayrshire, West Lothian and Glasgow. But he knew Johnston pretty well, the duo had attended various sponsorship functions in the past, and, according to Davie, if anybody had the balls and the bravado to ride out the storm, it was the former Celtic man:

"You have to be pretty tough to cope with all the publicity which he has faced in the last few months, but the best way of shutting up the critics is for Mo to do his talking on the pitch, and he seems to be doing that just fine. That is the one thing I don't miss about being at Rangers – all the hype and all the baggage which comes with the Old Firm matches and how you can be a hero one minute and a diddy the next. You would think that you would get used to it over the years, but you don't. If anything, it gets worse, because the longer you are in there, the more you find yourself at the fans' rallies and the supporters' meetings and you realise how much being a Ranger means to them."

By contrast, life at Fir Park offered a release from the old enmities and prejudices. The 'Well aficionados were as committed to their club as anybody, but they appreciated that their players were only human and that advancing to Cup semi-finals – or better – was an achievement to be cherished.

If he had been more ambitious, or more unscrupulous, Cooper might have gained the opportunity to bid farewell to Scotland at the 1990 World Cup in the United States, and he was certainly in the minds of the coaches, Andy Roxburgh and Craig Brown. But it was perhaps typical of Davie's low-key philosophy to his calling that his swansong for his country came during an underwhelming friendly fixture against Egypt at Pittodrie on 16 May, where the visitors served notice of their prowess by recording a well-deserved 3–1 victory, even as sections within the Tartan Army began to fear for the future of the national side. In what was only his twenty-second appearance for Scotland, Cooper played the whole match, and offered some telling touches, whilst being involved in the build-up to Ally McCoist's goal. But he was battling injury by this point of the season and he resolved that, having already sat through the best part of one World Cup campaign, it would be unfair for him to travel to America if he was less than 100 per cent fit. In the event, he could hardly been shown greater integrity – and, in doing so, managed to miss his compatriots' excruciating defeat to Costa Rica

– but his decision prompted some fresh soul searching from pundits who had once viewed Davie as a misfiring maverick, but now regarded him as some sort of Messiah.

The truth lay closer to the latter than the former, but as Brown told me, Cooper was invariably too honest and laid-back for his own good. He could have hidden his injury from the SFA's medical staff, but it wasn't in his nature to be deceitful or pursue selfish ends, even when his honesty actively counted against him. Instead, he informed his bosses that he would be ready for the Sweden game but would have to sit out the Costa Rican encounter. It cost him his place on the plane and terminated his involvement with his country, but as he spent the summer recuperating in Motherwell, Davie had no regrets about his course of action. As he confirmed later, he would have felt far worse if his dissembling had cost one of his confreres the opportunity to participate in a World Cup, because there was no greater honour in the sport. It summed up the man: as one former player after another told me, even his most bitter opponent could never have accused Davie of indulging in self interest or betraying mercenary instincts.

In any case, he had other challenges in front of him during what was to prove a momentous season for Motherwell FC. Under the beetle-browed gaze of Tommy McLean, the Steelmen had forged a burgeoning reputation in their homeland, but they had gone nearly forty years without winning any major honours and it was surely fanciful to imagine that they could halt that sequence, especially with Rangers spending like drunken yuppies. Yet when one glanced at their squad and weighed up the menace and potential within their ranks, this Fir Park collective boasted significant va va voom. And, particularly in the sphere of Cup confrontation, they were capable of beating anybody else in Scotland on any given afternoon. It was a tale which still stirs the blood.

They could hardly have faced a sterner examination of their credentials than beginning with an away trip to Pittodrie. This was in the days before the Dons suffered routine Cup humiliation at the hands of Livingston, Queen of the South, Raith Rovers and Tippethill Bottlewashers (all right, the last is a figment of my imagination, but you get the picture!). Yet, although Aberdeen began ominously with an Alex McLeish "goal" adjudged offside, as the prelude to Eoin Jess posing problems for Chris McCart and the rest of the visiting rearguard, Motherwell gradually regained the initiative, driven forward by the talismanic Cooper, who engineered chances for the likes of Jamie Dolan and Iain Ferguson.

As Tom Boyd told me, "There was a confidence about our team, a belief that if we performed to our potential, we could give anybody a decent run for their money." In which light, it was hardly surprising that as the contest raged on, with Theo Snelders forced to produce some excellent saves, the travelling fans grew increasingly confident that their personnel could register a historic victory.

With manager McLean ringing the changes and replacing Ferguson with Steve Kirk, who was already a cult figure among the Steelmen, there was a wondrous conclusion to the tussle for those who had braved the journey to the Granite City. In the words of one of the fans who knew their heroes best: "Kirk ambled on, as only he could, and when Davie Cooper squared the free kick, Stevie ran up and thumped it as hard as he could with his weaker foot. Now, I know that Stevie was a great player, but if he intended to curl the ball away from the goalie into the far corner at that speed with his left foot, then flying pigs should have carried him all the way home. When he looked as though he was going to hit it, I can remember thinking, 'Don't shoot, don't shoot, leave it to Cooper.' But how relieved I was that he ignored me.

"Having sent the 'Well fans wild, Kirkie then ran thirty-five yards to jump over the advertising hoardings and celebrate. He had been on the pitch for less than a minute, had one touch, scored a wonderful goal, and he was now getting booked. If it hadn't been Stevie, nobody would have believed it was possible." But it was, and that was good enough for his team to edge past Aberdeen and book their passage to the next round of the competition.

207

Nor could they have complained when the draw pitted them at home against Falkirk from the First Division. As if to illustrate the impact which the likes of Cooper, Russell and Boyd were having around the environs at Motherwell, a crowd of more than 10,000 supporters congregated to a match which turned into a feast of attacking football. In the early stages, Ferguson took a quick corner to Cooper, who promptly feinted past his would-be marker prior to feeding Nick Cusack, and it was 1–0 to the hosts. To their credit, Falkirk responded purposefully, pushing forward in a bid to level matters and although they were fortunate that Phil O'Donnell didn't punish them when presented with a couple of chances, the underdogs roared into contention once more when Sammy McGivern slotted the ball past Ally Maxwell. That was how matters stood at the interval, but although a few on the sidelines were worried as to how the script would unfold in the second period, they were reassured when a typically industrious foray from Ian Angus allowed Joe McLeod to grab his first – and only – goal for his club. Undaunted, though, Falkirk replied again with an exceptional effort from Alex Taylor, who latched on to Derek McWilliams' astute back-heel to level the tie at two-apiece.

It was excellent fare for neutrals, nerve-shredding stuff for the locals, but these Motherwell warriors refused to be fazed by the challenge, and just as it had done against Aberdeen, the entrance of Kirk saw his team's prayers being answered during a frenetic finale. First, the substitute profited from a mistake by John Hughes to score at close range. Then, with Cooper rampaging down the wing like a young filly rather than a thirty-five-year-old thoroughbred, the coup de grâce was applied by the elusive Cusack, who pounced on a blocked shot from Kirk to despatch the ball into the far corner. It had been a tough battle, but the look on Cooper's face at the climax spoke volumes for how he was lapping up these chaotic Cup collisions. Next up was Morton, again at Fir Park. Nobody was taking anything for granted, but that seemed to provide a safe route to the semi-finals.

However, sometimes the apparently easy pickings can provide the hardest tests. In advance of this tussle, Cooper was interviewed by a number of Scottish newspapers and his genial air of *joie de vivre* and confident body language was a world removed from the introverted individual who had once been intimidated by these press gatherings. He made all the right noises, spoke of how he and his teammates owed a debt to Tommy McLean, and described his life at Motherwell as a massive bonus, but Davie also warned that Morton would be no pushovers and he was justified in issuing that cautionary note. Indeed, they almost gate-crashed the home party during a nervy clash at Fir Park, which forced the clubs into a replay, and there were a few apprehensive souls on the buses which headed over to Greenock for the return meeting ten days later. If nobody remembers the semi-finalists in a Cup tournament, the losing quarter-finalists are even more anonymous, and McLean's troops briefly struggled with the expectations on their shoulders.

As it transpired, their butterflies seemed to have vanished in the opening moments when Cooper and Boyd were the catalysts for an exceptional assault on the home ramparts, encompassing the whole length of the pitch, which concluded with the youngster scoring a breath-taking goal. Yet if the visiting support thought that would ease their passage, they were in for a nasty surprise, as their opponents rallied with a marvellous, sustained sense of purpose. Ally Maxwell had to make two fine saves, whilst the Motherwell defence dug deep into their reserves, but Morton continued to press and were worthy of their sixty-second-minute equaliser from John Gaughan – a former 'Well player.

By now the tension had grown suffocating and it wouldn't have been a shock if Cooper and his colleagues had withered on the vine, particularly once the match went into extra time and thereafter to penalties. Derek McInnes converted Morton's first; Cooper, cool as Antarctica, followed suit. Then, Mark Pickering, aflutter with agitation, sclaffed his attempt into the crowd. Eyes were shut, fingers crossed and prayers delivered to the heavens by the more superstitious or religious of the throng, but there was no immediate respite as the penalty-takers on both sides retained their sangfroid. Eventually, it was left to Colin O'Neill, one of life's idiosyncratic characters, to complete the task for Motherwell and he did so with a ferocity which almost burst the net. It had been a fraught success, but Davie's side had eventually booked their place in the semis, and the news that they would tackle Celtic sent a frisson round the club for the next few weeks.

Unfortunately, from his perspective, Cooper was denied the opportunity to go toe-to-toe with the Hoops because of suspension. He had never been averse to letting referees know if he believed that he was being targeted for excessive abuse – and the Souness description of him as "Albert Tatlock" was appropriate in this instance, because Davie, in full spate with a grievance to argue about, was a fully paid-up member of the awkward squad. It was once remarked of Willie Miller that if football had adopted the same regulations as rugby in marching players back ten yards when they showed dissent, the Aberdeen maestro would have spent most of his career in Scandinavia. Cooper wasn't quite in that class, but his tendency to clash with officialdom increased as the years advanced. He was disconsolate at missing out on the chance to tackle Celtic again, but behind the scenes, his principal emotion was guilt at letting down his Fir Park teammates. He hoped fervently that his tongue would not come back to haunt him.

In his absence, Motherwell's epic Cup sequence unfolded with another torrent of twists throughout their brace of meetings with Celtic. In the first match, Phil O'Donnell might have conceded a penalty for handball, but the referee waved play on, as the precursor to a magnificent Iain Ferguson shot crashing off the woodwork with Pat Bonner beaten. At the denouement, even the more Panglossian 'Well partisans felt slightly deflated. The common perception was that "Celtic didn't lose replays", and although that was untrue, the Old Firm have long tended to pick opponents off in these circumstances.

Certainly nobody would have wagered against them maintaining their proud record at Hampden Park, on the evidence of the early action when the teams locked horns again. Amidst a series of frantic clearances and frazzled defending, Paul Elliott had one goal disallowed for offside, but the Englishman put his team in front shortly afterwards and the tie could have been out of sight during the first half an hour. Yet it was a measure of the camaraderie and unstinting endeavour of McLean's men that they never allowed their heads to droop, and once they had withstood that initial onslaught, they surged back into the mix when Dougie Arnott drilled the ball past Pat Bonner. As one might have anticipated from a Celtic collective of that period, they created plenty of chances, and Anton Rogan regained the lead for the Parkhead side. But, equally predictably, as they started to sink into mediocrity towards the end of the decade – a decline which almost saw them go out of business in the early 1990s – there was a vulnerability about their defence, which suggested that if Motherwell could keep the faith, they would gain opportunities, and the question was whether they could seize them and wrest the initiative from their adversaries. They did, in spectacular fashion, and on a momentous night in Glasgow, the Steelmen turned a 2–1 deficit into a stunning 4–2 triumph.

Parity was restored with a splendid Arnott header from a Luc Nijholt cross. Then, even as the balance ebbed and flowed, the suspicion grew that it would require something special for the Lanarkshire men to prevail. Quite how special, nobody could have foretold. But in the seventy-fifth minute, O'Neill, the fellow with a taste for unforgettable vignettes, suddenly unleashed a fabulous shot from at least thirty-five metres out, and despite Bonner's valiant efforts to prevent it finding the net, the ball crashed beyond him and the Motherwell followers went crazy. There was still plenty of time for Celtic to retrieve the situation, and Paul McStay came close to levelling matters again, but the outcome was settled conclusively when Kirk curled a terrific effort past Bonner and the Glaswegians' goose was cooked.

211

As these climactic scenes unfolded, Cooper could barely conceal his emotions. On the one hand, he hadn't been involved in what had been a marvellously spirited and inspirational performance from his club, and it would have been a sweet feeling had he been able to influence another success over his old foes. Yet, he was also mightily relieved that his absence hadn't weakened Motherwell's Cup bid. A lot of fuss had rightly been generated about the contributions of Davie and Tom Boyd, but there were a string of individuals – including such stalwarts as Kirk, O'Neill, Arnott, McCart, Ally Maxwell and John Philliben – whose yeoman exertions had been instrumental to the Fir Park side reaching the final. It meant that McLean faced a number of tough decisions while choosing his squad for their day in the sun and an extra soupcon of spice was added by the fact Tommy was up against Jim McLean's Dundee United at Hampden on that afternoon of 18 May 1991. In advance, it was billed as a battle between the "Brothers Grim". In the event, the teams conspired to narrate a fairytale to their audience, replete with enough drama and twists of fortune to fill up half a dozen of these occasions and demonstrate that there was lashings of life outwith the Old Firm's territory.

Less than two years after he had departed Ibrox, with the more cynical analysts spinning the line that he was effectively being put out to pasture, Cooper's career had gained a glorious Indian summer which must have left some of his former employers feeling a little shame-faced. The normal pattern in these stories was for the ex-Old Firm star to burble on about what a privilege it was to feature in another grand Cup occasion, while sticking to the clichés – "We are doing it for the gaffer," "We respect Dundee United and it will be difficult" and so on – but in this instance, Davie might have been a child who receives a letter inviting him to star in a Harry Potter film. He was genuinely thrilled, and his exuberance filtered through to his colleagues, even those who were unfortunate to miss out on selection for the Hampden squad. In purely pragmatic terms, he had been absent from the previous stage of the tournament, and it might have seemed like a big call for Tommy McLean to tinker with the side which had beaten Celtic, but, as Tom Boyd, Billy Davies and Bobby Russell told me, there was no prospect of any sane manager omitting Cooper from a high-profile final.

"Davie was the perfect man for these big matches because he had played in so many of them that he knew what to expect," said Davies. "He also realised that most of the players on both sides would be nervous at the start and that if he could dominate his rivals during that early period, he might be able to build up a momentum which they wouldn't be able to shake off." It was a prescient assessment from a chap who went on to enjoy rich pickings at Fir Park.

In that regard, all the anthems and the pre-match pomp and ceremony washed over Cooper's head. Whatever the sentimental tone of much of the coverage, he realised that these afternoons were bound to become increasingly rare and that he had better grasp the opportunity as if it was a winning Lottery ticket. In the back of his mind, he was also slightly apologetic about having booked his place at Hampden – "Some of the lads who have missed out will be gutted and I can sympathise with them 100 per cent" – but once the match commenced, there was no time for the participants to fret over side issues.

Dundee United were, of course, the bookies' favourites and deservedly so. They were an organisation which in the recent past had snaffled domestic trophies, reached a UEFA Cup final and had progressed to the semi-finals of the European Cup. They started with the confidence of a club which had jousted with giants and it was all that Motherwell could do to repel their early onslaught. A Hamish French "goal" was chalked off by the narrowest of margins, prior to a Freddy van der Hoorn shot rebounding off the post and rolling, agonisingly for the Tannadice man, along the goal line. Yet, much as they had done throughout the tournament, McLean's personnel weathered the storm and, as Cooper began to weave a mazy path through his opponents, chances arrived for the underdogs. McCart nearly broke the deadlock, but shortly afterwards Iain

Ferguson linked superbly with Griffin and the former's coruscating header pushed his side in front.

It had already been a thoroughly entertaining contest, yet there was little indication at the interval of the drama which lay in store, much of it revolving around the Fir Park keeper, Ally Maxwell, who went to collect a seemingly routine catch, only to clatter into United's redoubtable John Clark. The thud reverberated around Hampden, but these were doughty fellows: a couple of dabs with the magic sponge would suffice, although it later emerged that Maxwell had lacerated his stomach and broken two ribs. Nowadays, play would have been suspended and stretchers would have appeared on the pitch. Back then Ally had other, more pressing concerns to worry about than excruciating pain.

For Cooper, this was a throwback to an earlier vintage. One or two critics later alleged that he was off the pace, but his attacks still sparked panic in the United rearguard and left gaps elsewhere. When Dave Bowman served up a sparkling equaliser, it might have induced pangs of trepidation in lesser rivals, but Motherwell responded with the sort of high-class football which had defined their season and, as their supporters embarked on what sub-sequently proved to be premature celebrations, they surged 3–1 ahead. The first goal arrived when Davie delivered a resplendent free kick from thirty metres out and the teenager O'Donnell flung himself headlong into the melee to seize a memorable diving header. Then, with the Tayside personnel in the toils, the perennial substi-tute Kirk laid on the service for Ian Angus to unleash a scintillating shot into the bottom corner. On most occasions, that would have been that. But this was an extraordinary tussle.

Despite their cushion, Motherwell were increasingly rocked by Maxwell's travails: the keeper was in agony and, irrespective of his admirable perseverance, his incapacity allowed United a lifeline back into the match. John O'Neil launched their recovery when he stole in behind Nijholt and powered a great header into the net, and then, as the decibel level threatened to blow the roof off the stadium and with the contest advancing into injury time, a towering clearance from Alan Main found Darren Jackson with a sliver of space and he showed customary efficiency in levelling matters at three-apiece. It was a classic confrontation, encompassing old sweats and teenage wannabes, and by this stage, Cooper admitted that he was feeling absolutely knackered. He needed extra time the way that Marvin Gaye needed soul, but this game was destined to tax everybody's reserves, from the McLean brothers on either side of the managerial divide, to the thousands of supporters who could hardly bear to watch, yet were engrossed in the action.

There was nothing those on the periphery could do. Motherwell's followers reflected on how they had lost the Cup in similar circumstances, by failing to defend a two-goal advantage back in 1931. United, for their part, were becoming so accustomed to self-destructing in these scenarios that their fanzine bore the name *The Final Hurdle*. Yet there was nothing to be ashamed about as the respective combatants flung themselves into the fray, above and beyond the call of duty. Steve Kirk forced a wonderful save from Main, but a couple of minutes later, a typically well-directed corner from Davie provoked panic among the United players and Kirk, so often the hero on his team's golden Cup trail, stabbed the ball home from close range. Even at that juncture, with exhaustion seeping through the ranks of both collectives, Jim McLean's personnel were unstinting in their efforts to find another goal. Maxwell, so clearly in the wars, denied Jackson heroically, then as the second period of extra time raged on, United turned the screw even further, to the stage where even Cooper was forced into manning the barricades. Nine times out of ten, or ninety-nine out of 100, Maurice Malpas would have levelled the tie at 4–4, but his shot was parried away with remarkable fortitude by the ailing Maxwell, as the prelude to a last-gasp siege of the Motherwell ramparts. In the midst of the frenzy, Cooper was replaced by Colin O'Neill, but both sets of fans recognised the incredible shift which the veteran had offered his club and rose in acclaim as he hirpled off.

And then, it was all over. Boyd sought out Kirk, Tommy McLean rushed over to check on Maxwell and Davie dashed back onto the field as the victors enjoyed one of the most exhilarating experiences of their lives. "You never get tired of these days, and especially not when you are with a fantastic group of people," said Cooper in the aftermath. Inwardly, he must have realised that this might be his last tango in the spotlight, but considering that he had never envisaged he would bask in another Hampden triumph, there was nothing but ebullience, exuberance and elation in his post-match reaction.

The following morning, his aching joints testified to the fact that he would have to seek out another career, and sooner rather than later, but winning the Scottish Cup was a bonus, a boon and a blessing for him, and his performance had been a revelation to some of those who had dismissed him as incapable of tackling when the occasion demanded it.

Unsurprisingly, everything else which happened at the club thereafter was suffused with a mild sense of anti-climax for Cooper, yet he eventually amassed more than 150 appearances for Motherwell, and behind the scenes, a variety of individuals expressed gratitude for his guidance.

"The thing about Davie was that he wanted to help all the youngsters achieve their potential and I don't think anybody who approached him for advice ever left feeling disappointed," said Billy Davies, his former colleague at Rangers, who subsequently plied his trade at Motherwell. "He was a true professional. He knew that things change and that you have to keep encouraging the next generation. He was terrific at it and I have no doubt that he would have excelled in the role."

As the months passed at Fir Park, Cooper found added purpose from helping out with coaching the youths on the Motherwell books. He was excellent with these young men and he was fairly impressive in his dealings with young ladies as well. If they took the trouble to write to him, he always made the effort to respond, even if it was just with a scribbled note of encouragement. Yet as Karen

Reid, one of his fans, discovered, there were occasions where his attempts to please exceeded the normal call of duty:

"I wanted to meet Davie Cooper the footballer, but got to meet Davie Cooper the gentleman. He was down-to-earth and a wonderfully generous, kind person. Not what you would expect from an international superstar. Here's how it all came about.

"In 1991 I wrote to the *Daily Record* because I was desperate to meet Davie, but I had no idea how to go about meeting him. I felt that I had missed my chance when he left Rangers, but I asked them to pass my letter to Davie. I did not think that I would hear anything more about it, but a month or so later, I received a letter from Motherwell FC, inviting me to go and see the Scottish Cup trophy and meet Davie Cooper. I could not believe it. I had to phone to arrange a date and time, but I was just so excited.

"I took the train over and went to Fir Park, where I was taken in and offered a cup of tea in a dining room/canteen type room. There were a few players around, who were kidding me on, and I was so nervous. After about fifteen minutes, Davie arrived back from training and made me another cup of tea. We had a chat in the room, then he offered to take me on a tour of the stadium. I had my picture taken in the dugout and my photograph taken with him. He laughed because I was shaking so much, then he took me to the trophy room and I had my picture taken with the Scottish Cup. It was amazing.

"Afterwards, Davie offered to drop me off at the railway station. Wow! I got to ride in his Golf. He dropped me at Motherwell Station and said he would like to see the photos when they were developed. I thought he was just being polite, but I did as he asked and he was as good as his word. A few days later, I phoned the stadium and spoke to Davie to arrange a time to come and show him the pictures. I decided to make him a tape, as we had talked about music during our first meeting. (I was young and totally bowled over by him.) I never expected him to listen to the tape while I was there! But at our next meeting, he invited me along to Motherwell's next match and I told him that I would love that. He again dropped me off at Motherwell

Station and he put my tape on in the car – I was so embarrassed! But he was so kind. I collected the tickets for the game about half an hour before the kick off and sat in a Box with complimentary tickets. Then, at the end, he ran me to the station – his father and brother were both in the car and the alarm kept going off – but we talked and had a laugh and he was really fun to be around.

"I met him at the stadium quite a few times after that – I always phoned him to arrange it first – and it was more than a dream come true. My mother popped along to Fir Park on one occasion, and as she was walking away after we had arranged our plans for later in the evening, Coop walked round the corner. He must have seen her walking away, and asked who it was – I told him it was my mum – and he ran after her shouting, 'Mum, Mum, Mum . . . !' Then he took us into the stadium for a cup of tea and gave me a football top as a gift. That day he also asked my mother if it would be OK if he took me out for lunch. She said yes, so a few weeks later, Davie took me to the Santa Lucia restaurant and after we had enjoyed the meal, we went back to his parents' house to collect his wee dog, Misty. His mum asked if I would like cheese on toast. I was so excited.

"That was the last time I saw him because I didn't want to become a pest. I always planned to contact him again in the future, but time passed, then he left Motherwell for Clydebank and, well, I did not know that I would run out of time. I was at college and was literally in the process of writing a latter to say 'Hi' and asking him to a fundraising fashion show that some of us were organising. It would have been terrific to have heard from him. But things happened and I wish that I had kept in touch with him."

Sadly, she wasn't the only person to be shattered at the fashion in which matters unfolded once Davie left Fir Park at the end of 1993 and returned to his roots at Clydebank. In the normal course of events, this should have marked a fresh chapter and challenge in his life, among people he respected, and as a mentor to the new kids on the block in his heartland. But at a point when anything seemed possible, fate intervened with a vengeance.

13

A BANKIE FIRST AND LAST

The two things which made Davie Cooper tick were football and family. Fame was a by-product of the former, but throughout his career, he never chased the limelight and was occasionally embarrassed by it. Even at the height of his powers in the late 1970s and early 1980s, when he could have moved anywhere in Britain – as was demonstrated by the myriad offers which he attracted from a plethora of English clubs – he was at peace with his parochialism, more comfortable amongst the clientele of the Hamilton hotels and bookmakers' shops which he frequented than at any black-tie celebrity gathering.

Unsurprisingly, therefore, as the clock ticked down on his professional career, the notion of returning to his roots at Clydebank, the place where he had taken his initial steps on the ladder from tentative teenager to adulthood, was a compelling one. Davie had thoroughly enjoyed his period at Motherwell – "We were a happy dressing room and we fought our hearts out for one another" – and, latterly, he had augmented his playing appearances with the job of mentoring, in a coaching capacity, the Fir Park club's youth and reserve sides. But at the age of thirty-seven, coming on thirty-eight, he appreciated that his next task was to graduate from parading his talents to teaching others how to learn, absorb and emulate the same skills, and when he received an offer from New Kilbowie in

December 1993 to rejoin the Bankies as player and assistant coach, he required all of a couple of seconds to respond in the affirmative. Once again, the umbilical cord which kept him attached to the West of Scotland remained as secure as it had always been, but Davie felt a genuine debt to his first employers in the football domain and these next few months showed that the bond between him and Clydebank was as powerful as ever.

From a personal standpoint, he recognised that he could no longer dominate matches and terrorise opponents at the loftiest level, but he retained sufficient gifts with the ball at his feet to merit a place in the lower leagues and there was never a sense of him indulging in nostalgia or relying on sentiment from the moment he took the field against Ayr United on 4 January 1994. It was in a losing cause, with the visitors recording a 2–0 win, but as the weeks passed and Cooper became a regular fixture in the ranks – in the 1993–94 campaign, he made twenty appearances, including sixteen starts – the news spread throughout the community that Davie was back on the beat and a significant number of spectators, including the current president Gordon Robertson, were grateful for this opportunity to renew acquaintances with the man who had thrilled them nearly twenty years earlier:

"When Davie returned to Clydebank, it gave everybody a lift. To understand exactly why, you have to go back to his first spell at New Kilbowie Park, where he was the dynamic force behind successive promotion-winning seasons. We had a great team at the time, but he was the star, and when he left in the summer of 1977, it was a real blow. I remember it well, even though I was only eleven years old at the time. His departure cast a shadow over our first-ever season in the Premier Division and many fans are still convinced that if we had kept Cooper we would have stayed in the top flight.

"It is hard to overstate what he meant to Clydebank supporters of a certain age and it is certainly no coincidence that the current directors of the board all got hooked on the Bankies during that era. It was so exciting and we were easily lured away from the twin evils of Rangers and Celtic to support our local team. Davie was the reason for that devotion. Some of the goals he scored were terrific and the fans simply loved him.

"So when he came back in 1994 it was something special. When he took a bow before the first match [against Ayr], he received a standing ovation. The Bankies faithful welcomed him back with open arms and what was really memorable was the fact that he looked so pleased to be with us again. When the club launched our Hall of Fame recently, he and Jim Fallon – our longest-serving player – were the first inductees. There was no argument: Davie Cooper is considered to be the club's greatest-ever player. And although he has been dead eighteen years now, in our club shop we still sell a T-shirt with a picture of Coop beneath the words: 'A Bankie First and Last.' That says it all."

He still relished the chance to prepare in his normal fashion for the Saturdays, where he was just another member of a team which was striving to regain past glories. Sometimes in these circumstances, when tabloids resort to employing clichés such as the "return of the prodigal son" or "there wasn't a dry eye in the house", it distorts the true picture. At that juncture, far from being lachrymose, the Clydebank acolytes had smiles on their faces again. Behind the scenes, even if he couldn't reproduce the heroics of his adolescent incarnation, he imparted his wisdom with a dry wit and understanding that his young charges required patience, encouragement, a friendly word here and a consoling pat there, if they were to complete the process of transforming their fledgling promise into the hard-nosed professionalism they needed to graduate to senior football.

In that respect, Cooper's coaching ability brooked no dispute. On the pitch, he was an almost ubiquitous presence in the side during the 1994–95 season, from August until the start of February, when he turned out against Hearts in a Scottish Cup third-round replay at Tynecastle, although he was unable to prevent his club from slipping to defeat in Edinburgh. But away from the pitch, Davie's growing contribution to developing and nurturing kids was being noticed by increasing numbers of prominent observers. Expressed simply, he was a natural in the role. Children lapped up his skills and trickery, revelled in his self-deprecating manner of dealing with them – he never considered football to be that important – and he never talked down to his youthful pupils. On the contrary, there was ample evidence that Cooper possessed the requisite qualities to become a successful coach or manager at whatever level of the game he desired.

Sir Alex Ferguson doesn't do regret, or at least doesn't make a frequent habit of lapsing into *recherche du temps perdu*. Yet when we spoke about that period in the mid-1990s, his recollections of Davie were infused with a wistful strain which offered a telling contrast to the usual image of Ferguson as a footballing Mr Angry, forever chewing out assistants and reducing grown men to quivering heaps of jelly:

"Davie, ah yes Davie, he loved football and he loved doing his best to ensure that others enjoyed it as well. He was making the move into coaching in the mid-1990s and I have no doubt that he would have been magnificent in the role," said Ferguson, who had taken a break from piloting his Old Trafford charges towards fresh honours to pay homage to his former comrade. "When I look back, he had everything, really. There was a trend with Scotland to favour all-round players – midfielders who could play out wide if required – at the expense of real wingers, but Davie provided plenty of justification for ignoring that trend because he was blessed with qualities which most other people didn't have. He was never anything less than passionate about his football, too, and he was a hometown lad, without any airs or graces, whose enthusiasm never diminished. He was loss, a real loss . . . "

There is little point treading over the minutiae of how, less than five weeks after Davie had made his last appearance in a Clydebank jersey in a reserve fixture against Hamilton, he had been taken from us. There were no warnings, no indications that anything was amiss. If anything, those who came into contact with the thirty-nine-year-old spoke of how he was savouring the next chapter in his life. He had meetings planned with his former Rangers teammate, Gordon Smith and his long-term colleague, Bobby Russell, he had entered into an agreement with STV to record a coaching film for youngsters, which sounded exactly the right project to stimulate his mind, and even when he met up with Charlie Nicholas and Tommy Craig at Broadwood Stadium in March 1995, he was laughing and joking with the kids who were present, as bubbly and effervescent as one might have imagined from a man who was gazing optimistically into the future.

Yet the next twenty-four hours turned into an extended nightmare for Davie and his family, and the wider Scottish footballing community. One minute he was joshing with his colleagues and merrily exchanging banter; the next he was lying on the ground, the victim of a brain haemorrhage, whose effects were catastrophic. Initially, it was impossible to digest the scale of his illness, and Nicholas and Craig were understandably traumatised by the experience, even as Cooper was rushed into intensive care. Shortly afterwards, the miserable tidings started to filter through to newspaper sports desks and television studios and, very quickly, Davie was being spoken about in the past tense, even as the medical staff did their utmost for the stricken man in their midst. There was, of course, nothing they could do to steer him back from the brink and thus it was that a healthy fellow in his thirties perished the next day, to a backdrop of tears and tristesse.

The grief was overwhelming, the desire to acknowledge his passing all-pervasive. Around Scotland, thousands of football fans congregated outside Ibrox, Fir Park, New Kilbowie and at other grounds, to leave their scarves, flowers and messages of commiseration. Smith, who had been looking forward to a light-hearted meal with his old colleague, instead found himself delivering impromptu obituaries, and the media sought quotes, reaction and tributes from the great and good of the game.

At these times, perspective can occasionally fly out of the window, but while adjectives such as "terrific", "fantastic" and "world-class" were plastered all over the press in the next forty-eight hours, they seemed neither excessive nor extravagant. On the contrary, amidst the numbness there was a palpable feeling that Cooper had too long been a prophet without honour in his own land and that his prodigious gifts had, to a degree, been squandered by the country he called home. Some of the obits recognised that twenty-two international caps was insufficient for somebody of his talent, but there again, Jimmy Johnstone only gained twenty-three in his career. Within a team setting, genius is often an uneasy bedfellow with graft.

At the offices of *Scotland on Sunday*, the shock was followed by a need to flesh out Davie's story and attempt to do justice to his powers. One of my former colleagues penned a powerful tribute, in the course of which he expressed his relief that he had been granted a few days to recover his equilibrium. Yet there was no disguising the mixture of guilt and horror which enveloped the sport before and after Davie's emotional funeral service at Hillhouse Parish Church in Hamilton, where Walter Smith delivered a moving paean to his compatriot, striking the right tone between solemnity and mawkishness:

"God gave Davie Cooper a talent. He would not be disappointed with how it was used," said the Rangers manager, even as the likes of Sir Alex Ferguson, Kenny Dalglish and Ally McCoist tried to hold back the tears. Plenty of these were shed while his body was laid to rest in the town's cemetery. And plenty more as the initial shock was replaced by the remembrance of things past: the grand theatrical flourish of the 1979 Drybrough Cup goal, his poise under pressure, even as Jock Stein was near to death in Wales in 1985, the violent majesty of his free kick past Jim Leighton in 1987 and the belated splendour of his contributions to Motherwell's Scottish Cup victory in 1991. At least in the modern era we have pictures of these exploits, readily accessible on the Internet, and every generation can flick back to the past and discover for themselves just why Davie was capable of making grown men and women feel like little kids at the Yuletide.

McCoist, typically, spoke with poignancy and fluency about his sadness: "Coop was the consummate entertainer. Whether it was the swivel of the hips or the forty-yard pass, he entertained, no matter the fixture or the surroundings. The highest tribute I can pay him is to say that I worked many times with Ruud Gullit on TV and he was always raving about Davie and his talent. I like the idea of a lasting tribute to Davie in Clydebank, because I first became aware of him in 1976 when the Bankies took Rangers to four games in the League Cup before we got rid of them. I won't name names, but there were two of our full-backs who tried swapping sides during the first of these matches because one of them was getting such a chasing from this young kid.

"Coop was, first and foremost, a humble man, but when people talk about him, they don't mention his medals, they talk about his skills. I remember when it was Davie's testimonial year and we were racking our brains for a gift. Then one of the lads had a brain-wave and got the right leg off a tailor's dummy and wrapped it up in brown paper with the message: 'What do you give the man who has got everything?' I couldn't put a price on what that left peg of his would be worth in today's transfer market."

Tragedies occur every day, whether within one's own community or on the wider international stage. When they involve the deaths of thousands of people or tens of thousands of victims, such as happened during 9/11 or the Asian tsunami, they are beyond the comprehension of the majority of us. We view the pictures on our screens, dig deep to help, however modestly, with the charity efforts, and thank our lucky stars that we will never find ourselves trapped in such a maelstrom of horror.

By comparison, football these days is synonymous with WAGs, players demanding six-figure advances for their (usually) bland autobiographies, and men behaving all too frequently as though they never really escaped the mentality of the playground. When supposed adults refuse to shake their opponent's hand before a match, when managers in their fifties and sixties indulge in yah-boo-sucks tantrums with their rivals, and when millionaires with mince for brains casually flick V-signs as they sit, huffily, on the sidelines at a Scotland match, it is clear that soccer has an image problem, which won't be easily remedied.

Thankfully though, the game usually transcends these concerns with spectacular pieces of theatre which reinforce the faith and convince the doubters of its merits. It wouldn't do to portray Davie Cooper as some kind of latter-day Angel Gabriel. He *could* be moody and querulous in the early years. He *could* lose the rag at referees if he felt that they were permitting rivals to scythe through him. And he *could* resemble a dog in the manger, when one considered his refusal to leave Rangers in the midst of the Greig deep freeze of the early 1980s, even though it must have been evident to him that his prospects of gaining a regular starting berth would have been significantly enhanced by moving elsewhere, even if only for a few years.

Yet in the final analysis, the virtues far outweighed these minor vices. He was a magician when in the right mood, a Sinatra or Ella Fitzgerald of the wing, capable of soaring above the humdrum tedium of any match and lifting it into a different, rarefied sphere, with some of the silkiest touches ever witnessed in the chronicles of Scottish football. His desire not to stray far from the nest might have limited his earning potential, but Davie was never bothered about chasing a cheap buck or screwing the fans, and the latter adored him for it. Ultimately, he was one of them from beginning to end, and there are websites in his memory scattered all over the globe, from Australia to Canada and obscure parts of Europe. That was the effect of his pizzazz: it inspired a generation of Scots who were too young to recollect Jimmy Johnstone or Jim Baxter but found a natural heir to that sublime duo in the guise of the trickster from Hamilton.

Of course he was snatched away too soon. His former Motherwell teammate Phil O'Donnell also died in his thirties, during a Premier League tussle against Dundee United in 2007. Indeed, four members of Tommy McLean's Cup-winning squad from just over twenty years ago are no longer with us. In anybody's language, that is too many, and especially when one considers the unfettered exuberance, panache and sheer enthusiasm which embodied those who pulled together to ensure that trophy was paraded at Fir Park.

But if you are of a mind to feel depressed at the state of Scottish football, cast your gaze over the footage from that 1991 denouement. If our country was once capable of producing individuals of the calibre of Cooper, Bobby Russell, Tom Boyd, Phil O'Donnell, Darren Jackson and Maurice Malpas and pitting them in a prime-time encounter which didn't involve the Old Firm, it can surely do so again.

As for Davie, the beatific expression on his face at the conclusion of that against-the-odds success testified to his sport's enduring ability to throw up the most unlikely results in the most improbable of settings. On his way up to collect his medal, he gazed around at the fans, and you can see him soaking in the atmosphere, imprinting the images on his mind and locking them away safely for posterity. It might be the case that, had he survived and advanced into management, as many of his peers predicted, there would have been other triumphs on his CV in the future. But ifs and buts count for nothing in the end. What matters is what you do with the gifts in your repertoire and how you enhance the gaiety of nations if you are born with a talent which can command a wider audience.

On that score, Davie's deeds will never be forgotten by anybody who witnessed them. It isn't a bad legacy for a small-town Scot with an international pedigree.

14

ENIGMA VARIATIONS

It is nearly twenty years since Davie Cooper's star burned out, yet one would never guess that from visiting the locales in the West of Scotland where he once revelled in his anonymity. Wherever one ventures, there are no shortages of apostles prepared to pay homage to Davie's football magic and who seem willing to converse with a stranger about the qualities he brought to the game. In the course of writing this book, I visited several of the communities where Cooper left an indelible mark – Hamilton, Motherwell, Clydebank, Fauldhouse and Larkhall – and spoke to many Rangers fans whose conversation encompassed the whole gamut of emotions from pride at how Davie wore the blue jersey with such distinction, to exasperation at the memory of how his gifts were so often squandered by those around him in the dank days of the early 1980s.

This is a familiar theme. It can be heard from those who admire John Greig as a player, but describe his managerial tenure at Ibrox with a variety of f-words, including fiasco, farce and feckless failure. It can be discerned among those who revere Graeme Souness and Walter Smith for their part in effecting a revolution at Ibrox, yet still shake their heads in bemusement at how they could have allowed Davie to escape from their grasp, en route to Motherwell for a paltry £50,000.

"I reckon Tommy McLean must have thought that he had won the Lottery," said forty-five-year-old Bob McKenzie from Bellshill.

"I never understood why the Rangers guys were so reluctant to pick Coop in 1987 and 1988. When he did play, there would usually be some magic stuff, but he was allowed to fade out of the picture too soon. Did he want to go to Fir Park in the first place? Not according to what I have heard. But when he moved on, he made the Gers look bloody stupid."

Everybody has a theory. If they didn't, this would hardly be the land in which the Old Firm reign supreme. But while there remains a sense of disbelief at the fate which befell Cooper, his legacy is a story of positive developments and of fitting tributes to one of the most exceptional performers of his generation. There is the Davie Cooper Stand at Fir Park, then there was the 2005 CIS Insurance Cup final between Motherwell and Rangers [which the latter won 5–1], which allowed both sets of supporters to recognise their hero's myriad abilities, and, most importantly, there is the emergence of the Davie Cooper Centre in Clydebank, which is committed to helping special needs children and their families and enjoys the backing of such individuals as Ally McCoist, Neil Lennon, Davie Moyes and Willie Miller. It is almost as if the Caledonian community is determined to heed the lessons from Davie's demise and channel negative thoughts into positive initiatives.

In sporting terms, his legacy is most definitely secure. In 2010 STV broadcast a series of programmes, highlighting the best exponents of football in their country's football history, and invited supporters to vote for their greatest-ever XI. These sorts of concepts are inevitably biased towards the modern generation – on the basis that we don't have many pictures of the Wembley Wizards in their pomp – and, consequently, one should always treat the findings with a pinch of salt. And yet . . . the team selected was Andy Goram in goal, a defensive quartet of Danny McGrain, Alex McLeish, Willie Miller and Sandy Jardine, a midfield comprising Graeme Souness, Billy Bremner and the twin threats of Jimmy Johnstone and Davie Cooper, with Kenny Dalglish and Denis Law providing the striking threat for the personnel under Jock Stein's tutelage.

In anybody's language, this is a formation which would offer any opponents a run for their money, not least because few but the most foolhardy of rivals would dare meddle with Cooper and Johnstone, whilst Souness and Bremner were ready to inflict retribution in much the same fashion which made them such feared figures at Liverpool and Leeds United. It oozes class, purpose, attacking potency, rock-solid defence . . . and the mouth waters at the thought of the refulgent Davie and Jinky orchestrating their full repertoire of trickery and cutting a merry swathe on the flanks prior to unleashing King Kenny and the Lawman.

Of course, in the bigger picture, it is a purely hypothetical exercise, a triumph of wishful thinking over tangible achievement. But, there again, isn't that what we do best in Scotland?

One or two final thoughts will suffice to emphasise the impact which Cooper had on so many people's lives, from the Ibrox diehards to the Fir Park faithful, and even those who used to curse his influence during Old Firm tussles. There were fresh flowers at Davie's grave on the day I visited it in March 2013. I don't know whether I was surprised by that or not, but I had been hoping the grave would be a fitting monument and it certainly was. If there is one thing designed to dampen the soul, it is the experience of standing shivering in a Scottish cemetery, but the solitude allowed me to think a while and focus again on the rich array of qualities which this man brought to his life. There was sporting talent, of course, copious amounts of athleticism, balletic balance, close control and dexterity of movement, allied to a confidence, which manifested itself on the pitch despite Coop's innate reserve away from the field of conflict. There was an eternal loyalty to his club, to his friends and family, and a close-knit camaraderie with his contemporaries on his short journeys between his environs in the west of his homeland.

It might be true that he would never have bothered obtaining a passport if he hadn't been selected for Scotland duty, but that should not be depicted as some major character weakness. On the contrary, it is surely heartening to reflect that, despite all the temptations and vices which are available to those who populate the modern football milieu, Coop's only human frailty off the pitch was a predilection for backing the wrong horse in the 2.30 at Plumpton or Carlisle. The demons which plagued George Best and continue to pervade Paul Gascoigne were mercifully absent.

From the early stage, one aspect which shone through was the contrast between his dominance on the pitch and diffidence off it. David Mason, the official Rangers historian, conveyed this to me with a series of evocative reminiscences. "I recall him playing against us in October 1976, in the third replay of the seemingly endless League Cup quarter-final tussle against Clydebank. Cooper scored against us that night – his third of the tie – and although it was insufficient to stop the Bankies slipping out of the tournament, my abiding memory of that game was of his graceful gliding around the pitch," said Mason.

"He was seemingly sylph-like as he teased the Rangers defenders with a ball which rarely left his immediate control and it appeared that there was nothing which he couldn't do with it while he controlled the play. His performance was reminiscent of the great Johan Cruyff, who had similarly tormented the Rangers defence three years earlier in the Super Cup.

"No matter that he was clearly playing at a level far above his teammates, Coop was an enigma, even to the Clydebank boss, Bill Munro. We are related and have shared many a story about Davie, but possibly the best story that highlights the inconsistency he displayed, even then, related to his demeanour when he walked into training every day. Munro said, 'I could always tell if Davie was going to have a good day by the way that he carried his newspaper in the morning. If it was under his arm, he was ready for business. If he was carrying it in his hand, I tended to get another Cooper.'"

One of these was jovial and upbeat, the other was introspective and occasionally morose. Yet what was evident from Mason's testimony was how much greater his sense of authority once he was in his chosen sphere.

"One of the best anecdotes about Davie revolves around his first game at Ibrox, where he waited at the mouth of the tunnel for Tom Forsyth to come across the field. Moments earlier, big Tam had unleashed, in his mind, the pass of his life into space ahead of Cooper on the wing. However, when Forsyth arrived at the tunnel, Coop pointed to his feet and said, 'Play the ball to my feet, big man!' As you might expect, Tom wasn't impressed by this response, but he eventually realised that Davie was a player who nurtured the ball but did not chase it. That was Coop."

Mason isn't the only observer to believe that the winger was treated shabbily by the Ibrox club in the early 1980s. Indeed, he considers that Cooper grew heavy-legged, and it was almost as if the battle of wills between him and Greig was one of those personal vendettas where common sense came a distant third behind ego and obstinacy. Thankfully, though, the arrival of Graeme Souness transformed the climate around the Govan milieu, even if, as it transpired, it was for too short a period.

"Graeme was a world-class player and he knew how best to operate with Coop. The latter was an individual who thrived on having quality around him – players whose brain and skill could match the alertness he had for an opening," recalled Mason. "It was around that time that I first had the opportunity to meet him, in the foyer of the Main Stand, as he prepared to leave after training. I met him often thereafter, exchanging pleasantries or sharing a blether. He was always willing to chat, offering a view on a past game or the next contest. At Ibrox, [the former manager] Bill Struth had instilled a tradition that players should always look like Rangers players. Cooper was always immaculately dressed and he had the air of a real star.

"He loved Old Firm matches, but he once confessed to me that he encountered much more bitterness in games against Hibernian at the time. He was not any more inspired against them than Celtic, because he was a Rangers man through and through, and to him defeat against the Parkhead side was unthinkable. But as much as he relished playing against them, he just loved football, and during the early part of his career, he displayed some naïveté about the star status which he had assumed.

"As one of his close friends told me, Coop just could not understand why anybody would have any special interest in him because he was a football player. And that summed him up. He was born just nine days after me and the shocking news of his death highlighted my own vulnerability. How could a fit man die so young – in the prime of his life? Every year I celebrate another birthday I think of Davie, who was robbed of the same celebrations."

Munro, the man who coached and managed Clydebank all the way to the top flight of Scottish football, has never forgotten the youthful insouciance with which the teenage Cooper stamped his imprint on the sport from the mid-1970s. But equally, he can recollect the idiosyncrasies which mystified many observers.

"Davie could do anything with a football, but he wasn't very ambitious. He could leave opponents trailing in his wake, yet he never believed his own publicity or that of the media. Week in, week out, he was excelling for Clydebank and the press soon got wind of it. Tommy Cooper was a big star at the time and they [the papers] tried to persuade Davie to wear a fez, but he never wanted to play these games.

"In fact, he wasn't obsessed with football at all. I remember when we went off on a pre-season trip to Spain that Davie didn't want to come because he told me he was keen to stay at home and play tennis. I pointed out that he could play tennis in Spain, but it was an effort to get him on the plane. And that was just his way.

"Yet my abiding memory of Coop was how he ripped Rangers apart in the three matches of the League Cup. Obviously, football's a team game, and there were other lads trying their hearts out, but Davie ran the show, he was pretty much in a class of his own and I suppose I knew he had to leave Clydebank to realise his potential. But, you know, there was never any great urgency on his part to move elsewhere. He wasn't interested in fame. He wasn't bothered by publicity. He could have gone anywhere, but he didn't. I still wonder where he might have ended up if he had been really ambitious . . ."

That failure to crack the enigma by even the sharpest soccer sages permeates the whole Cooper saga. It nags away like a persistent toothache at some of those whom I interviewed. Yet, at this distance, it is an unfathomable mystery. What truly matters to his countless aficionados are his acts of brilliance and, even at this distance, the recollections flood off the tongue, from those who paid their admission money to be entertained and duly marvelled at Coop. "There was a League Cup semi-final against Hibs in 1985. We had lost the first leg 2–0, but he gave us hope at Ibrox with a searing thirty-five-yard free kick that tore the flesh off the normally excellent Alan Rough's eyebrows as it ripped into the top corner," recalls Alister Campbell, another forty-something with a photographic memory of Davie's best moments. "Then, a year later, with the influence of Souness galvanising the club, we played Hearts at Tynecastle and Coop went on a run, beating man after man, and then eventually slipping the ball past Henry Smith. Sensational!

"Moving on to the terrible time when he died, I found out the news when I was on the phone to the BBC. The station was doing a series of programmes called *Voices of the Old Firm*, about fans' memories of various Rangers and Celtic games. Unfortunately, my tape recorder had packed in the night before, and I had failed to record it, so I was on the phone trying, and succeeding, in sweet-talking Victoria Darbyshire into sending me a copy.

"But then she told me a piece of breaking news about how Davie had suffered a brain haemorrhage and added that the prognosis wasn't looking good. She asked me if I wanted to go on the radio and give a comment from a fan's perspective, but I couldn't even speak. At the time I worked in London with two other Rangers supporters and they were as stunned as I was when I told them. And then when he died the next day, a piece of my childhood died with him. I am not ashamed to say that I cried."

This is a common refrain among those of us from Davie's generation. Namely that while we were joyously privileged to behold him in full flight, there is still a tiny part of us which feels that he didn't earn his due while he was alive. It might be irrational, but his exploits are precious and the effect of these feats is indelibly locked inside us.

That was what Coop was all about. He made you glad to be in the same space as him while he cracked through the carapace of mediocrity and marched into a rarefied realm when he was in the mood.

As somebody once remarked, on hearing of the demise of Duke Ellington, "I don't have to believe it if I don't want to." And for as long as we can click onto our computers and watch Coop embark on that mazy run at Hampden Park in 1979, he is never truly dead.